What the critics said about *Tiger*
Pacific

'. . . stands out as much for its sh[...]
observations.'
Singapore *Sunday Straits Times*

'There is nothing by an American writer to match it.'
R.W. Apple, *New York Times*

'. . . interesting, informative and extremely well written. It is a
must for many readers.'
F. Gerard Adams, *Asian Pacific Economic Literature*

'. . . an important book, a skilful mix of narrative and opinion.'
Milton Osborne, *The Australian*

'. . . an informative, provocative and readable book.'
Melbourne *Age*

'No journalist in contemporary times has done more than Greg Sheridan, not just to report Asia, but to interpret it to us. This book may be his most useful and enjoyable contribution yet to that vital task.'

Paul Keating
FORMER PRIME MINISTER
OF AUSTRALIA

'Greg Sheridan understands the highly varied societies of Asia at a depth that few commentators can match. He is at home with their heads of state; with their rising young professionals; with their poor. The result is a vital analysis of the post-boom region of the '90s. Immensely readable and provocative, this book is essential reading, exploding any number of cliches.'

Christopher Koch
AUTHOR OF *THE YEAR*
OF LIVING DANGEROUSLY

'*Asian Values, Western Dreams* is a remarkable journey of cultural exposure and intellectual understanding. From an identity-seeking Philippines to a switched on Singapore to a frenetic China, Greg Sheridan presents a vivid collage of atmosphere, ethnicity and insight. For Americans and Australians there are great lessons. We Americans consider ourselves an Asian nation, but for 224 years, my nation has been a democracy in progress—one which took 89 years to end slavery, 144 years to give women a vote and 188 years to make all citizens equal under law. Mr Sheridan reminds us we need to all lighten-up on the moralizing and begin to appreciate that there is more to Asian values than simply ascribed authoritarianism.'

Richard L. Armitage
FORMER US ASSISTANT
SECRETARY OF DEFENCE

'Greg Sheridan recovers the idea of Asian values from the oblivion to which Western triumphalism would have us consign it, to show its continuing relevance to understanding East Asian societies . . . he supports his argument through Asian voices he has heard and reported over a decade and a half in many East Asian countries, in many settings, from pubs to presidential palaces . . . His basic point is irrefutable—that Asian values are what Asian people value and that these may stack up differently from the way they do in the West and both reflect and determine different attitudes, behavioural patterns, and cultures. This book should encourage renewed attention to this issue, and that would be a major service to the cause of more layered analysis, sophisticated understanding and nuanced reporting of East Asian societies in the West.'

Stephen FitzGerald
CHAIRMAN, ASIA–AUSTRALIA
INSTITUTE

GREG SHERIDAN first began writing about Asia during a five year post at the *Bulletin*. His involvement developed following the story of Vietnamese boat people in the late 1970s; his first trips into Asia were to report on refugee camps. Since 1984 he has worked at *The Australian*, having held the positions of chief editorial writer, columnist, Beijing correspondent, Washington correspondent, Canberra diplomatic correspondent and, since 1992, foreign editor.

Greg Sheridan has written for the *Sunday Times* of London, the *Asian Wall Street Journal,* the *Jakarta Post* and the *South China Morning Post*. He is the author of *Tigers: Leaders of the New Asia Pacific* (1997) and editor and co-author of *Living with Dragons: Australia Confronts its Asian Destiny* (1995). His work has been anthologised in numerous books.

When he's not travelling in Asia, Greg Sheridan lives in Sydney. He is married to Jasbir Kaur Sheridan and has three sons, Ajay, Lakhvinder and Jagdave.

ASIAN VALUES WESTERN DREAMS

Understanding the new Asia

Greg Sheridan

ALLEN & UNWIN

First published in 1999 by
Allen & Unwin
9 Atchison Street,
St Leonards NSW 1590 Australia
Phone: (61 2) 8425 0100
Fax: (61 2) 9906 2218
E-mail: frontdesk@allen-unwin.com.au
Web: http://www.allen-unwin.com.au

National Library of Australia
Cataloguing-in-Publication entry:

Sheridan Greg, 1956– .
  Asian values, western dreams: understanding the new Asia.

  Includes index.
  ISBN 1 86448 496 9.

  1. Intercultural communication—Asia. 2. Cultural relations.
  3. Cultural relativism—Asia. 4. Social values—Asia. I. Title.

303.4825

Set in 10.5/13pt Arrus by DOCUPRO, Sydney
Printed by Australian Print Group, Maryborough

10 9 8 7 6 5 4 3 2 1

CONTENTS

I wish to dedicate this book to my wife, Jasbir Kaur Sheridan, the true light in my life, and to our three sons, Ajaypal, Lakhvinder and Jagdave, and respectfully to Rich Armitage, who always tells it like it is

FOREWORD

I T WAS THE NOVELIST Christopher Koch who first took me to
Asia, almost literally though not personally, some twenty years
ago. Reading *The Year of Living Dangerously*, his magnificent novel
of Indonesia and Sukarno and Western journalists, convinced me
that I wanted to spend a lot of time in Asia, that this was the
story for me. Since then I've made dozens, perhaps hundreds, of
journeys across Asia. It was quite clear to me that the re-emergence of East Asia, and more recently South Asia, into the front
ranks of history was worth a lifetime's work.

This book is the fruit of many such journeys. It asks a simple
question: how do Asian societies reconcile their desire to celebrate
their distinctive local cultures with the overwhelming forces of
globalisation? This is not a book about the Asian economic crisis,
which broke out in Thailand in the second half of 1997. But the
crisis is an essential backdrop (and a backdrop often discussed)
to everything that happens in the book.

This is a journalistic book, a book about people. In many
ways it is a book about countless small victories. It draws on
hundreds of interviews with all manner of people right across
Asia and in America. It examines the central issue of 'Asian
values', which I believe to be of fundamental importance to the
21st century, through the oldest journalistic technique known to
man—asking people about it.

I have decided to spare innocent people in the street whom
I interviewed a notoriety they may not want, by disguising most
of the names. But anyone with any public position at all, from

a nation's president to a company executive to a professor, is identified by his or her real name.

Too many people helped me in the preparation of this book for me to thank them individually. Every single one of the hundreds of men and women heard in these pages has my gratitude for making the time to talk to me. Beyond that I would like to thank my editor-in-chief at *The Australian*, David Armstrong, for his advice, forbearance, guidance and friendship. I should also thank my wife Jasbir, whose labours on behalf of this book were at least as burdensome as mine, and our sons Ajay, Lakhvinder and Jagdave, for putting up with a frequently absent dad.

Of course, no one but me is responsible for this book's opinions or any of its mistakes.

1

INTRODUCTION: ASIAN VALUES LIVE!

BEIJING, 1985: A CHINESE friend takes me to the home of an art professor from the Central China Art Academy. It is a bare and tiny two-room apartment; the kitchen seems to be on the narrow walkway that forms a balcony outside. But the professor is delighted to welcome a visitor. He offers me a watermelon and a fruit drink. Unfortunately, I am suffering from a truly epic bout of Beijing belly and must refuse all food.

I don't blame you, he says, China is a backward country with low standards of hygiene. He thinks I am right to refuse his food.

Mortified, I explain that this is not the case at all. Normally I would be delighted to accept his kind offer of food. I add that, far from being a backward country, China is a great and ancient civilisation with much to teach the West.

No, he says, yours is an advanced country, while we are backward. It is we who have much to learn from you.

This goes on for a long time, perhaps literally half an hour, a kind of conversational politeness ping-pong, with each of us patting the encomiums gently back across the net to the other. I find the experience, after the initial embarrassment wears off, charming yet slightly off-key. Despite the goodwill on either side of the net, there is something not quite right about it.

Bangkok, 1998: I am sitting in the coffee shop of a swank, downtown hotel, with another professor, a Thai academic who has been a senior politician as well. He is surveying the wreckage of the Thai economy, and the wreckage of the hopes and ambitions he once held for his society, in the wake of the economic tsunami that has recently devastated the region.

He is brutally honest: 'Now when I see a *farang* (a white person) in Bangkok I feel ashamed, especially when I see them coming from the International Monetary Fund to tell our government what to do. I feel ashamed that we made such a mess of it.'

Asians and Westerners, politeness and embarrassment, misunderstanding and power, wrecked dreams and shame—two scenes, more than a decade apart, that take us to the heart of the Asian values debate. Are we allowed to have that debate any more after the great East Asian economic crash of 1997 and beyond? There will of course be a host of nitpicking and semantic objections. Whatever values we can identify as Asian can also be identified in other traditions and therefore they are not exclusively Asian, one line of argument has it. How can we suggest, this argument continues, a commonality across Asia, implied in the term 'Asian values', when Asia itself is so diverse? The Asian values trumpeted by leaders such as Malaysia's Dr Mahathir, or Singapore's Lee Kuan Yew, the proponents of this line will say, cannot be up to much after all if they produced not just decades of economic growth but the great crash of 1997 and all the subsequent economic difficulties.

But it would be a fundamental misreading of Asia, whether by outsiders or Asians themselves, to take that approach—to believe that the Asian economic turmoil of the late 1990s means that the Asian values debate is over and that the West won. Indeed, for Western analysts to take that approach would not only confirm the smug, ingrained and irrelevant assumption of superiority on the part of the West; it would be to misread altogether what the Asian values debate is all about. Plotting what the debate really is about, seeing it at work in a variety of Asian societies and Asian lives, is the subject of this book.

Asian values have an obviously political dimension but they are not just about politics. They have an obviously anti-Western tinge in the sense that they are often defined in contrast with the West, but that is not really what drives them either. They are much more to do with an internal Asian debate about the nature of the good life, about regional community, about the dynamics of modernisation, about whether modernisation means Westernisation, about the civic dimension of life, about the reconciliation of indigenous traditions with new cosmopolitan dynamics, about the challenges of globalisation.

Kishore Mahbubani, a distinguished Singapore diplomat and a key figure in the Asian values debate, captures this reality directly in his marvellous essay, *Can Asians Think?*, which has had several lives but most recently appeared in his book by the same name. We will examine his ideas in a little more detail in Chapter 4 on Singapore, but the key argument he makes about Asian values is that it is not just about, or even primarily about, politics. Instead it is part of an attempt to renew societies, to reconnect them with their past, to overcome the legacy of colonialism and the old assumption of white supremacy, to find a way of life that is both modern and yet true to the traditions of Asian societies.

Mahbubani's candour in referring to the sometimes unconscious, sometimes very conscious, assumption by many Asians as well as Westerners that somehow or other they were inferior beings in a white man's universe is a delicate, but important, aspect of Asian values. In 1998 Lee Kuan Yew published the first volume of his memoirs, *The Singapore Story*. They are as direct, compelling and uncompromising as the man himself and full of all manner of delicious insights. But the most compelling chapters of all are those that deal with Lee's childhood and then the period of Japanese occupation of Singapore. Lee makes it clear that before the war he and his fellow educated Chinese assumed that the white man, in Singapore's case the Englishman, was the big boss, and that while there were greater and lesser big bosses there was no doubt that the Englishman had the best life and wielded the most power. The prestige of the British Empire, to the maintenance of which every state effort was bent, was intimately linked to the racial prestige of the white man. These assumptions were utterly shattered by Japan's rapid, ruthless invasion of Singapore. Lee describes in brutal frankness the cruel behaviour of the Japanese when they ruled Singapore and nothing could ever justify that behaviour. But the fall of Singapore to an Asian power was the fall of the white man's pedestal in South East Asia.

Much of the Asian values debate, as Mahbubani suggests, is about finding a psychological equilibrium, based on neither inferiority nor superiority but on common humanity. Indeed, the most interesting part of the Asian values debate is not necessarily the political part, and much of this book is about non-political values, or at least values that are not directly and predominantly linked to politics. Of course, the search for psychological equilibrium with the West is not the whole story of Asian values either. While the encounter with the West is a profoundly important part of the story of Asia's development over the last hundred years, Asian values are not primarily a contest between Asia and the West. It was Chesterton who observed that Christianity is best approached as a poem not a syllogism, and he wrote many books attempting to find the rhyme in the poem, the rhythm in the verse. Constructing syllogisms he left for someone else. Asian values, similarly, cannot be reduced to a syllogism, but can be found in the lives, the human poetry, of Asians themselves. The approach of this book, accordingly, is empirical in the journalistic sense and also discursive in the journalistic sense.

Some Asian leaders *have* phrased the debate in an anti-Western fashion, but even this defensiveness or much of it is a reaction to the routine Western assumption that the West knows everything and everyone else must learn what the West knows. Harvard scholar Sam Huntington, in his now immensely famous book *The Clash of Civilizations and the Remaking of World Order*, argues that Western civilisation is not universal and ought to give up its universal pretensions. But far from being a generous act of cultural humility—the notion that we might all have something to learn from each other—Huntington's view seems akin to that underlying a very old form of colonialism. The West has the best and most humane values, he argues, but the Rest (Asia, Africa etc), because of their ineradicable cultural limitations, just aren't capable of implementing such values in their own societies. Therefore the West should stop trying to spread those values to societies incapable of receiving them. This is just the old Western superiority complex but now made brutally exclusive, implying an unpleasant cultural determinism and a serious limitation on the idea of friendship across civilisations.

There are of course universal values of good and evil, but different societies and different traditions mediate them in vastly different ways. Yet culture is not static, it is open to substantial reinterpretation and reinvention. The renewed attention to Asian values is an attention to the question of how to draw the best out of Asian traditions, how to preserve something of those traditions while experiencing ultra-rapid modernisation, how to achieve a sense of psychological parity and self-confidence in the great world, and how to draw out something of the wisdom in Asian traditions for the benefit of the broad human discourse on pursuit of the good life.

Perversely, one of the most frequent objections to the notion of Asian values comes from many Western scholars of Asia, especially single-country specialists and especially Sinologists. These people have spent a lifetime working on one particular country and have come to love, or sometimes to hate, its particularities. They don't want it subsumed in any larger identity, they don't want it understood through some other conceptual or even political grid. Most especially they don't want anyone talking about *their* particular country who hasn't spent decades exclusively devoted to it.

A related objection comes from the professional South Asianists. What about India, they not unreasonably ask—Asia's second largest nation, the world's second largest nation for that matter, home of one of the world's oldest continuous civilisations, source of much of the world's cultural richness, and so on.

These two arguments are best dealt with together. The Asian values debate has so far mainly concerned East Asia, by which I mean North East Asia and South East Asia. The easiest way to define these regions is just to define them. North East Asia comprises China, Hong Kong, Taiwan, Japan, South Korea, North Korea and Mongolia. South East Asia consists of Indonesia, Thailand, the Philippines, Malaysia, Singapore, Brunei, Vietnam, Myanmar (formerly Burma), Laos and Cambodia.

Both North East Asia and South East Asia are more diverse—culturally, politically, religiously, economically—than, say, Western Europe, yet each is still meaningfully a region. The extent of their regionality varies and is certainly debatable. Yet there is, in both cases, a regional dynamic. All North East Asian societies are 'chopstick societies'. All owe a massive cultural debt to Confucianism. While there is vast linguistic diversity, there is a unifying force in their character-based writing systems.

South East Asia is more diverse. Yet the Association of South East Asian Nations (ASEAN) has produced an intimate political network striving towards a shared regional identity, notwithstanding plenty of disagreements. This is evident too in the efforts to create a South East Asian common market. While there is great religious diversity, much of the region shares a broad Malay ethnic identity with substantial Chinese, Indian and indigenous minorities.

What then about India? The attempt of India and East Asia to engage more closely with each other—attempts which have been recent, fitful, episodic—is infinitely intriguing and promising. It is one reason why there is a chapter on India in this book. But India serves more as a fascinating, non-Western cultural counterpoint in the Asian values debate. If India and East Asia come much closer together they are both likely to benefit, but that is a development for the future. The Asian values debate so far has been about East Asia.

Increasingly, North East Asia and South East Asia are coming to recognise some commonalities. East Asians are talking more and more of a broader identity and regional context which embraces both their sub-regions. Sometimes they talk of this in terms of practical organisations, such as Dr Mahathir's proposed East Asia Economic Caucus, or the Asia-Europe summit process. Even the Asia-Pacific Economic Cooperation (APEC) forum, in its Asian membership, recognises an emerging East Asian sphere. The former Australian foreign minister, Gareth Evans, tried to promote the idea of an 'East Asian hemisphere' as an obvious way of both recognising this dynamic and defining it in a way that included Australia. Alas, the concept died when he left office in 1996.

In any event, much more important than practical organisational issues is the increasing sense of cultural interconnection of East Asian societies. Yoichi Funabashi, of the Japanese newspaper *Asahi Shimbun* and one of Japan's most acute observers of the wider Asian scene, comments in his book *Asia Pacific Fusion* on the 'Asianisation of Asia'. Many writers have addressed this same phenomenon in different ways. In 1967, when ASEAN was formed, it was a somewhat revolutionary idea to include ethnic Chinese societies like Singapore with ethnically Malay nations, such as Indonesia and Malaysia, in the one organisation. Now there is undeniably a much closer connection between all the founding nations of ASEAN. When most of the South East Asian nations gained independence their education systems were replicas of those of the European metropolitan powers from which they had just become independent, and had little local content, much less regional content.

Looking now from the end of the 1990s, all that has changed. The educational experience of most Asians has changed fundamentally, and now contains much more about their own society and about those of their neighbours—much more about Asian languages too. In popular culture and in deeper senses of identity, from Japanese comics to Hong Kong movies, from Taiwanese pop songs to Indonesian singers, there is now infinitely greater cultural interchange between East Asian societies. As Ian Buruma has argued, even in their encounter with Western culture the East Asian societies influence each other. Japan often plays the role of transmission belt for numerous Western trends in popular culture, but softening and 'Asianising' those trends along the way.

Organisationally and politically, East Asian societies are bound together in ASEAN and APEC. Their citizens travel in huge numbers to each other's countries as tourists or businessmen. The Asian values debate proceeds in this context, and in the context of East Asia's broad success in defusing most of the territorial disputes which once riddled the region.

In terms of the Asian values debate, as others have pointed out, we might compare the region to a family. It is often possible to see the clear family resemblance among siblings, even cousins, yet impossible to nominate a single feature which they all share, or which only they share. Some are short, some are tall, some are blonde, some dark—yet they are all recognisably of one family. This is substantially true of East Asia. It is the sort of resemblance that would never satisfy an academic definition—every characteristic involved would bring forth exceptions and compromises— and yet there is a resemblance there and the resemblance is important.

None of this is invalidated by the economic crisis that hit the region in 1997 and 1998. At the same time, the regional leadership, which is overwhelmingly pragmatic, is looking to the experience of the West for both positive and negative lessons. Regional leaders understand very deeply the power—military, economic and cultural—of the West, in particular of the United States. They want to emulate much of what they recognise as Western success, and much of the system that produces that success. But at the same time they do not want an explosion in the rate of teenage pregnancies, the ready availability of crack cocaine, the breakdown of marriage, the erosion of traditional patterns of authority, chronic high unemployment, the gun culture and other pathologies associated with the West (however unfairly in specific cases) in the Asian mind.

Lee Kuan Yew, in a famous interview carried in the influential journal, *Foreign Affairs* in 1994, in commenting on the culture of the United States—much of which he admired—summed up the Asian fear of Western-style development thus: 'As a total system I find parts of it totally unacceptable: guns, drugs, violent crime, unbecoming behaviour in public—in sum the breakdown of civil society . . . '

Since then conditions in America have improved, of course, with unemployment in particular falling through the 1990s. But Lee believes his basic point about the intractable problems of the American underclass remains valid.

Han Sung-Joo, a former South Korean foreign minister, has argued: 'For the first time in human history, Western civilisation stressing pre-eminence of the individual is encountering Sinic civilisation emphasising social harmony.' Han gave a short-hand description of the potential cultural clash as being that between the activist impulse of the West and the passive impulses of Asia: 'What will happen when the passive Sinic golden rule meets the active Western golden rule? The East will say: "Do not do unto others what thou dost not want them to do unto you." The West will respond: "All things you would have men do to you, do even so to them." . . . The West will say: "You are the light of the world, you give light to everyone in the house." The East will respond: "Mud is used to make celadons but it is the emptiness of the celadon that becomes useful."'

Of course, these epigrammatic civilisational summaries are of limited utility. Certainly there could be a million quibbles with any generalisation that sweeps carelessly across a civilisation. But human beings are required to integrate these concerns into their real lives and to do so in real time and generally without the luxury of a hundred academic lifetimes in which to debate the categories. In an increasingly globalising world people are making cultural and even civilisational decisions in cross-cultural contexts all the time. They need terms of some kind in order to find a purchase on the issues. As George Orwell pointed out so long ago, you cannot think about something if there is no name for it. If we are to think about civilisations we need short-hand descriptions of them.

What about Asian values, though, as a positive social force in their own right, something more substantial than the emptiness of the celadon? What do they embody?

Again the redoubtable Lee Kuan Yew offers an answer, based in his view of Confucianism. Confucianism is a profound historical influence in all of North East Asia, in Singapore and Vietnam in South East Asia, and also among the overseas Chinese communities who dominate most South East Asian economies. In this book the Analects of Confucius are considered in Chapter 6 on China, and Lee Kuan Yew's interpretation of Confucianism is considered in Chapter 4 on Singapore.

For our present purposes it is sufficient to note Lee's view that the conservative conception of family in Confucian tradition, in which a wise and benevolent father rules over a respectful wife and children, is both a social ideal and a metaphor—more than that, the chief operating principle—for the state's relationship to the citizen. The citizen stands in relation to the state in something like the situation of the son in relation to the father. More generally, Lee sees the Confucian stress on authority, filial piety, harmony within the home and within the society, thrift and education as key positive values.

Traditionally, in analyses of East Asian economic success made before the 1997 crash, a common set of economic virtues were often cited. These included:

- a capitalist economy
- high savings rate

- propensity to defer consumption, even across generations
- strong work ethic
- bias towards the interests of producers as opposed to consumers
- export-oriented industries which enforce efficiency
- generally weak trade unions or unions that, in a reflection of the stress on authority, are actually allied closely to the companies employing the workers the unions represent
- general stress on the maintenance of social and political stability
- stress on the interests of the group and willingness to sublimate individual interests to those of the group

The American analyst, David Hitchkok, in one of very few surveys done in this area, asked East Asians and Americans to choose six societal values. The East Asians chose, in order, an orderly society, social harmony, accountability of public officials, openness to new ideas and respect for authority. Americans chose freedom of expression, the rights of the individual, personal freedom, open debate, thinking for oneself and the accountability of public officials. In the personal values area, Asians tended to stress education more highly than Americans did. Such surveys may not be statistically significant, but they are suggestive.

Of course, the ways in which certain of these and other values are played out by individuals in individual societies differ enormously. And since the economic crisis began, some aspects of traditional East Asian economic behaviour, such as always favouring the producer's interests over those of the consumer, have had to be re-evaluated. This tendency reinforced massive over-investment and resultant over-capacity and removed, in consumer choice, what now appears to have been a necessary discipline on the disposition of capital.

But the East Asian economic miracle was not a mirage. It involved, in nations like South Korea and Taiwan, the most rapid sustained economic growth in human history and the most rapid large-scale exit from poverty. In Indonesia tens of millions of people rose out of absolute poverty. A certain amount of the miracle has been undone by the crisis, but by no means all, by no means most. The Asian values that enabled the miracle to happen remain overwhelmingly positive in themselves.

That is not the view of most Western analysts. Sebastian Mallaby of *The Economist* offered a high-gloss but substantially representative sample of the Western commentariat's reaction in the Summer 1998 issue of the American journal *The National Interest*. Mallaby claimed that the challenge to the West of Asian values had been totally destroyed by the Asian economic crisis. This challenge had taken two primary forms: the challenge in practice of the North East Asian economic model, specifically Japan Inc; and the rhetorical challenge of assertive South East Asian leaders such as Lee Kuan Yew and Dr Mahathir.

Mallaby argued that not only had the Asian economic crisis decisively ended both those challenges in favour of the West, specifically the United States, but that the US was being absurdly restrained in not proclaiming its victory over Asian values. This, I believe, is an almost wholly destructive triumphalism. But worse, it is not really accurate. It is at best wildly premature, not least in its judgement of North East Asian economies. Moreover, as I have argued, the Asian values debate has never been wholly, or even primarily, about challenging the West. It is much more interesting and worthwhile to explore the debate within Asia than to posit a simple, but phoney, complete opposition between the West and Asia as the sum total of the Asian values debate.

Kim Dae Jung, the elected president of South Korea, a nation of 45 million people, believes it is not only possible but intellectually compelling to find the democratic instinct lodged firmly within the major Asian traditions. And surely such a process is of immense importance if Asians are to own their own democracies. Anwar Ibrahim, the former deputy prime minister of Malaysia, pioneered a useful Islamic–Confucian dialogue within his own country which sought common ground between those two great traditions of South East Asia. The Thai citizens who forced the end of a military government in 1992, the Filipinos who did the same in 1986, were as deeply committed to democracy as any Western democrat. Many paid for this commitment with their lives. Indeed, what was the anti-colonial struggle in Asia but an assertion of democratic principles of self-determination? And of course there are countless democratic heroes in modern Asia— names like Benigno Aquino, Aung San Suu Kyi, Wei Jing Sheng, Martin Lee. Not all of them end in prison, either. Some authentic heroes of the democratic struggle, like Corazon Aquino or Kim Dae Jung himself, became president of their country.

In Anwar Ibrahim's lovely little book, *The Asian Renaissance*, he suggests that the primary role of religion in Asian societies will distinguish them sharply from Western societies, in which the long historical processes following the Enlightenment have left religion drained as an energising factor in Western culture. Anwar's view, his ideal, is not all that different from that of the Puritan founding fathers of the United States. It is more difficult to apply Anwar's ideas directly to more predominantly Sinic societies, or even Japan, which do not appear overly religious. Indeed, where formal Confucianism is strong, transcendental religion seems correspondingly weak. But in identifying a powerful influence for religion as something he wants to hang on to, without of course being remotely fundamentalist or obscurantist, Anwar lays down an important marker. Nonetheless, it is instructive that in a book which argues for an Asian cultural and political renaissance, Anwar could find plenty of Western exemplars (and plenty of Asian ones as well of course) for the type of values he wants for his own society.

Serious Western scholars are increasingly responding to the Asian values debate, even as some question its intellectual legitimacy. The sheer vitality of the debate, its propensity to turn up in all parts of East Asia, are making this happen. Michael Vatikiotis of the *Far Eastern Economic Review* is a distinguished chronicler of South East Asia. His book, *Political Change in South East Asia: Trimming the Banyan Tree*, was written before the economic crisis and before the fall of the Suharto Government in Indonesia. But it remains relevant to a consideration of politico-cultural trends in South East Asia. He tells us that the book was partly provoked by the growing Asian values debate.

Vatikiotis thought that the re-legitimisation of indigenous cultural traditions in South East Asia would be used by the elites of those societies to beat off challenges for more democracy. As it turns out, this prediction was wrong, at least in the short term. But it may well have been right had the economic crisis not intervened. However, it rests on another deep insight of Vatikiotis, and that is the important role of nationalism in the evolution of the political cultures of South East Asia.

Sometimes this nationalism is deeply intertwined with the Asian values debate. 'This may not be the way Western powers want us to do things but this is the way we do them here' is a refrain which was heard throughout South East Asia in the 1980s and 1990s, before the eruption of the economic crisis. After the crisis broke out, with a loss of regional self-confidence, it was heard less often.

However, Vatikiotis offers us another important insight. He argued that the political cultures of the authoritarian countries in South East Asia that had also experienced rapid economic development, especially Indonesia, were failing to keep pace with the dynamism and diversity of their own societies. He resolved this contradiction by suggesting that authoritarianism, dressed up as local, national or Asian values, would triumph over demands for democracy. Certainly the economic crisis shook everything up and accelerated political change. But even without the crisis there was increasing demand within South East Asia for political change anyway.

Western commentators, and Western governments, should always have been more alive to this. It is not up to the West—the United States or any other part of the West—to determine the political culture of nations in South East Asia. Vatikiotis thought that South East Asian leaders would be able to defeat demands for democracy by painting demands for democracy as Western interference.

This whole process has a long way to run yet before anything like a stable resolution can emerge. But the political arguments in most South East Asian societies are about universal values mediated through local traditions. Filipinos (and sometimes other South East Asians) when they talk of freedom often evoke José Rizal, the great independence leader of a century ago. The point is that there is plenty within each Asian cultural and national tradition to support the democracy option. Vatikiotis argues that the South East Asian bourgeoisie is more interested in stability than in democracy and therefore may not play the politically liberalising role ascribed to it in classical Western political theory. That is at least an arguable proposition, but in any event democracy of some kind is increasingly seen as the friend of stability, not least because it promotes modern and transparent financial practices, but more importantly because it confers a unique degree of legitimacy on the political leadership.

Nonetheless, the more rigorous examination of Asian traditions for their own ideas of freedom is welcome and overdue. There is much in Confucius, after all, to give pause to an authoritarian and heart to a democrat, notwithstanding the great philosopher's stress on authority. People power is a term found in Mencius. *Asian Freedoms*, edited by David Kelly and Anthony Reid, is an early if imperfect example of what is necessary in the way of such examination. Using an admittedly somewhat perverse methodology, it attempts to locate ideas of freedom, especially political freedom, in the classical traditions of China, Japan, Thailand, Indonesia, Myanmar and Vietnam.

One of the book's most interesting lines of argument is that it was the very success of the Chinese state that historically left little room for the idea of civic freedom to grow. The ramshackle states of pre-modern Europe, which were far less well organised and effective than the historical state in China, left much more space for the development of independent sources of power and of limits on the sovereign's authority.

In the case of Buddhism, according to *Asian Freedoms*, we find a system that is pro-freedom in the way that it values all life but anti-political in that it regards all worldly things as lacking in substance.

Other scholars have pointed out that much of the idea of modern freedom in former colonial states in Asia depended on accidents of linguistics. How you talk about something profoundly influences how you think about it. Thus those states that in the struggle for independence used the English word 'democracy', effectively importing that word into their language, tended to end up, mentally, with something approaching the Western meaning of that word. Those nations that used a word already in their own language, with some kind of roughly equivalent meaning, ended up with a guiding concept that was quite different. Thus in Indonesia and Malaysia the word *demokrasi* was used; in Thailand, which was never a colony, the Thai word *prachatipatai*, which initially meant 'republic' in a pejorative sense, came to mean 'democracy'. The blends within the various Asian societies of Western influence and the indigenous traditions—of consultation, legitimacy, reciprocity of obligation between ruler and ruled, limits on the powers of rulers—together constitute the heart of the Asian values debate in its political dimension. As David Kelly wrote: 'If Asia is the Antarctica of freedom it is thought to be, like the real Antarctica it turns out to be teeming with life under the forbidding coat of ice.'

But as this Introduction has argued, and as this whole book suggests, Asian values are much more than political values. The Asian values debate is alive and well. Asian values themselves are alive and well. The debate, if anything, is set to intensify. It is not rendered redundant by the economic turmoil, just as it was never to be found wholly residing in the economic success and high growth rates of the past. Indeed, it is a debate much more concerned with the future than with the past. It is a great adventure, a journey of the human spirit, an aspiration for cultural renewal and social integration, a debate the more challenging because it is without definitional straitjackets.

And it has only just begun.

2

California Dreaming:
The Philippines in
South East Asia

IN MANILA IT'S EASY to panic, even when things are going
relatively well. Jo Jo and I are sitting at a tiny, squalid outdoor
cafe on the edge of Makati, the capital's glitzy business district,
Manila's version of Hong Kong. The cafe is on the edge of a
building site. It caters for workers like Jo Jo from that and another
huge building site nearby. It is nothing more than a few formica
tables and a couple of pieces of shadecloth. Building workers
taking their break sit around, most of them stripped to the waist,
sipping soft drinks and smoking; a mother and baby sleep under
a piece of shadecloth, avoiding the baking sun; and a small dog,
tethered to an old car, barks incessantly.

Suddenly there are screams and shouts and everyone runs out
to the street. Two men have drawn handguns on each other and
everyone races out in anticipation of witnessing a gunfight. Ah,
here, I think, is the old Hispanic macho culture at work. But the
dispute is over a car space, somehow involving a car-watch boy.
And while gunplay is threatened no shots are actually fired. So
just which cultural influence is at work here? Is this really the
macho Spanish inheritance? Is it the Malay phenomenon of
running 'amok'? Or is it more just a high stress Asian version of
modern Los Angeles, where road rage has often led to gunplay
and death?

Listen to Jessica Zaffra, one of Manila's most popular newspaper columnists: 'Let me tell you something about myself. I am
a city dweller. My lungs are filled to bursting with car exhausts,
factory emissions and other noxious gases which in time shall

16

kill me. My stress level resembles a frayed piece of rope with which a piano is being lowered down the side of a ten-storey building. My idea of exercise is getting up and switching TV channels manually instead of using the remote control clicker. When the building elevator is on the blink, I don't give a sigh of resignation and take the stairs, I find the person in charge and yell at him to fix it.'

There speaks a gal with angst. But it's the kind of angst you might find in any big city in the world. In the great debate about Asian values the Philippines has figured too little. Probably the least important aspect of the debate is the question of which values are Asian and which are Western. Many values are universal but their particular application within a living culture, their particular weighting within a scale of national values, is the elusive yet defining question for each nation.

But the term 'Asian values' has another meaning too. It's the attempt by societies which are rapidly modernising and experiencing fast social change to hold on to something of their traditional cultures, their traditional patterns of thought and behaviour—in particular to find a future which is wholly modern but which does not lead to inner-city decay, drug use, high rates of illegitimacy, unemployment, welfare dependency or the other social pathologies associated with the downside of contemporary Western societies. It's not that Asian societies have stopped admiring the achievements of the West but that they want to learn from the West's mistakes as well as its achievements.

What better place to start an investigation into Asian values than this extraordinary place called the Philippines, this nation of 70 million people, predominantly Catholic, named after a Spanish king, ethnically Malay (though arguably Eurasian) and parked in the middle of South East Asia?

Filipinos are great jokers, not least about their own heritage. But the Philippines has been the butt of too many jokes, not just in Asia but also in the West, where the Philippines is almost universally depicted as irredeemably corrupt and degenerate. It has its corrupt and degenerate side, of course. Most countries do. But the Philippines is also a nation of heroes, and in particular a heroic commitment to democracy, as the People's Power revolution of 1986 demonstrated. Of course, all kinds of vote-buying and rough trade go on in the elections, but the Philippines people are nonetheless deeply wedded to their democracy. It's a similar feeling to that which you find in India. Filipinos do not appear to regard democracy as some alien system foisted on them by an interfering West, but as their natural birthright as Filipinos, an integral part of their national culture.

Then, too, in the 1990s the Philippines appeared to rejoin the high economic growth rates club of East Asia. Having had a later and smaller boom, it was not as heavily devastated in the regional economic crash that began in Thailand in mid-1997. Certainly its growth stalled, but not nearly so badly as among most of its South East Asian neighbours. Democracy and a better economic performance should underline its right to a bigger say in all the great regional debates, including the debate on Asian values.

Delia, single, in her early 30s, impeccably groomed, works as an economist at the grossly and gauchely plush headquarters of an international aid agency in Manila. On her desk is a photograph of herself on holiday in Austria and a book with a characteristically Asian title, *Building a Success Culture*. She thinks being Asian is a plus for Filipinos: 'When I hear the term "Asian values" I usually think of things like discipline and loyalty. Maybe these are more Chinese or Japanese characteristics. We Filipinos still lack discipline and we're not as loyal, to a company, say, as the Japanese. Perhaps another Asian value is being hardworking. Filipinos certainly have that hardworking virtue, especially if they go overseas to work. But people here, too, have a feeling of entrepreneurship. They love to set up small businesses. But in other things we're very American.'

This diverse (to put it mildly), view of the Philippines national identity is typical of countless conversations I've had with Filipinos. They acknowledge everything, accept everything, but it does not necessarily lead to an easy conclusion, or indeed to any conclusion. Delia's own life experience bears out her point. She comes from a middle-class Filipino family and attended a private religious school and then the University of the Philippines. She and her family speak Tagalog, the national language, at home.

At school and university the language of instruction was English; as with millions of Filipinos, Delia's English is perfect.

And, although she now regards it as a waste of time, she took Spanish in high school and college because it was then compulsory (though that is no longer so). In her professional life she has had some training and exposure to French and Russian. When she reads for pleasure it is in English.

Overall that is a prodigious linguistic effort, but the truly remarkable aspect of it is that none of that additional linguistic training involved an Asian language. The sense of Asianness in the Philippines is attenuated for people such as Delia, although it is fair to say that under the presidency of Fidel Ramos (1992 to 1998) membership of the Association of South East Asian Nations became much more important to the Philippines. So too did the desire not to be the only one of ASEAN's founding members (Indonesia, Malaysia, Thailand, Singapore and the Philippines founded ASEAN in 1967) that did not achieve, at least before the regional crisis hit, rapid economic growth and consequent improvement in its people's living standards.

Neighbouring Singapore's former leader, Lee Kuan Yew, upset Filipinos in 1992 by telling them that they had too much democracy and too little discipline. Behind the rebarbative Singaporean view was a deeper feeling that the Philippines was, at the very least, an odd man out in Asia, that its mental universe was focused on the United States, that it was psychologically an extension of southern California displaced a couple of thousand kilometres into the Pacific. Benigno Aquino, Cory's late husband who was assassinated at Manila Airport on his return to the Philippines in 1983, once famously wrote: 'The Filipinos were an Asian people not Asian in the eyes of their fellow Asians, not Western in the eyes of the West.'

One of the country's greatest novelists, Francisco Sionil José, in 1996 wrote an elegiac essay on his country's identity in which he argued that, if it were possible to put a referendum question to the Philippines people on the proposition that the Philippines should become a state of the United States of America, it would pass overwhelmingly. He cited surveys which showed Filipino children wishing they were Americans.

A great deal of this is just a question of poverty and the perception of American wealth. But now you get the feeling that the Philippines is changing and a greater sense of Asianness, and

Asian pride, are taking hold. Just as many Asian nations fear becoming Westernised culturally through their engagement in the global economy, the Philippines, while wishing to get closer to Asia, does not want to sacrifice any of its own distinctive national traits—traits that some other Asians might find uncomfortable, such as the commitment to democracy, or the commitment to the most rambunctious freedom of speech anywhere in Asia.

Zaffra, the feisty columnist, recounts a typical experience: 'I was in Indonesia at a writers conference. Everyone from South East Asia was talking about how to get around censorship. I had absolutely nothing to contribute to the discussion because we don't have censorship here. If we see ourselves as part of ASEAN it's more as part of the growth area, not historically or culturally. Families and family ties are very strong, and that's typically Asian, but in many ways we're very Westernised. It's not a good thing or a bad thing. It's just the way we are.'

Other Filipinos argue aggressively that their version of Asian-ness is just as Asian as anyone else's, that they have as much right, and as much intellectual legitimacy, in claiming their distinctive national culture as Asian as does anyone else. An articulate if moderate defender of this view is Roberto De Ocampo, who was Finance Secretary when I met him in Manila in his formal, Spanish-style office, with its sombre wood panel-ling, high-backed chairs and dark, sepulchral tones. Bobby, as he's known to his friends, is himself a mixture of Asian and Western influences. He did his first degree at Ateneo de Manila University, but has postgraduate qualifications from the London School of Economics and Michigan University and worked for ten years at the World Bank in Washington, DC.

He became a powerful figure in Philippines politics after his return. I have interviewed him several times and find him this day his usual mixture of low-key charm and hardheaded business sense. 'Asian values does mean something to the Philippines—in two ways,' he says. 'One, we've become a lot more sensitive to being part of Asia. Partly through our own fault our neighbours regarded us as more in tune with New York than with Asia or even ASEAN in particular. Now we see a lot of ASEAN invest-ment coming into the Philippines. The suspicion of us as not really Asian has declined. We are as Asian as Singapore, or even

Malaysia, with all their Western influences. We do uphold some values which are considered Asian, such as respect for elders, whereas in the West there is a tendency to glorify youth. Too often in the West elders are regarded as doddering bumpkins. We also place a high emphasis on education. But if there's anything we're trying to emphasise in our economic strategy it's the creation of a new model for Asian economic development which combines the best of Asian values with Western traditions of democracy. It's an advantage we've long had but little used, but it will be particularly important in a globalising world.'

Many rank and file Filipinos are at least as passionate about keeping their democracy as De Ocampo. Maria, a young woman who was working for a foreign embassy when I met her, had been active in the anti-Marcos student movements. She remembers the soldiers in her university classrooms in the early 1980s, when Marcos was president, monitoring what the teachers were saying. Growing up, she had no sense of the wider Asian region: 'As a student there was no feeling of being Asian. There was none. Now it's more important. There's a tendency for us to discover what we have in common with our Asian neighbours. Asian Studies and Asian languages are becoming more important. But the influence of the US is still very strong.'

She also points out that the Philippines is subject to strong internal regionalism. She once went to Cebu, in the southern Philippines, and felt like a foreigner. Now she is learning the Cebuano language, which is quite different from Tagalog, because she would like to get involved in the economic development in Mindanao, in the south. Like many Filipinos, she does not want a return to flamboyant or ideological politics, and for her this attitude is born out of bitter personal experience. At the end of our discussion, in her office canteen, I rise to pay the bill for our two cups of tea. She touches my arm, asks me to wait. 'There's something I haven't told you about.' She pauses. Some kind of emotional turmoil is going on inside her, a little struggle to retain self-possession. Then comes the explanation: 'My boyfriend was killed in an anti-Marcos demonstration in 1984. We were being dispersed and he was hit on the head by a policeman's truncheon.'

Maria has not married since and even at this distance of years her eyes fill with tears at the memory. She draws a lesson from the incident that must have been drawn by countless enthusiasts who once flirted with dramatic Leftist politics: 'At first it made me very bitter with the government and the police, but eventually it made me lose faith in the anti-imperialist cause, in the Leftist cause. I never attended demonstrations after that. We were demonstrating on behalf of a group of poor people, but the poor people themselves didn't join the demonstration. It was just the students. If you want to help the poor, you teach them how to work and make a living, you don't give up your life.'

It is easy to be brought up short in the Philippines by tragedy. For tragedy is ever present—in the Manila slums, in the *barrios* of the countryside, in lives rich and poor. The Philippines is a land of exceptional cruelty and violence, of layer upon layer of cruelty and suffering, and yet it is also a land of routine kindness and warmth.

Manila, as every visitor knows, is a dangerous city. Foreigners routinely record the registration numbers of taxis their friends enter, because crimes by cab drivers against passengers, especially tourists, are common. It happened to a friend of mine. On his first visit to Manila he boarded a taxi at the airport and asked to be taken to his hotel. Instead he was driven to a distant location and robbed at knife-point of his money, luggage, passport and even some of his clothes by the taxi driver. Yet the story has a typical Philippines coda. My friend, penniless and shoeless and with no clue as to where he was, was shortly thereafter picked up by a truck driver who sympathised, cheered him up and drove him, at no charge, all the way to his hotel.

On a more serious level, throughout the 1970s and 1980s Vietnamese boat people were the prey of pirates of many nation-alities in the South China Sea. Yet almost invariably when they entered Philippines waters they were helped by local fishermen. All through the Philippines, of course, families help each other survive through poverty which seems endless. But amidst all the tragedy the sense of fun seems never very far away.

Perhaps, though, what gives the Philippines an extra dimen-sion of suffering is the sense of almost shameless corruption in the society, corruption which, until the presidency of Fidel Ramos, did not even result in much economic growth or trickle-down benefit for the people at the bottom.

Occasionally the corruption is farcical. I remember once walking out of an airconditioned shopping mall in Manila just across the road from the Justice Department. As usual there were two policemen guarding the entrance. One motioned me over to him. I wonder what he wants, I thought, unaware of any possible infraction on my part. What he wanted was to sell me his official police badge for 500 pesos. The Philippines police, as you might guess, are ludicrously underpaid.

Corruption and tragedy stalk the Philippines' Chinese community especially, a community ostensibly doing very well from the economic upturn, although in ferocious competition with the traditional Mestizo land-owning oligarchy.

David Chang is the president of a mid-sized industrial company at the tender age of 30. He is a typical Chinese-Filipino workaholic. He now takes two whole days off at the weekend but spends most of those days with his friends on their common hobby, which is a computer shop they have founded together just for the fun of it. We meet at night at the San Mig Bar in a Makati restaurant complex. The joint, the district, is hopping. Manila's beautiful young people are out to play, showing off their wealth. But there is still a fragility about this wealth, as about so many things in the Philippines. In this case the fragility comes not least from the envy this wealth arouses among other Filipinos. David, for example, observes a private curfew, lives in a secure compound, varies his daily routine and never talks in detail about what he is doing. Why? Because the Chinese business community is the target of so many kidnappings that Manila has been dubbed 'Asia's kidnap capital'.

Although he is optimistic about the Philippines, and says he would never live anywhere else, David is nonetheless totally realistic about the risks this situation presents: 'There are three or four kidnappings a month [of Chinese] and maybe only a quarter are reported. So some Chinese leave to invest elsewhere. The general belief is that the kidnappers are either Chinese themselves or in with the military.

'Some Chinese are involved in the illegal drugs trade here.

The military can do nothing. People are in their pay. Among the Chinese there are a lot of connections to Hong Kong and the first people Hong Kong Chinese look for are Chinese connections.'

David describes himself as '75 per cent Chinese, 25 per cent Spanish and 100 per cent Filipino'. He lives at home with his parents and already regrets, a little, that he has devoted so much of his life's energy to business and so little to matters of the spirit. He values Chinese traditions but would be happy, when he has children and they grow up, for them to marry non-Chinese—although it is not likely that he himself would marry a non-Chinese, for if he did his mother would disown him.

Life presents very different challenges for Jo Jo, the building worker with whom I nearly witnessed a shooting. Jo Jo is a dark-skinned, lean, muscular man who knows how to look after himself and his family. He's not without curiosity but he's not too fussed about whether he's Asian or Western or anything else. National identity, as others have told me, is overwhelmingly a middle-class issue and in the Philippines the middle class is still relatively small. But Jo Jo does like the upturn in the economy in the 1990s. He doesn't feel it's led to any great wage rises, although the statistics suggest that this has been the case, but rather it means he can find work more easily in Manila if he wants to, and thus spend more time with his wife and six daughters.

Jo Jo didn't plan to have so many children; like most Filipino men he wanted a son but his wife kept having daughters. Before the economic upturn of the 1990s Jo Jo saw his family only on home leave. Like so many of his countrymen he was forced to find work overseas, to find enough money to give his family a chance at a decent life. That is often the key to everything in the Philippines: If we can just get enough money for the family to lead a proper life. Jo Jo worked for eight years in Saudi Arabia. That wasn't too bad, he says. Seventy per cent of his pay was automatically deducted for his family and he came home for a month's holiday each year. He was badly ripped off once by a labour contractor in Micronesia, but he would go back to the Middle East to work if he got the right offer. But he doesn't have to. Now he has a choice. Now there is work for him in Manila.

Jo Jo is himself as much a product of globalisation as Delia, the multilingual economist at the Asian Development Bank. He is almost unbearably proud of his eldest daughter, who is going to university. He hopes some of his younger daughters will too. Jo Jo himself, though with very little formal education, speaks quite functional English, Tagalog of course, passable Arabic, Spanish and a smattering of other languages—skills, commercially useful to him, that he has picked up on his roaming quest for sustenance for his family.

Official estimates have it that four million Filipinos live and work overseas, mainly as contract labourers and domestic servants, although there is also a goodly number of Filipino professionals working all through Asia and in parts of the United States. In truth the real figure is probably nearer six million. At least a couple of million must be separated spouses, separated for work or education reasons. This must impose an immense cost on the families involved, yet these families are the lucky ones: at least they can get enough money to live more or less decently, the perennial bottom line for millions of Filipinos.

Historically, the mass of the Philippines people have not been well served by their political system, which, even before Ferdinand Marcos installed martial law and made himself a dictator, was dominated by a land-owning oligarchy that alternated power among its constituent factions and clans but always prevented substantial reform, especially land reform. A decisive break came in 1986 when Corazon Aquino put herself at the head of a movement of popular disgust at Marcos and became president herself. But her presidency was a dismal disappointment. She was heroic in achieving democracy but ineffectual as president. The Philippines really began to change only when Fidel Ramos, who had been a central figure in the People's Power revolt against Marcos, became president. Ramos had served Mrs Aquino as chief of the armed forces and defence secretary and had protected her from numerous coup attempts.

In 1997 I spent some time with Ramos and with a number of other Filipino politicians and observed a political style that is unique. Ramos was the most straightforwardly sensible president the Philippines had had in a long time. His priorities were prosaic—things like solving Manila's ruinous 'brown-out' power shortages, attracting investment, providing jobs. When, in late

1997, Cardinal Jamie Sin and Mrs Aquino herself dragged several hundred thousand citizens on to the street (partly by the cardinal's cancelling Sunday mass in Manila except for the mass celebrated at his approved rally) for a demonstration to oppose the idea of changing the constitution so that Ramos could run for president a second time, Ramos riposted tartly that Cardinal Sin should be encouraging young Filipinos to learn how to use computers rather than how to demonstrate.

Although the oligarchy has never really lost its power, the Philippines has had a flamboyant, ideological and melodramatic style of politics, highly personalised, highly ideological, but without much serious policy content. Political parties have been mere breezes in the wind, serving the interests of various powerful figures in the oligarchy, forever dissolving and re-forming as power flowed from one oligarch to another. Patronage has been the organising principle of real power, though conflicts have been dressed up in the most soaring and passionate rhetoric.

Ramos was a magnificent circuit-breaker because of his resolute concentration on the practical. In June of 1997 I spent two days as Ramos's shadow, following him wherever he went, eating meals with him, sitting next to him at the grand functions of state and in the presidential helicopter which took us around Luzon.

I arrive at the Presidential Security Group compound in the golf course at Malacanang Palace at 6.00 am as directed, for a typically early Ramos start. Malacanang itself is a symbol of the many discordant cultural influences in the Philippines' past. Built 200 years ago by the Spanish, it was used successively by the Americans, the Japanese and the Filipinos. It is a vast, white and genuinely beautiful building, surrounded by exquisite gardens. Ramos, like Aquino before him, didn't live there because of its unpalatable associations with the Marcos excesses. Inside it is dominated by heavy Spanish formalism, chandeliers, vast curtains, dark wood panelling. This is an undeniable part of the Philippines' cultural inheritance but it seems at odds with the informality and jocularity that characterise the Philippines.

Malacanang is a vastly curious establishment. It houses a little mosque which Marcos built when he planned to host Libya's

Colonel Gaddafi, who never came. Under Marcos it was a military fortress. Even the riverbank at the back was strewn with land mines and the streets around the palace were fortified and closed to the public. Now the political atmosphere is much more relaxed and Malacanang and its environs, like Ramos himself, are much more approachable.

The palace golf course, which houses the Presidential Security Group, is a little nine-hole charmer, with holes named after Greg Norman and other famous visitors. Ramos uses the course as a helipad. Today half a dozen cabinet secretaries and sundry other officials have gathered to fly to the provinces with the president. I have met them all the previous day and now we are like old friends, sitting around the Golf House exchanging gossip. Coffee and rice are served. While we chat in a desultory, bleary-eyed fashion, all eyes stray to the TV where the Chicago Bulls are playing the Utah Jazz—American basketball, a national obsession in the Philippines.

The president's arrival is announced and we are directed to our helicopters. I am sent to Helicopter Two but there is an odd delay. Eventually a security man comes running across the fairway. The president wants me to travel in his chopper with him and the defence secretary, Renato de Villa. Ramos, it soon becomes clear, loves these visits to the provinces. (In his presidential term he visited all 78 provinces at least twice. The visits were part of his perpetual campaigning but also part of an attempt to stay in touch, to bring the government to the people, to liberate it from the confines of Manila's artificial wealth and urbanisation, in what is still a poor and predominantly rural country).

We fly to Nueva Ecija province in northern Luzon. There is one sense in which Ramos reveals himself to me as an absolutely typical South East Asian leader. As we soar above Manila, he enthusiastically points down at factories and real estate developments and industrial parks and auto assembly plants and transport constructions. Like numerous regional leaders, he seems to know and love individually every new factory, every new piece of infrastructure, that provides amenities and jobs for his people. Ramos is an attentive host. For two exhausting days I am never more than a few feet away from the president. Most usefully, in our frequent bus and helicopter rides, at occasional meal breaks and in a final discussion, I have the chance to talk to him at length about Asian values and the Philippines.

We fly north for an hour and arrive at Fort Magsaysay, in Nueva Ecija. We leave the helicopter and walk a few hundred metres to the village of Bagong Buhay. This is the rural Philippines of legend, plenty of cows wandering around, untarred roads and seemingly countless children, cute as can be. There is some dispute, which will be much discussed during the day, about the use of some of the land at Fort Magsaysay. Local villagers use it, as well as people resettled in the area after the eruption at Mount Pinatubo. But it is also a military base and live ammunition is used in training. The combination of the two causes problems.

Ramos tells me the area is a stronghold of the Iglesia Ni Christo church, a millenarian Protestant sect whose churches are designed to function as spaceships on the day of salvation. They had been fierce fighters against the communist Huk rebellion in the 1950s. Today, at our first function in Bagong Buhay, a Protestant pastor starts the meeting with an hortatory, evangelical prayer. Most Philippines civic functions are begun by Catholic priests or bishops muttering the traditional Roman prayers but here, in this little rural village, the style is more Billy Graham in Tagalog.

The mayor (pronounced by Filipinos may-or), a feisty little woman wearing something that looks like a ten-pin bowling outfit, gives a stirring speech of welcome. Ramos, after various ground-breakings and inaugurations, thanks the village for taking in victims of Pinatubo, tells them how much they will benefit economically from the penitentiary to be built in their area, and deals with the land disputes between the army and the villagers. He departs from his written text in one major riff, which he produces whenever the audience contains children: 'You must study hard. Concentrate on your studies, especially maths, English, science and technology.' It is a message that Ramos, an engineer himself who loves gadgets and new technology and communicates with all sorts of people through e-mail, repeats again and again. The previous day, invoking the spirit of the great Philippines nationalist leader, José Rizal, who was executed by the Spanish 100 years ago, Ramos had declared: 'Dr Rizal said we must not be lazy, we must not be indolent, we must educate ourselves.' When he visits the provinces Ramos is a little like the Pope visiting outposts of the Catholic Church, constantly exhorting his countrymen to strive harder, to take up the spiritual struggle, to better themselves. Ramos has crafted all these messages quite consciously during his presidency, wanting to redefine the notion of what is romantic, what is achievement. He wants his countrymen, he tells me, to stop feeling sorry for themselves.

After Bagong Buhay we board buses. I ask Ramos about one of my pet obsessions. Is a free press consistent with Asian values? Will a free press, as exists in the Philippines, ever come to the rest of East Asia? His answer is revealing in its mixture of self-confidence and national self-criticism: 'Yes, it's inevitable. It comes in through the Internet, through TV, even through printed material. I see it everywhere. I even see its beginnings in China. But our press in the Philippines has this problem. There was a survey in Singapore of expatriates which showed that we are considered to have the freest press in the region. But also the worst press. Our press needs to address its quality. It's too dramatic all the time, too ideological, too much based on rumours and opinions. The writing is good but the reporting is poor. That's why too many of our journalists are killed. They concentrate on rumours and melodramatic revelations and derogatory information about people. And their facts are often wrong.'

Our day of traversing the vast tracts of Fort Magsaysay takes us to a firing range, where Ramos answers impromptu questions from the troops, mainly concerning pay and conditions, and then to a huge oval where a vast display of anti-terrorist manoeuvres and firepower is put on for our benefit. Ramos is very approachable, talking freely to whoever is around. He holds an impromptu press conference for local and travelling journalists. The rambunctious Philippines press is certainly unconstrained in what it asks him.

Ramos's presidential term was successful and important, both for the Philippines and for the region. It was important for the Philippines because it got the process of economic growth going for the first time in many years, while preserving the nation's democracy. It gave hope and self-respect back to the Philippines. It was important to the region because it demonstrated that a

poor nation can kickstart development while still a democracy.
By bringing the Philippines back to a position of esteem in the
region the Ramos era reinforced the standing of democracy in
South East Asia. It meant that the Philippines perspective, a
democratic perspective, was added into regional debates and
institutions.

The other figures at the top of Philippines politics are routinely more exotic than Ramos. I went to interview his vice-
president, Joseph Estrada, in his lavish Manila home towards the
end of 1997. Estrada, of course, would win the presidential
election of 1998 handsomely in his own right. (The president
and vice-president are elected separately in the Philippines;
Ramos and Estrada ran on different tickets in 1992.) For a time
Ramos gave Estrada the job of running the Presidential Anti-
Crime Commission, which Estrada did with mixed results. But
later Ramos gave Estrada no job at all and, as Estrada says,
unless the president gives the incumbent a specific task the
vice-president is like 'a spare tyre' in the Philippines system.

It is rather brave, I think, of the generously proportioned
Estrada to talk of a 'spare tyre'. Joseph 'Erap' Estrada became
famous in the Philippines as a movie actor, playing sympathetic
gangsters and good-guy rebel cops in action movies. He went into
politics when he became mayor of San Juan, a town inside
Manila. He is a populist through and through, who tells me he
came to understand Philippines social conditions by doing 'research' for his diverse movie roles. At times he opposed Marcos,
at other times he was a member of Marcos's New Society
Movement. He opposed the presence of the US bases in the
Philippines and for a time called on the Philippines Government
to repudiate its national debt.

When I meet him economic reform is all the go and Estrada
says he will continue, as president, with the liberal economic
policies of his predecessor, Ramos. His primary election promises,
though, are to provide food security for Filipinos and to clean
up crime and corruption, highly worthy but somewhat vague
goals. But the biggest issues hanging over Estrada as a senior
politician are those of character. Estrada has the reputation of a
playboy, which he acquired, along with a number of children from
different women, during his movie star days.

Estrada's San Juan home, like the homes of most of Manila's elite, is in a walled suburb, with access points manned by armed security guards. There are two main buildings in Estrada's residential compound. One building he uses as an office and one as his residence. His staff are as friendly and informal as Filipinos always seem to be. His chief of staff is reading a magazine about jeans as I enter. He is an amiable fellow and tells me there will be a little delay as the vice-president is upstairs 'freshening up'.

This can mean many things. Estrada sometimes takes a massage during the afternoon. Sometimes he likes a nap. He is a late-night person rather than an early riser. Eventually we meet in a lavish sitting room overlooking the courtyard. Estrada strolls in, a roly-poly man, his features seeming an odd contrivance of various bits of various movie stars—his hair looks like Elvis Presley's, there is an Errol Flynn moustache, an open-neck shirt in the style of a John Wayne western, a cigarette in his hand much as Humphrey Bogart had in *Casablanca*. Here is a man who looks the parts. He is disarmingly direct about the playboy stuff: 'I don't deny it. I'm not a hypocrite. I was a movie actor and a young man—you have your flings. But it's an old, recycled issue. What is important is that for seventeen years as mayor, five years as a senator, five years as vice-president, my name was never linked to any corruption or scandal.'

It is one of Estrada's political strengths that he makes a joke of the charges against him. He once quipped: 'It's better to be drunk on liquor than drunk on power.' Now he says of that quip: 'I took it as a slogan. But I'm not a drunkard, I'm a social drinker.' Some of his countrymen find Estrada an irresistible rogue, others a champion of the poor, others find him very frightening. It's certainly unusual to find a senior politician, a contender for his country's highest office, with an image quite like Estrada's. And without wishing to be unfair to him, it does suggest a certain immaturity in the Philippines national political culture.

For a contrast, that same day I go to see another leading presidential contender, Senator Gloria Macapagal-Arroyo, who in 1998 won the election for vice-president. Philippines politics often seems, even these days, to be a game played out by a few dozen families from the landed oligarchy. The diminutive senator has all the right dynastic and familial connections. Her father, Diasdado Macapagal, was the last president before Marcos took over in 1965. We meet in her simultaneously antiseptic and bustling office in the Senate building. Different versions of a painting of herself with her father adorn both her inner and outer office and she says her program is almost identical to that of her father, who has become popular in hindsight, although he was pretty ineffectual as president and failed in his bid for a second term.

There is nothing remarkable in the content of our discussion. She says mostly orthodox things, claiming to emphasise poverty alleviation, moral rejuvenation and the fighting of corruption. Her most passionate comments are about the alleged plots of her opponents to bring her undone. But Macapagal-Arroyo is also a perfect representative of the distinctive Philippines national culture, although she could not be a greater contrast to Estrada. While we talk we sit by an almost life-size statue of the Virgin with votive candles burning at its base. Again, an unusual touch in most political offices, this gesture seems entirely in character in the Philippines.

The Philippines milieu is certainly quite unlike any other in the world. This hybrid nation is unique—and not only unique but seemingly more culturally-distant from any other nation than anywhere else in the world is. Its intimate connections, with Spain, with the United States, seem somehow to have created their own sense of isolation, as though the Philippines' connections are increasingly fossilised elements of history, which do not inform a vibrant contemporary culture. James Fallows in a famous *Atlantic Monthly* article once witheringly described the Philippines as a 'damaged culture'.

This seems a harsh judgement (which culture is not damaged after all?), yet Filipinos themselves can be brutally critical of their own country. Francisco Sionil José is one his country's most distinguished novelists. We meet in a plush coffee shop in Mandalouyong, a rapidly developing business centre which takes some of the overflow of Manila's Makati. José is a portly man in his 70s, balding, immensely friendly and helpful to a foreigner looking to learn something of the Philippines. Most of his novels, including a grand, five novel sequence, are historical. His ambition as a novelist is nothing less than to give his countrymen a national memory.

'There is no memory in this country,' he says. 'Where in the world can you get someone like Imelda Marcos coming back to the hosannas of hundreds of thousands, with hundreds of thousands of people even voting for her? Our departments of history are dying. In my novels I want to give my countrymen an historic memory.

'We suffer from a terrific American hangover, unlike the Indonesians who have no hangover from the Dutch. Forty years of very benign American rule have given us this terrific American hangover.'

The Philippines' relationship with America is infinitely complex and vexatious. The United States originally took control of the Philippines at the end of the 19th century as a result of the Spanish–American war. At the outset, the Americans were brutal. The first use of the term 'gook' was by American soldiers subduing Philippines independentists. But compared to Europeans the Americans were benign colonisers. They realised from the start that their colony would eventually become independent and self-governing, and thus their great historic project was to institute education and development such that the Philippines would be able to undertake independence. The Americans in their way were idealistic colonisers, wanting to spread the democratic idea of the American dream to their subject people. European colonisers did not acknowledge until much later that their subject people were intrinsically their equals and had the right ultimately to independence.

But it is as much as anything the period after the Philippines achieved independence that produced the American hangover. The Americans granted the Filipinos independence immediately after World War II, during which the Filipinos had suffered a savage Japanese occupation and had mounted a particularly courageous anti-Japanese resistance. But power in independence went to the landed oligarchy, most of whom had collaborated with the Japanese. The Americans retained giant military bases in the Philippines and a degree of de facto control over its security and foreign policies. Then, during the Cold War, the Philippines were an important ally for the US in South East Asia. Their bases were 'unsinkable aircraft carriers' and the Philippines Government could be relied on to support controversial American positions. As a result there was never really a decisive psychological break between the Philippines and the US, at least until the Americans closed their giant bases at Subic Bay and Clark Field.

It is this period, from 1945 until 1992, that produced an unhealthy relationship between the Philippines and the US. While the other nations of South East Asia were establishing their independent identities, institutions and habits of regional cooperation the Philippines' gaze was firmly and lovingly fixed on California. It was a relationship not of direct colonisation but de facto colonisation, the same yearning of the distant colony for the metropolitan power, the same sense of mutual proprietorship, special obligation and intimacy. But it also produced a corruption of the Philippines national spirit. Power may well be corrupting but the lack of power is also corrupting. It induces irresponsibility and a cargo-cult mentality.

This has changed through the 1990s. And in any event it is not only the American connection that has distressed thoughtful Philippines nationalists. Frank José is in some ways a representative Philippines intellectual who has been forced by circumstances to adopt what seem many and varying positions on the ideological spectrum. He runs a magazine, *Solidaridad*, which grew out of the postwar international liberal anti-communist organisation, the Congress for Cultural Freedom. It was later revealed that the Congress for Cultural Freedom had been partly funded by the American Central Intelligence Agency, so José is sometimes accused of being a CIA agent.

On the other hand, he describes his politics as radical because he favours a revolution in power relations in the Philippines. For a time under Marcos he supported the communist New People's Army, as the only effective way to oppose Marcos. His novels were seen as subversive and Leftist and he was forbidden foreign travel. And he has always had a lot of friends on the Left.

Yet naturally when Mrs Aquino ran against Marcos for the presidency in 1986 he supported her bid, dismissing the NPA's boycott of the electoral process as a waste of time. Like virtually everyone else he thought Mrs Aquino's presidency a dreadful disappointment. Though a nationalist, he was, late in the debate, opposed to the removal of the American bases simply because of the unemployment it would cause. Then he found the Ramos presidency 'a thousand times better than Aquino'. The oligarchy called José a communist, the Left said he was a CIA agent. So this eclectic intellectual could look as though his ideological positions have been unstable, that he is a gadfly. But in truth José was responding as any intelligent, sensitive man might in the face of unreasonable and desperately urgent political choices. The Philippines often presents you with unreasonable choices.

José sees the greatest problem of his country as a species of moral breakdown. 'This moral breakdown goes way back to when we failed to condemn those who collaborated with the colonisers,' he says. 'The higher up you go the whiter it gets in the Philippines; the mestizos have no faith in the indios.' This is reminiscent of John Le Carré's sad joke about Panamanian society: that the premium on European blood means there is an 'altitude sickness' at work in the society—the higher you go the paler you get.

'No wealthy Filipino has ever been put on trial for collaborating,' José continues. 'Look at those who collaborated with Marcos, they're everywhere again.' Similarly, the Americans, and the Filipinos themselves, failed to punish or demote those who had collaborated with the Japanese during World War II. The portrait of the wartime collaborationist president, José Laurel, occupies a place of honour in Malacanang Palace. In some ways this can be seen as a strength in Philippines national life, a prodigious power of forgiveness and a willingness to acknowledge and accept every aspect of their past. Others see it as a lack of moral judgement and moral commitment.

José sees moral decay in many aspects of contemporary Philippines life: 'The parents of those girls who go to Japan as domestics know they are going to end up as prostitutes. Who pimps for the young boys in Manila? Their parents. There is vast consumerism in this country now. There are no social goals among wealthy Filipinos. I'm at heart a capitalist but capitalism should dignify its profits. Look at the burst of the Japanese bubble. It should have given us the clue. But still much of the investment here went into condominiums and golf courses.

'I would like to see the transfer of power from the oligarchy to the people. Cory Aquino says she restored democracy. That's bullshit! We have empty institutions. The essence of democracy is the stomach. The taxi driver in Washington can eat the same sort of meat as the president. That's not the case here.'

The moral breakdown contributes to a national lack of self-esteem, José believes. 'All Philippines writers want to be published in America. Our doctors proudly display their American qualifications. We call our entertainers Elvis Presleys. Young Filipino-Americans, living in America, have very low self-esteem. They are influenced by so many negative stories from this century. They are culturally weak. They are not well organised politically. They should have terrific clout on the west coast.'

Part of the problem, José argues, is the lack of a classical tradition in Philippines culture. Much of the culture has a folk art quality to it. 'There is not enough good writing,' José says. 'Many of our writers don't work hard enough at what they are doing, unlike the Japanese. It's true what James Fallows said about our damaged culture. We have inherited the vices of our colonisers but not their virtues. In the Iberian peninsula, for example, there is a lack of respect for manual labour. From the Americans we got their megalomania but not their work ethic.'

So much of Filipino conversation automatically assumes an American frame of reference. But what about the process of Asianisation in the Philippines? 'Asianisation is proceeding,' says José. 'But it is not as widespread as it should be. Most people are not very conscious of the Asian environment. I *am* conscious of it. My feeling is that all of South East Asia will eventually be Sinicised.'

José is thinking here of the very long term, perhaps a hundred years away. Yet it's difficult to imagine South East Asian nations acquiescing in cultural Sinicisation, although the Chinese communities certainly provide commercial leadership for the region. Militarily, China's future role is uncertain, but again it seems extremely unlikely that Beijing would be able to gain any undue benefit from the existence of ethnic Chinese minorities in South East Asia. Yet there is a certain fragility in South East Asian culture compared with either the global dominance of the United States or the vast historic and population resources of China.

José is also critical of the national style in the Philippines: 'We're a nation of braggarts and showoffs. Imelda Marcos is the epitome of the Filipino woman. And where in the world do you find men wearing diamond rings, gold necklaces, manicured nails? In the lobby of the Peninsula Hotel in Hong Kong you can tell, if you see an ethnic Malay come in, whether he is a Filipino or an Indonesian. The Filipino swaggers in as if he owns the place. The Indonesian carries himself like a waiter.'

But for all that, José loves his country and does see signs of hope over the long term: 'In spite of my pessimism, in the long run I think we'll be all right. We're a heroic people, very patient, and there is a lot of talent here. Look at all the Filipinos working as managers in Indonesia and Hong Kong. Eventually we'll resolve our contradictions through education. Education is the real answer.'

It is important to all of South East Asia that the Philippines succeed. Along with Thailand, it is the most overtly democratic nation in the region. South East Asia needs successful democracies. But the whole world will be influenced by the Philippines' fate. It is a quintessential cultural mixing pot. As the culturally mixed nations succeed or fail, so the prestige of cultural mixing rises and falls. The Philippines has the ingredients for success: a well-educated people; useful skills such as widespread English literacy; good connections to the West; a useful location in a dynamic region. Its people's particular verbal skills should be most useful in the information age.

The only thing that can really prevent its success over the long term is its sometimes wilfully shortsighted political caste. Its Asian values can be a strength, its Western values can be a strength. In the immensely important Asian values debate, the world needs a Filipino contribution.

3

A TRAGEDY OF SHADOWS:
RETRIBUTION AND
RECONSTRUCTION IN
INDONESIA AMOK

SLEEP. FITFUL. INTERMITTENT. STACCATO. Occupied by lurid dreams and punctuated by violent awakenings.

I am staying in a government-owned hotel in Jakarta. The year is 1991, in the late Suharto period. Outside my room an all-night performance of a Wayang Kulit play—the traditional Javanese theatre of shadows and puppets and Hindu mysticism mixed with Javanese folklore—is taking place. Every so often a loud gong is beaten, disturbing an already disturbed slumber, more exhausting in its way than the half drug-like consciousness of the long, languid, tropical days.

I am a guest of the Indonesian Government, part of a group of Asian journalists touring a seemingly endless succession of factories and government facilities, in Jakarta, Bandung, Jogjakarta. It is exactly like the tours that the mainland Chinese Government provides. Hospitality is lavish, political questions are avoided, countless guides look after us and all that is required of us is that we show up and smile.

Slowly I drift back to sleep. But again a loud interruption. I come to with a start, but this time the gong won't stop. After a few seconds I realise it is not the Wayang gong but the insistent ringing of the telephone. It is late—who can be ringing at this hour? I pick up the receiver to hear a distressed female voice. A Miss Xu, the Chinese delegate on the journalistic mission, is in a room a few doors away.

'Mr Sheridan, please come to my room immediately.'

I dress and walk along to her room. She is a young woman

on her first trip away from China and is deeply upset. It turns out that an unidentified man has been ringing her and asking her to go out with him. He even came and knocked on her door and tried to get into her room. She is very scared and, as she knows no one locally, has decided to call me for assistance.

I follow the obvious route and take her down to reception. We ask to speak to hotel security and after seemingly endless palaver the staff decide that the calls have been coming from a member of a visiting sports team. They will block her line for the rest of the night and place a hotel security man on our floor. Surely this is sufficient to reassure her? But she does not trust the hotel security. Indeed, the visiting journalist from Brunei tells us, the next morning, that the hotel security guards have been pestering him, under the false but common misapprehension that all Bruneians are wealthy, and offering him a girl for the night. He too had had nuisance calls that night.

Finally, after Miss Xu is settled down, her door securely locked, her phone barred, the security man, for what he is worth, posted outside, I give up the unequal struggle for sleep and go downstairs to watch the Wayang for a while. I cannot understand the words but the conflict of the characters, the comedy and drama of their situations, alternately hilarious and desperate, feverish then languid, and the strange rhythms of the drums and other sound effects, are compelling in their way. After a while the play's spell diminishes and I wander off for a breath of air. A luridly made-up young person, garishly bewigged, displaying muscular thighs emerging from beneath a tight miniskirt, perched upon tiny stiletto heels, approaches from the night's shadows and declares in a deep, throaty, unmistakably masculine voice: 'Hullo, sir, I am a girl!'

Ah, Jakarta, city of shadows and deceptions, city of boundless corruption, ubiquitous dereliction, pathos upon pathos. This was Suharto's Jakarta, the other side of the gleaming office towers and new factories; according to some international studies the most corrupt society on Earth.

And yet, of course, it was so much more. As the former United States ambassador to Indonesia, Paul Wolfowitz, has rightly observed, there is no other nation so big or so important about which the US knows so little. With 210 million people, Indonesia is the world's fourth most populous nation. With 85–90 per cent of those being Muslims, it is the world's largest Islamic nation. A vast chain of 13 000 islands stretching out at the bottom of South East Asia, it is also the greatest archipelagic nation.

It has an ancient and intricate history. Hindu and Buddhist kingdoms of great antiquity gradually gave way to the dominance of Islam and subsequently the spread of Western colonialism. From the 16th century the Dutch gradually established their predominance, suffering periodic reverses. The Japanese invaded in 1942 and, as in much of South East Asia, discredited European power even as they came to be opposed by local forces themselves. After the war a bitter independence struggle against renewed Dutch colonialism produced not only an independent Indonesia but the country's first president, the charismatic but erratic Sukarno.

The unity of the Indonesian nation derived only from the common colonial experience. Indonesia was the successor state to the Dutch East Indies. But it embraced hundreds of widely divergent ethnic groups and dozens of different languages. It has been wisely said that every nation tries to become a state and every state tries to become a nation. Indonesia's history, in part, has been that of a state struggling to become a nation.

Sukarno led Indonesia down many strange and unproductive diplomatic and political byways. He tried to oversee a coalition of nationalism, communism and Islam. In the great struggle between the Indonesian Communist Party (PKI) and the Army (ABRI) for control of Indonesia in the 1960s he sided, albeit ambiguously, with the PKI. Sukarno had some notable achievements, among them wresting control of West New Guinea, or Irian Jaya, from the Dutch in 1963. And he was a rallying and symbolically unifying figure for a period. But he suspended Indonesian democracy, disastrously pursued confrontation against Malaysia, led Indonesia out of the United Nations and oversaw the near total wreckage of the Indonesian economy.

An abortive coup involving the communists in 1965 led in due course to Sukarno's overthrow and the gradual assumption of authority by Suharto, a former army general, who went on to rule Indonesia for more than 30 years. Suharto's rule was full of paradox. In the period after the 1965 coup, gruesome

bloodletting, directed primarily at the PKI but much of it uncontrolled and anti-Chinese, resulted in perhaps half a million
deaths. Suharto gradually restored order. At first his regime, the
New Order Government, consulted widely across Indonesian
society. Although it revived elections it did not institute real
democracy. But Suharto substantially handed over the running
of the economy to the so-called 'Berekely mafia', a group of
Western-trained technocrats who reformed the economy along
orthodox, free market lines. Hardly ever has orthodox policy been
so well rewarded. Tens of millions of Indonesians were lifted out
of poverty. The economy diversified away from its reliance on
natural resources and grew a substantial manufacturing and
export sector. Indonesia rejoined the UN and was central in
establishing the Association of South East Asian Nations in 1967.
Its decision to content itself with being merely *primus inter pares*
within ASEAN was an essential ingredient in the stability and
economic growth that the ASEAN states enjoyed from the 1960s
through to the mid-1990s.

But in a pattern familiar to many authoritarian leaders,
Suharto's success contained a paradox which encapsulated its own
destruction. For the rapid economic development that Suharto
oversaw, and by which Indonesia indisputably joined the ranks
of the Asian tigers in the 1980s, with year after year of economic growth of better than 7 per cent, created ultimately
uncontrollable social change which in turn led to a demand for
political change. To visit Indonesia in the 1980s and 1990s, as
I did frequently, was to witness a new civic society yearning to
burst free but kept in check at every point only by crude
authoritarianism.

Indonesians in this period were becoming increasingly cosmopolitan, affluent, diverse and sophisticated. But, as they were
becoming thus, by the early 1990s Suharto was retreating from
his earlier policies of openness and was restricting political life
more and more. Yet it was not really working. You didn't meet
an Indonesian intellectual, official or rank and file civilian beyond
those intimately involved with the administration in this period
who didn't acknowledge the corruption at the heart of the system
or its political dishonesty, even as many of them appreciated the
economic development. The growing influence and business

interests of Suharto's children made things infinitely worse. Only continued rapid economic growth could contain the contradiction inherent in all this.

When that condition evaporated in late 1997 an explosion became inevitable. Suharto's legitimacy had rested on rapid economic growth, social stability and improving economic circumstances for the majority of the population. When all this disappeared so did the legitimacy of the New Order Government. But Suharto ploughed on, relentless and heedless, sacrificing so much that should have been honourable in his legacy. He had himself unanimously re-elected president by the People's Consultative Assembly in March 1998 and appointed a cabinet of cronies, sycophants and relatives. It couldn't last. It didn't last. Protests escalated and amidst looting and rioting of sickening violence, Suharto finally resigned on 21 May 1998, to be replaced by his vice-president and long-time protégé, B. J. Habibie.

Suharto's historic achievements were great but his historic failure was threefold. First, his regime had a bad and unnecessarily brutal approach to human rights, in East Timor, Aceh and Irian Jaya, but also more generally. Second, from the early 1990s, when he reversed his earlier policies of gradual political liberalisation, he intensified the gap between the reality of Indonesian society and the sclerotic political system which could neither reflect nor manage that society.

And third, in combination with this, he refused to make any coherent plan for presidential succession. Thus, with a severely dysfunctional political system, when the economic crisis forced adjustment Suharto had sacrificed the ability of himself or those around him to manage a transition to a more democratic and representative system—as, say, the Kuomintang did in Taiwan while remaining in power, even as it introduced and won fully democratic elections. In this sense Suharto was an unsuccessful authoritarian and one with a limited vision, a limited political imagination.

I went back to Indonesia a few months after Suharto's fall, to see how this nation, which I love so much, was putting itself back together.

There is no getting away from the fact that Indonesia is a very sensuous place . . . the smell of the clove cigarettes, the evening calls to prayer broadcast on Jakarta's countless loudspeakers, the graceful Javanese architectural designs, the constant press of human beings in every state of opulence and squalor. It is impossible not to be moved by Indonesia.

Two little boys, aged maybe five and six, one lying atop the other, perfectly still in the gutter of a main road in the centre of Jakarta. Are they dead?, I wondered for a shocked second. But then they moved and I saw that their momentary stillness, like much stillness in Jakarta, was a product of that perfect tension that two struggling bodies can achieve for an instant.

They were wrestling with each other. Doing so in the gutter, in the middle of the huge traffic roundabout in the front of the Hotel Indonesia, was to risk their lives in the most immediate way. When they saw me looking at them they jumped up and ran over and started shaking little metal tambourine-like devices. The idea, by no means unreasonable, was that I should pay them for bringing this music into my life.

They were two of Jakarta's beggars, whose ranks had been monstrously bloated by the economic crash. Indeed, this was one of the most immediately noticeable changes from the old Suharto days—many more beggars and much more desperation. One of the worst consequences of the economic crisis is the decline in schooling rates it has brought about. Once a kid is taken out of school he or she is most unlikely to go back. Even when the economy picks up again the options of such kids will be severely curtailed, for they will lack the education and skills that the global economy now so ruthlessly demands.

These two were cute kids. Their innocence, and the innocent pleasure they took in playing and wrestling with each other, would break your heart. Perplexed, flummoxed even, by their frank approaches, I hurried on. But I found I couldn't get them out of my mind. Surely these kids had the right to a childhood. In any event, they certainly had a better claim to the few thousand rupiah in my pocket than did any alternative use I could put the money to.

Later that day I was passing the same way, but couldn't see the boys. Instead I gave a few thousand 'roops', barely a couple of dollars, to a mother and infant begging team. As I feared, this meant I got a lot of attention from other beggars on the way back to my hotel. Some of these beggars were pretty sizeable teenagers. The experience was a little disconcerting, but no worse than that, not really threatening. My first reaction was, I suspect, fairly typical. See, I thought to myself, you give money to beggars, you inevitably get hassled.

But then I realised that this attitude was no good. So what if you're hassled. This is Indonesia. The government was saying at the time that, as a result of the economic crisis, something like a hundred million Indonesians were living below the poverty line (although that figure was later revised downwards). Some 40 million were said to be living on less than a dollar a day. A dollar a day! A few dollars and these kids just might eat decently for a week. It's not much but it's better than nothing.

Next day, walking in the same area, the older of the two little boys came running up to me, walked beside me playing his little metallic instrument, smiling a big, toothy grin, as self-confident as you like. Somehow you could just see that this was an intelligent kid. What order has decreed that he should be begging here in Jakarta? Why does he have any less of a right to feel secure and valued, to be at home watching cartoons, having a drink of milk with mum, playing with a toy truck in the backyard, than any American or European or Australian boy? The global financial markets might be as wise as Solomon and as inevitable as the sun, but why did they have to punish him? What did he ever do to the hedge fund managers?

I decided to wait till the pedestrian lights changed to green, then give him a 50 000 rupiah note (less than $10) and walk quickly across the road before a new crowd of beggars could gather. But while I was waiting for the lights to change and looking away pretending to ignore him, I felt some movement near my trouser pocket and turned round to see him trying to extract my wallet. That's fair enough, I thought. I'm sure I'd do the same in his position. I put my hand over my wallet and thought, I'll just wait for the green light and give him the money then.

Unfortunately, a kindly Indonesian woman standing behind me, looking out for an innocent westerner (*bule* in Indonesian), told the kid to leave me alone or she'd tell the policeman. That was nice of her but I wish she hadn't spoken. To my infinite sadness the little boy ran away. He didn't run very far. He was obviously following someone else's rules: his field of operation was limited. This sign of adult supervision didn't act as a consolation—the knowledge that he was not wholly alone—but rather seemed to me an unbearable distortion of what childhood should be; that the adult supervision he was subject to had no better purpose than begging.

I never saw him again. He didn't get his 50 000 rupiah, although he had certainly brought some music with him. I guess he's probably still based at that same roundabout, waiting for traffic or disease or malnutrition to get the better of him.

The proliferation of beggars was merely the most immediate sign of the changes that had taken place. The city's scars from the upheavals of May were evident elsewhere. One morning I drove through the Kota section of town, near the Glodok shopping area, north of the city centre. Much of this precinct was burnt out during the May 1998 riots and looting. Five months later burnt-out cars still littered the streets, building after building was still blackened and deserted.

Astonishingly, a few ethnic Chinese electronics retailers, displaying the almost infinite resilience of the Chinese trader, had got going again. Their character, their courage, in this enterprise were astounding. With a colleague who speaks Indonesian, I asked one shopkeeper whether he supported President Habibie, or one of the main Opposition leaders, Megawati Sukarnoputri (daughter of the late Sukarno), or Amien Rais, leader of the modernist Muslims, or Abdurrahman Wahid, popularly known as Gus Dur, leader of the traditional Muslim Nadhlatul Ulama, as president.

'It doesn't matter who I support,' he said. 'It's no good being Chinese.'

During the riots, in violence against which the authorities took no effective action, hundreds of Chinese shopkeepers were burnt out and looted, perhaps dozens of ethnic Chinese lost their lives and many ethnic Chinese women—officially at least 66 but probably four or five hundred—were systematically gang-raped. The dark forces behind all this were not wholly spontaneous. There was a degree of manipulation by ruthless figures in the military seeking to provoke a chaotic situation such that a heavyhanded military intervention would be justified. But the violence was not wholly orchestrated either. There is still a deep vein of anti-Chinese sentiment among many Indonesians, a sentiment which was never extinguished in the Suharto years. Indeed by favouring a few ethnic Chinese conglomerate bosses, but keeping all Chinese away from political participation, Suharto if anything possibly exacerbated popular anti-Chinese sentiment.

In the course of the May riots some Chinese took shelter for a night or two in one of the five star hotels, all of which the security forces did manage to protect. When the violence died down some left the country. In the wake of all this the courage of the shopkeepers I saw reassembling their businesses and their lives in Kota and Glodok was overwhelming. What was worse was to see in a few weeks time a new burst of looting and burning in the same sections of Jakarta, in the wake of protests at the special session of the People's Consultative Assembly and the killing of some student protesters by soldiers. It seemed that no security was more than very temporary for the city's Chinese.

Shadows. Puppets. Rumours. Whispers. Suggestions.

And conspiracies. Endless, endless conspiracies.

Jakarta's contrasts are multitudinous. Its personality, even at the worst of times, is not only intense but strangely elusive. There is something dreamlike and frequently unreal about the political discourse.

In the elegant, affluent and rarefied surrounds of Menteng, Jakarta's richest inner-city residential precinct, I went for lunch at a friend's house with a small group of Indonesia's political elite. It was a representative sample—a pro-military modernist Muslim, a supporter of Megawati, a couple of journalistic commentators of differing political persuasions, a liberal economist. The conversation turned to one of the most perplexing and distressing subjects of the day—who or what was behind the killings of nearly 200 Muslims, mostly Muslim teachers, in East Java. Many of the victims were members of Gus Dur's Nadhlatul Ulama (NU), which, with 30 million members, is the largest Muslim organisation in the world. It is a traditional, Malay, syncretic and tolerant organisation. Its leader, Gus Dur, is the grandson of its founder and his consistent moderation and political courage throughout the Suharto years have given him immense prestige. NU is bound to be a big player in Indonesian politics and society in the years to come. In the early days after Suharto's overthrow NU formed a powerful alliance with Megawati's Parti Demokrasi Indonesia (PDI).

My interlocutors offered a range of explanations for the killings. The first, a hardy perennial in Indonesia, was to blame it on the remnants of the old Indonesian Communist Party, the PKI.

The PKI had once been one of the great mass-based communist parties of the world. In East Java, where the killings of the Muslim teachers were concentrated, whole villages had been loyal to the PKI, living cheek by jowl with NU villages. In the bloodletting of the mid-1960s, thousands upon thousands of PKI members and supporters were killed. Could the new killings be the work of children and grandchildren of the old PKI stalwarts using this opportunity to wreak revenge? The theory seemed implausible. The PKI throughout the Suharto years had been the great scapegoat of Indonesian politics, a phantasmagorical entity, something like Emmanuel Goldstein in George Orwell's *1984*. It was alleged to be behind labour unrest, student activism, foreign press criticism—a sprawling, shadowy, menacing presence, at once ethereal and deadly.

And yet, hugely unlikely as the theory was as a primary explanation of the killings, the scars of the mid-1960s were still present, the consequences still ran deep, the psychological impact had never been wholly faced. Could there be something in the PKI theory—at least as an important background to the killings? The great virtue of the theory, of course, was that it left every player in contemporary Indonesian politics innocent of blame.

If not the PKI, could it be forces loyal to the former president, Suharto, reaching out from retirement? What would be their purpose? To show their continuing power, to warn that they must not be trifled with? There was no real evidence for this theory, though it was held with great force by some, but like the PKI theory it absolved all the current players from blame.

Could it be that forces connected with Suharto's son-in-law, former special forces commander, Prabowo Subianto, were involved? Ah, no, one luncheon guest replied, Prabowo's name is just being used as a smokescreen to divert attention from Suharto. Perhaps both Suharto and Prabowo would come to occupy the status of a new PKI, able to be invoked and blamed on all occasions and for every purpose.

NU's natural rivals for the loyalty of the Muslims of East Java were various modernist Muslim groups. Could some extreme faction of modernist Muslims be behind the killings? To believe this would be to believe very hard things indeed about the modernist Muslims, or at least some faction of them.

Could it be that the killings were not wholly political? It is difficult for outsiders to grasp just how thoroughly mysticism pervades the lives of people throughout the vast Malay archipelago, embracing Indonesia, Malaysia and the Philippines. Many of those killed had been accused of practising black magic. Many of the killers were identified as blackclad 'ninjas', and so perhaps a whole round of revenge, and even allegedly preventative, killings had been touched off, sometimes against strangers merely wearing black, sometimes against the mentally ill.

Could local score-settling be at work: individuals and groups taking the opportunity to eliminate enemies under the cover of the wider phenomenon? Could the phenomenon be regional? Could regional forces, perhaps criminal networks, be determined to disrupt NU so that it in turn could not become the dominant political force in East Java and disturb existing patterns of influence, patronage and corruption? Could this all be happening without much central coordination at all? And were there other dark forces of which we knew nothing?

All of these possibilities were explored at my Menteng lunch. The reasons for each theory were advanced and rebutted. The discussion was civilised and rational. And at the end of it I was convinced only of how very difficult it is for the outsider, or even the insider, to know with certainty what is really going on at any moment in the vast nation of Indonesia—just how many shadows, how many layers of psychological repression and tribal animosity, overlay what seem to be ideological or even economic cleavages.

Nonetheless, Indonesia was undoubtedly thrown into a crucial ideological debate following the departure of Suharto. At one level, there was a certain apparent ideological unanimity. Everyone in Indonesia post-Suharto was in favour of reform. Everyone was in favour of democracy and a basically free market economy. But if you looked just a little below the surface you saw an infinitely more complex ideological debate taking shape, a debate all the more urgent because of the economic straits into which Indonesia had fallen and the resulting need to reassure international capital markets that the nation was stable enough to consider investing in once more.

Unhedged foreign debt was the heart of Indonesia's economic vulnerability and resolving bad debt proved one of the most difficult tasks for the post-Suharto Government. It was also an acutely important political question, because the resolution of debt would involve the disposal of vast assets which backed the debt. Control of those assets would be an immense financial and political strength as Indonesia started to recover. And so a debate broke out about how bad debt should be resolved.

The orthodox International Monetary Fund (IMF) approach held that the value of the assets should be maximised by having them disposed of in an orderly fashion over a reasonable period of time. This contrasted with an ethnic-nationalist approach which above all wanted to see the assets pass from ethnic Chinese hands into *pribumi* (indigenous) hands. And then there was the populist, political Islam camp which wanted to see at least a substantial share of the assets go to cooperatives with an Islamic flavour.

Apart from general disarray, the impression that Habibie's Government gave, and indeed the impression that most of the Indonesian political elite gave, was of being committed to the IMF reform program (admittedly in its modified, more people-friendly version) purely on pragmatic grounds. There was nowhere else to get the necessary money from, and when Suharto had opposed the IMF he had lost power.

On the other hand, there was a widespread desire to change and reform the conglomerate-dominated economy of Java. Indonesia's outer islands, less heavily populated, less industrialised, more agricultural or natural resource based, did not suffer from the crash of 1997 and its aftermath nearly as badly as Java, where the industrial economy collapsed, leading to millions of newly unemployed.

Mari Pangestu, the immensely sophisticated chief economist at the Centre for Strategic and International Studies in Jakarta, has identified three broad ideological strands in the economic debate. First, political Islam, which, while it might use the rhetoric of the free market, has had a basically socialist inclination and has wanted a more orderly economy with a more egalitarian distribution of income. Second, the socialist democrats, organised around labour unions and often averse to foreign ownership of Indonesian assets. And third, the secular nationalists, who have also tended to emphasise national self-sufficiency. Each of these three strands has had a strong anti-capital and anti-foreign wing and could easily challenge the basic free market orientation of the economy.

In some respects the ideological divisions over the economy are a subset of broader ideological and social divisions within Indonesia. It is worth exploring these briefly. Political Islam has consisted of at least three segments. There have been the modernist Muslims associated with the Muhammadiyah movement, an urban-based grouping of some 25 million members. These have been mostly moderate in terms of an Islamic political idiom and have wanted a modern economy, but they could be stirred up into chauvinistic feelings based on race or religion. Amien Rais emerged as their leader. Then there have been the traditional Muslims, mostly rural, associated particularly with NU and Gus Dur. Although more traditional, more respectful of authority, more 'feudal' according to their detractors, these too have been basically moderate politically and have blended traditional Malay mysticism and Javanese cultural identity in with their Islam. The third grouping might be regarded as a more militant, even extremist, element, although their numbers have appeared rather small.

Certainly a more democratic Indonesia will have a more Islamic flavour. The natural Islamic flavour of Indonesia has been suppressed by the demobilisation and depoliticisation of the Suharto years, and especially its forced secularism under the anodyne mantra of Pancasila, the official state ideology, which stresses belief in one God but does not prescribe Islam as the state religion.

Beyond the Muslim groupings the secular nationalists associated with Megawati Sukarnoputri's PDI have been important inheritors of much of the idealism of the independence struggle. They too have drawn the bulk of their support from at least nominal Muslims but their motivation has been more nationalistic, and frequently more democratic, than that of other groups. They have also gained a lot of support from the 3–5 per cent of Indonesia's population that are ethnically Chinese although, sensibly, numbers of Chinese have felt they should become active in other parties as well.

Beyond these ideological groups there have been two other powerful forces. One is the whole apparatus of patronage and power that was built up under Suharto's New Order. This found its formal political expression in the ongoing Golkar party and in the apparatus of much of the state bureaucracy. How longstanding a force this might be in Indonesian life is unclear, however.

The other major force is the military, which underwrote the political changes. The prestige of the military declined sharply in the post-Suharto period, especially after its brutality in the May 1998 riots (in which sections of the army were implicated in the worst violence) and then in the riots of November 1998 accompanying the special session of the People's Consultative Assembly. During these riots a number of student protesters were killed by soldiers and this increased the contempt in which the forces were held by much of the population. The army's prestige had previously rested on its role both in the struggle for independence and in its guise as a guarantor of stability. The Indonesians, having lived through the terror of the mid-1960s, resemble the Chinese who have lived through the Cultural Revolution. They have a deep horror of big disorder and the terror that can accompany it. That gives them a certain sympathy for the forces of law and order. But the army lost much of its prestige by its spasmodic brutality. Nonetheless, it is difficult to imagine an Indonesia in the near future in which the military is not a significant political force in its own right.

The military's poor human rights record has led, of course, to deep alienation in East Timor, in the northern Sumatran province of Aceh and in Irian Jaya. The greatest brutality, and the greatest disaffection, have been in East Timor.

However, the disaffection felt in particular provinces has

reflected a more general phenomenon: a desire for greater local and regional autonomy. The Indonesian state under Suharto had become hugely centralised in Jakarta and decision making within Jakarta had become centralised in the person of Suharto himself. Some new kind of balance would need to be found between Jakarta and the provinces. This will be a perennial problem for Indonesia. It is so astonishingly diverse a nation that the fissiparous tendencies will probably always need to be countered by some strong centralising and unifying elements of policy and structure. It was with these considerations very much in mind that Indonesia's independence leaders did not choose the majority language, Javanese, as the national language but chose Malay, or, as it is known in Indonesia, Bahasa Indonesia, as the national language. To have chosen Javanese would have been seen by the non-Javanese as a clear act of cultural imperialism. The idealism and the daring, the courage, the romance of the Indonesian national experiment should never be forgotten. Once the Suharto legacy is disposed of perhaps it can be properly celebrated again.

The Islamic populist approach has been associated with the powerful Adi Sosono, who was minister for cooperatives in the Habibie Government and also secretary-general of the Association of Muslim Intellectuals, the group that Habibie himself has used as his power base. Sosono is seen as a ruthless player in Indonesian politics, a man well able to mobilise support in the streets as well as in the mosques and in elite circles.

I interviewed him in his spacious Jakarta office and found him suave, self-confident and plausible. He preached the cause of Islamic cooperatives in terms of economic democracy: 'We have had in the past a concentrated economy which resulted from concentrated political management. Under Suharto this was designed to maintain the status quo. We have to move away from elitism in both politics and economics. We have to move away from an economy in which conglomerates control basic commodities that the people need.'

Sosono wanted Indonesia's cooperatives, of which there are some 7000, to play a much bigger role in its economy. His program of subsidies, interest rate breaks for farmers and import substitution for agricultural production sounded distinctly old-fashioned. I asked him how he planned to finance such expenditures. 'The cost of purchasing rice, if it's produced here, is less than importing it,' he said. 'So we can save on imports. Promoting small business is also good economics. This financial crisis was not the fault of small business but the result of actions taken by big business, so why punish the small businessman?'

None of that sounded like IMF orthodoxy. Rather it was a sign of a vast ideological debate which was under way in Indonesia and which Indonesia must have.

I went one day to interview the strangely confusing figure at the centre of much of the debate, the man who succeeded Suharto as president, B. J. Habibie. We met at the Merdeka Istana, the independence palace, a grand, white, colonial Dutch building in the centre of Jakarta. Manicured lawns, voluptuous gardens, high-ceilinged rooms, chandeliers, the haunting paintings of Indonesian scenes from the late President Sukarno's art collection—it couldn't have been less like the teeming, febrile city outside.

On this day the city is throbbing with threat and fear. Hundreds of heavily armed troops are conspicuous at key points—at the parliament building, at Merdeka Square, at the Hotel Indonesia circle and at the gleaming Merdeka Istana itself.

But, inside, freneticism of a totally different kind reigns. 'Look at these computers. I am the first president to have three computers in my office. Look at my desk. This is the first time in Indonesia's history that this office has been like this. That one is for the stock market, that one is for e-mail, and that's for the Internet.' Bacharudin Jusuf Habibie, a small bundle of atomic energy spinning and buzzing atop the vast nation of Indonesia, explains how he approaches the job of president: 'I was too long in the cockpit. I can read the statistics. I'm running this country like a chief executive . . . But it's not my achievement alone. It's not the performance of one man, but of the whole nation, including those who make demonstrations. They make a contribution too.'

Small, a dapper dresser, voluble, excitable, informal, accessible, Habibie is certainly the ultimate contrast to the aloof and enigmatic persona his predecessor, Suharto, cultivated for so long. There is something indefinably but unmistakably eccentric about his body language. He is always about to giggle nervously, his body is always wriggling and squirming, his hands seem a constant problem. Like everyone else in post-Suharto Indonesia, Habibie talks grandly of democracy: 'I see a system based on human rights and a free market economy. We'll make the only legitimate power the system of the law.'

Indonesia's democrats have always been suspicious of Habibie because for so long he was a protégé of Suharto's, going back to his childhood and a period of military service undertaken by Suharto in Habibie's home province of Sulawesi. For a long time Habibie's affectionate nickname for his old boss was SGS—Super Genius Suharto. Suharto apparently didn't hold quite the same opinion of Habibie, for although he had appointed Habibie as vice-president, in his last-ditch effort to hang on to office Suharto said that one reason he could not resign was that people would not accept Habibie as president and he too would be forced to resign. Another ground for distrust of Habibie was his 20-year record as technology minister, during which time he mostly rejected orthodox free market ideas and focused instead on the development of strategic high-tech industries, which were regarded by his critics as being of dubious quality, highly expensive, inefficient and a drain on scarce state resources.

But at our meeting Habibie portrays himself as a logical progression from Sukarno and Suharto: 'The first president [Sukarno] had a mission to implement the independence declaration of the people and the constitution. But 95 per cent of the people were illiterate and there was no infrastructure for them, no information infrastructure or education or whatever. So the only way to avoid counterproductive fights was to concentrate all power in one man, which was not incompatible with the constitution. Then in 1955 he tried to make the first election in a democracy. But there was no infrastructure etc, so in 1958 he returned back to power concentrated in one man. So power-brokers grew up around him and the compromises between them were not always the best solution.

'So he faced the abortive coup in 1965 and two years later he had to step down and in came President Suharto. He had to follow a similar system of power concentrated in one man because the nation was facing big instability. Under the first president, illiterate people had been reduced to 60 per cent. So Suharto surrounded himself with technocrats and he himself was a technocrat. He could operate with them effectively because he was a very, very rational person . . . Based on this system we Indonesian people enjoyed sustainable economic growth and this contributed to the Indonesian miracle. But since power was still concentrated in Mr Suharto he found himself surrounded by political brokers; then, after about ten years, by business brokers as well. For the first 20 years political brokers and business brokers did not make accommodations between themselves. They were two different types and not connected to each other. Mr Suharto could face them because he was very rational and very influenced by the technocrats up until the last ten years of his rule.

'He had a big family of six children and they became used by brokers for power. So for the first time there was not a rational but an emotional basis for power. There were only six avenues for power. So for the first time the business and political brokers coincided and thus you have collusion. This creates more problems. His wife passed away and the interwoven system became more complex. Then we had what happened in May [the riots which deposed Suharto]. Then I came into the picture.

'The picture was different. The illiterate were only 4 per cent, intellectuals were 10 to 20 per cent. For the first time a president could implement systematically what was in the constitution. So today is a result of 53 years of marching of all the people.'

Habibie's interpretation of history is certainly contestable. But it puts him in a process of political evolution. Unlike Suharto, he points out, he had had 20 years in parliament before becoming president. But the Indonesian parliament under Suharto was such a tame beast that it is not clear that service there really helped anyone develop the type of political skills necessary in a democracy.

The contradiction in Habibie's outlook in some ways mirrors the contradiction in Indonesia's political system: wanting to identify with reform, wanting to be seen as brand new, but still mired in all the old, and for many Indonesians unacceptable, practices of the past. For example, he has supported a continuing, overt political role for the military in Indonesia's political life, the notorious *dwifungsi* or dual function, in which the military play a civic/political as well as a military role. 'You have to look at the military in Indonesia with different spectacles,' he says. 'The military was established out of the people's struggle for independence. The armed forces were born from their mother, the people, who were 95 per cent illiterate and had suffered 350 years of colonisation. The armed forces had three roles—to protect the people, to defend the people and to help the people overcome their innocent, helpless situation because they are illiterate. These three values became their soul and you cannot change your soul. Even if you talk about a company like IBM it has a corporate culture, and this is the military's soul. The military is the only organisation in the history of my country which has always been loyal to the constitution and proactive in taking care of the unity of the nation.'

These comments of Habibie's seem seriously at odds with the reputation that Indonesia's military has earnt by its brutality in Timor, Aceh and Irian Jaya, by its heavy involvement in business activities, by the involvement of some of its special forces in human rights abuses in Jakarta and elsewhere in Java, and by its heavyhanded and clumsy dealing with demonstrators throughout 1998.

At the same time, it would be wrong to think that all Indonesian civilians hold the military in contempt. Many think of it, despite its past lapses, as the only guarantee of stability. This view emerges when I gather a group of young professionals together to see how they are coping with the economic crisis and to learn what they think of their country's future.

'I loved New York but I could never live there permanently,' says Mata. She is a young Indonesian woman, in her mid-20s, short-cropped hair, smartly groomed, a professional working for a local advertising company. We meet in a Jakarta coffee shop in a five star hotel. She is eating a burger and chips, I am having nasi goreng. Outside, the usual trouble and violence are rolling around the city.

But I can understand her desire to be in Indonesia—its warm, sensuous charms, the characteristic smells, the daily Muslim calls to prayer, loyalty to her family, the ineluctable call of ancestral voices . . .

Why, I ask, expecting some such more or less romantic answer, would she not live permanently in America?

'New York would be a hardship post for me. I couldn't have a maid.'

The practicalities of everyday life are uppermost in most people's minds in most places most of the time, even in Jakarta, even at a time of riots, perhaps especially at a time of riots. For several days during the riots which brought down Suharto, people could not get out of their homes and just getting food from a supermarket became a big issue for many middle-class families.

I ask Robby how he feels about the new spirit of democracy and openness in Indonesia, especially in the Indonesian press. Also in his 20s, Robby, slim, bespectacled, dapper, working for a commercial firm in the city, unlike Mata has never lived abroad. He is a sophisticated young man with good English and I expect an enthusiastic endorsement at least of Indonesia's new press freedoms. But once again the answer is not exactly according to my script: 'Yes, it's more open now, but it's like a teenager who is let loose, let out of their house for the first time. There's a feeling of madness and chaos about it. I don't find the press anymore interesting. They offer no solutions.'

Mata chimes in: 'My mother's an avid reader now because our tabloid press is full of "I was Tommy Suharto's girlfriend" type stories, but it's all negative, it's all trashing the former president. Now the press is able to open boxes of secret stories. It's like an Indonesian *X-Files* every day.'

Nonetheless, Mata and Robby want the new openness of the press to continue. But they were shocked by the violence that accompanied Suharto's overthrow and they are suffering from the difficulties imposed by the economic crisis, and Mata says openly that she would dearly love to return to the stability and amenity of the past.

They are both Muslims but differ sharply on the role Islam should play in Indonesia. 'From the point of view of a Muslim, I would have to say that the role of Islam should be bigger,' says Robby. 'The flavour of Islam in everyday life is declining now. I don't want to have Islamic law enforced but I would like to see the Islamic spirit of Indonesia back to what it was when I was younger, with people visiting each other's homes on Muslim festivals, for example.'

Mata disagrees: 'I hope life doesn't get more Islamic. I'm Muslim but I like religion to be private. I don't want Islam to be more of a political force. But the majority of people are Muslims living outside the big cities. The majority hold the traditional view that Islam is exclusively right and other religions are wrong.'

Jusuf Wanandi, one of Indonesia's most distinguished and influential intellectuals, and the moving force behind the Centre for Strategic and International Studies, tells me that if Islamic law were ever enforced even only for Muslims (which was envisaged when the state ideology of Pancasila was first drafted, but after much debate was left out of the final formulation and is roughly the situation in Malaysia), it would lead to non-Muslims becoming second-class citizens.

Habibie too had been cautious about any change in the role of religion in Indonesia, telling me: 'All the people living in this state are very close to God. However, we are not a government based on religion even though we are a very religious people. We are not an Islamic state even though 90 per cent of our people are Muslim. We are not a kingdom but a republic. But we are not a secular state either but a state based on Pancasila.'

Pancasila has for more than 50 years been the official state ideology of Indonesia, first proclaimed by Sukarno in 1945. It prescribes belief in one God (though no state religion), humanism, nationalism, democracy and social justice as its five guiding principles. It became content-free, an anodyne collection of platitudes, under Suharto, except for its use as a device to justify repressing Islamic political expression.

However, in many long discussions with Indonesians other than government officials, I almost never hear Pancasila mentioned. Even when talking with government officials it is rare to hear it raised.

But nationalism, and the desire to find an accommodation in politics, business and culture that retains distinctively Indonesian attributes, are frequently raised. Robby and Mata and their friends are committed to the global economy but they don't like the way it tends to override local culture. Says Mata: 'I hate it that my nephews and nieces collect Mickey Mouse and are hooked on *MTV*, but don't know the Wayang characters.' Wayang Kulit, the traditional Javanese puppet theatre, has become a universal symbol of Indonesian culture.

Ida, a slightly older friend of Mata and Robby, is a Christian and works in public relations. She agrees with Mata: 'My seven-year-old nephew said of Princess Diana's death that Princes William and Harry would grow up and take revenge on the paparazzi. I told him in the Bible there is forgiveness, but he said, what about in the *Lion King*—Simba grows up thinking of revenge on the hyena who killed his father. It's so hard for us to stop them from watching the *Lion King*. They like Tom and Jerry too, but do they really have any cultural choice? Why aren't there Indonesian cartoons? When they are made they are popular but there are so few of them.'

Robby doesn't worry so much about Western cultural influences, thinking that attentive parents can screen in the good and screen out the bad. Not only that, he prefers elements of the Western approach to child-rearing: 'Take the relationship between children and parents. Specifically in Java, but also all over Asia, children can't express themselves as well as American kids and that's not a good thing. In the West they have a dialogue with their parents, whereas here they have only a monologue from their parents. I'm a product of the system of not being able to express myself as a kid, so that at work even now I tend not to be assertive.'

Robby thinks he is a bit better off in this respect than some of his fellow Indonesians, however, because he originally came from Sumatra, and Sumatrans are proverbially more forthright than Javanese, who are characteristically reluctant to say no or to force a social confrontation directly.

Frans Winata, a well-known human rights lawyer, believes Indonesians badly want democratic change and a more open system, but he acknowledges that there are elements of traditional Indonesian culture that support authoritarianism: 'Indonesian culture is very feudalistic and paternalistic. The idea was that the leaders can do anything they like. Javanese kings were served by the people, they didn't serve the people. Even under Dutch colonialism the thinking was very state-oriented.'

But Mata, Robby and Ida remain optimistic about Indonesia's future, long-term. Says Robby: 'This crisis won't last and anyway we are coping with it. I still believe my children will have a bright future, though perhaps not as opulent as in the years just past.'

All three agree that they want to see an Indonesia in which ethnic origin plays no role in civic life and in which all are considered Indonesians pure and simple. But the jealousy and hostility towards Indonesia's ethnic Chinese minority seem almost ineradicable. This stands in stark contrast to a neighbour like Thailand, where the ethnic Chinese have blended in and been accepted much more. The treatment of the ethnic Chinese in Indonesia has been worse than in other parts of South East Asia. Moreover, their situation is consistently exploited by political forces for political ends. Way back in the 1960s, when mainland China was giving moral support to the communists in Indonesia, the military in particular linked ethnic Chinese Indonesians with the mainland Chinese Government and stirred up anti-Chinese sentiment.

Frans Winata believes the process was continued, in a different way, under Suharto. Winata himself is a third generation Indonesian on his mother's side and a fifth generation Indonesian on his father's side, and he does not speak any Chinese language, but no one would consider him anything other than an ethnic Chinese Indonesian.

'The problem of Suharto's New Order Government was that it worked on slogans,' he says. 'Unity is very important but the regime refused to openly discuss issues of pluralism and multiculturalism. Suharto always discussed Indonesian politics as though it were Javanese politics. He used Javanese symbols. Since 1965 the Chinese have been the target of every episode of social unrest. Suharto groomed Chinese-owned conglomerates but this only increased the envy and jealousy of the pribumis. But at the same time Suharto refused the political rights of the Chinese. There were no Chinese ministers or legislators and few Chinese judges. The Chinese were allowed to participate in the economy but were seen only as economic animals. Anywhere in the world, if you're politically weak but economically strong you're in danger.'

Winata refers to periodic anti-Chinese remarks by Indonesian leaders to show how easily they revert to the anti-Chinese tactic when they are under pressure, or when they need to rouse populist sentiment and polarise political emotions. He thinks perhaps 100 000 Chinese have in recent years left Indonesia to live abroad. This is greatly damaging to the Indonesian economy and to Indonesian society, but in any event departure is an option not available to most ethnic Chinese. 'It's quite clear that the rapes [of ethnic Chinese women in May 1998] occurred on a systematic basis. They were done by professional terrorists and they were systematically done. Ethnic Chinese Indonesians are scared and paranoid. I've spoken to victims of the gang rapes; they are terrified, some want to give up, some want to commit suicide.'

Winata believes it is crucial for Indonesia's future that ethnic Chinese become politically active and politically visible: 'The most realistic thing would be to join the big political parties and fight all discrimination, not only against Chinese but against other minorities like the East Timorese and the Papuans.'

Amien Rais, former leader of Muhammadiyah and a recognised leader of the modernist Muslims, expresses sympathy for the Chinese Indonesians. At a meeting he tells me: 'I can understand, because of their experiences in May 1998, my Chinese brothers and sisters feeling abandoned. Not a single policeman defended their property. The people of Indonesia were stunned and couldn't believe they had witnessed such acts of ethnic hostility, such unbelievably disruptive acts against people of different race or creed. But I still believe the social explosion was caused not by religion or race but by the widening differences between rich and poor. A hungry man is an angry man. There were many hungry people in Indonesia provoked by irresponsible politicians and especially the Suharto Government. But in the rich and poor conflict the rich happened to be Chinese.'

Rais himself has in the past made comments that ethnic Chinese Indonesians found unhelpful, but in his contemporary guise he is liberal on issues of race. He was the key figure in leading, organising and controlling the demonstrations that ultimately were crucial in bringing down Suharto. I have interviewed him and heard him speak on several occasions and find him a highly skilled politician, adept at crafting the nuances of his message to his audience while sticking to an essential common theme.

Like Winata, he believes Indonesians will have to overcome elements of their traditional culture if they are to become fully democratic: 'There is a cultural handicap to having a flourishing democracy in Indonesia. The Indonesian people still have a paternalistic and feudalistic view. Equality before the law, the basic idea of equality of all people, is quite new. So what we need is a two-pronged process—to establish free elections, freedom of the press and so on but also to try to cultivate a new paradigm of culture among our people, a paradigm which is democratic and egalitarian.'

Rais is one Asian leader who does not see much merit in the term Asian Values: 'Asian Values are a kind of protection on the part of Asian leaders, to justify behaviour which is not democratic. To me, democratic values are universal. Asian Values were really a ploy to defend undemocratic actions.'

Like many other Indonesians, Rais is confident that Islamic extremism will not be a determining factor in Indonesia's future: 'Look back at our history. Indonesian Muslim leaders accepted Pancasila and helped formulate its principles. That was a very strong indication that Muslim leaders did not want to force Islam on others. The prospect of an Islamic state can be put away altogether. The mainstream is very moderate and Muslims accept democracy as fully in accordance with Islamic teachings. I lived and studied in Chicago for seven years—I know some of the weaknesses of democracy and also its strengths. No political system is perfect but democracy is best.'

Rather dangerously, many reform-minded Indonesians have enlisted international opinion as an actor in domestic politics in favour of reform and democracy. This is understandable and international opinion can have a beneficial effect, as in the case of South Africa when it was moving towards dismantling apartheid. But to be long-term and effective, political reform must come from within. It must not be seen to be forced on the society from outside. There is no doubt a desire within Indonesia for political reform and a much more open and representative civic society. But the long years of Suharto stunted all political development. As Winata put it: 'Sukarno thought that if you solved the political problem then everything else would work out of its own accord. Suharto thought that if you solved the economic problem everything else would be OK. But really the economy, politics, social life and the law all have to be developed simultaneously. They all have to go together.'

The issues to be resolved in Indonesia are fundamental—the role of Islam, the shape of a long-term political system, the place of the ethnic Chinese, the balance between the centre and the provinces, the place of other ethnic minorities such as the Timorese and Papuans, the nature of the economic system, Indonesia's place within the global economy. The long years of stability under Suharto were as deceptive as an Alpine snow mass, which from its vast impassivity can suddenly come crashing down in a frightening and transforming avalanche. The task of reconstruction, not the sterile pleasures of revenge, must be the priority, not only for Indonesia's sake but for the sake of her neighbours, and indeed for all of us, who need the contribution of the Indonesian genius to the great human discourse.

4

SINGAPORE: ORIGIN, EPICENTRE, EXEMPLAR

IN 1994 AN AMERICAN student, Michael Fay, was convicted in Singapore of vandalism and of writing graffiti on cars. He was sentenced to six strokes of the rotan, later reduced to four. Despite intervention from the American president himself, and an accompanying vast international uproar, the Singapore Government went ahead with the punishment.

Although basically a trivial incident, the caning aroused uproar in both Asia and the United States. Here in some ways was a perfect clash between Asian values and Western values. If there has been a single unifying theme in popular Western culture since the 1960s it has been the youth cult, the glorification of youth itself, and the accompanying glorification of rebellion against authority, an attitude of permanent scepticism towards established patterns of command. The loner rebelling against the norms of the group is the archetypal Western hero, the figure locked in some existential dilemma of self-expression, with full self-realisation as the only psychologically approved goal.

What could be further from the Asian ideal? If there is one unifying idea in Asian values it is the idea of authority, especially the deference due from the young to the old, and above all the authority of the legitimate organs of state power over the citizen. Michael Fay's offence could thus be seen as both a revolt of the young against the old and a denial of the legitimate authority of the state in which he was a guest.

Moreover, there was a clash of power here. Although the use of the rotan had not previously exercised American public opinion as a human rights issue when it was used only against Singaporeans, the 'usual suspects' in the Western human rights debate (especially the *New York Times*) were inflamed with righteous anger at the Singaporean authorities daring to enforce their own law in their own country against an American.

That the American Government bought into such a matter at such a level—the president, for goodness sake!—was preposterous and in its way a low point of American standing in the region. Washington could not help but look a bully, and its bullying was ineffective anyway. The Singapore Government itself would have looked intolerably supine had it given in to official US pressure.

But one of the most perplexing aspects of the case, for those who posit simple Western–Asian dichotomies, was the degree of support Singapore won in Western public opinion—including, perhaps especially, American public opinion—for the action it took. From the crime-filled streets of American cities came the single, resounding cry: Give us (or at least our uncontrollable teenage males) the firm smack of Singapore-style government.

Importantly, the fracas was not allowed by either side, Washington or Singapore, to disturb the de facto strategic partnership between these two hugely unequal states although, again preposterously, it did lead Washington to argue, ineffectually, against Singapore's hosting the first ministerial meeting of the World Trade Organisation. But this was seen by hardheads in both countries as little more than falderal. For although it avoids a formal alliance relationship with the United States, Singapore is the single most enthusiastic proponent of the necessity and overall benefit of deep American security involvement in the region.

The Michael Fay case was essentially trivial but because it evoked responses concerning issues of relevance to both Asians and Americans (and other Westerners)—namely crime and punishment, youth rebellion and authority—it became for a while the focus of the Asian values debate. But this itself was only possible because Singapore more broadly is the epicentre of that debate. Singapore's redoubtable long-time leader, Lee Kuan Yew, who formally retired as prime minister in 1990 but retains enormous influence in Singapore and throughout the region, has been one of the two Asian leaders most associated with the idea that Asian values are different from the West's values and perhaps superior to them, or at least not inferior, and certainly worthy of consideration. The other leader is Malaysia's Dr Mahathir.

But to confine Singapore's contribution to the Asian values debate to Lee Kuan Yew would be a serious injustice. First, it would unfairly diminish the contribution of Lee's successor as prime minister, Goh Chok Tong, other ministers such as George Yeo, thinktank leaders like Tommy Koh and senior civil servants like Kishore Mabubhani, who defended the Singapore way in a series of articles in the influential journal *Foreign Affairs*. And second, Singapore itself, its society, has become a central exhibit in the argument about Asian values.

I have been a frequent visitor to Singapore for nearly 20 years and I must say that when I am there I don't recognise the Western stereotype of the place at all. Those who don't travel in South East Asia are likely to be aware of Singapore in only one or two respects—apart from its status as a shopping destination. They may have heard of Lee Kuan Yew, and the legend of his strategic sagacity. Or they may have heard about some of the numerous minor and occasionally irksome social regulations that Singapore has enacted—things such as banning cigarette smoking in public places, the heavy fines for littering, regulations about the length of men's hair, fines for not flushing public toilets, or the banning of chewing gum. In the Western stereotype of Singapore these restrictions have a quite undue prominence. They distort the image.

The chewing gum regulation, as Kishore Mabubhani has pointed out, is the source of endless ridicule among the *bien pensants* of the West. Yet, he tartly observes, in virtually every major American city crack cocaine is freely, if illegally, available. So which is the real transgression of human freedom—the crime and destruction involved in the ready availability of crack, or the sense of social order coded into the marginal loss of personal freedom in the chewing gum ban? Which city in the end is more concerned for its citizens?

I have heard George Yeo, a senior Singapore minister, and one of the leading intellectuals in the Singapore Government, argue that the question of Singapore's smallness has to be factored into these considerations. Many of Singapore's social regulations are akin to a small American city's deciding that it will not have the Playboy Channel as part of its cable TV mix. It's not really the end of civil liberties as we know it.

Of course, there are limitations in Singapore on the Opposition and it is not a liberal democracy in the accepted Western sense. Nonetheless its democracy is real, it is not a sham. Its elections are clean and honest. More importantly, freedoms, all kinds of freedoms, abound in Singapore. There is no sense at all that the government is illegitimate, that the population wishes it had another government. There is absolute freedom of religion in Singapore, there is of course freedom of movement. And very many of Singapore's prosperous, well-educated population could gain acceptance as emigrants to other countries if they wished to, so this is not an empty freedom. There is certainly freedom of commerce and the reliable rule of law, such that Singapore is one of the least corrupt and fairest business environments in Asia.

Moreover, Singapore does not have the feel of authoritarianism about it. From the vast temples to shopping in Orchard Road, to the night life of Buggis Street and the island's seemingly countless discos and bars, to the steaming curries of Serangoon Road and Little India, to the street that specialises in Arab carpets, from the chilli prawns at Ponggol Point to the decent, orderly home units provided by the Housing Development Board, to the vast financial reserves so many Singaporeans build up through the Central Provident Fund, to the almost universal affluence of the place, Singapore does not look or feel like a society groaning under political authoritarianism. Most of all it does not feel authoritarian when you meet and talk to Singapore's people. They are opinionated, diverse and forthcoming, from the taxi driver to the stockbroker. More than that, they are extremely well informed. Singapore is technologically a very switched-on society and technology these days means information. It is also a very well-travelled society. Nestled in the heart of South East Asia, it is almost impossible to meet a Singaporean who has not been outside his own country and seen some other version of the good life to compare with Singapore's.

Yet the boldness of Lee Kuan Yew's complex intellectual challenge to the idea that Western social norms are universal and

must be automatically regarded as the best, while at the same time
Lee profoundly appreciates the American contribution to strategic
stability in his region, makes Singapore perplexing to Western
triumphalists. It also makes it intriguing to many other Asians.
The mainland Chinese leadership, for example, used to be highly
critical and downright dismissive of Singapore. Not any longer.
Singapore is an attractive model for the mainland Chinese, for it
has combined a thoroughly successful contemporary capitalist
economy with social order, hierarchy and authority. Beijing finds
the combination much more attractive than what it used to see
as a kind of moral anarchy in Hong Kong and Taiwan (though of
course now that Hong Kong has returned to the motherland,
Beijing can take pride in Hong Kong's achievements).

Of course, all this can be overstated. Singapore is an island
nation of three million people. China is an almost unimaginably
populous nation of 1.2 billion. Nonetheless, Singapore as a social
experiment—from Beijing's point of view highly successful in all
the things that make the West desirable, yet unlike the West in
critical respects—is endlessly fascinating.

The same attitude applies in a different way among the
Vietnamese. They believe there may be lessons to learn from
Singapore.

Lee Kuan Yew has provided us with such a splendid discourse
on values, culture, economics and strategic issues over the decades
that there is a temptation simply to plunder his speeches for
endless bon mots. That temptation should be resisted, but he
has also provided in succinct form an excellent definition of what
he regards as the essential elements of Asian values.

In a speech entitled 'Changes in Singapore: The Obvious and
the Imperceptible', which he delivered to students of the National
University of Singapore and Nanyang Technological Institute in
1988, Lee directly addressed the core of Asian values, as he saw
them, before the term came into vogue. First he drew some
comparisons among the three main cultures of Singapore—
Chinese, Indian and Malay:

> I am not familiar with basic Malay and Indian values as much
> as I am with Chinese values. But I do not believe there's all that

much disparity between the Asian cultures. The Malays are least under assault because they have religion—Islam. The strongest single factor in any culture is your religion. It is the book by which you live, your behaviour, your rituals, your prayers, the things you say and do, your day of remembrances. And theirs is strong and resurgent. The Indians, more than the Chinese, attend their temples, keep to custom. I agree . . . that Indians have changed less than Chinese. Malays, least of all. Indians still observe their customs, still have arranged marriages.

But then Lee, having made a praiseworthy attempt to link the three main Asian traditions of Singapore, moved on to what he really saw as the core of everything—Confucianism, or traditional Chinese values. He said:

What is it that we should consider core values? I don't think how you dress, whether you wear shorts or ties or open-neck shirts, or wear your hair short or long, makes the slightest difference. Unless it's a manifestation of an inner urge. But these core values, I believe, are basic. Do you consider your basic values to be fundamental? The human relationships. What Confucius described as the five critical relationships. Mencius epigrammatised it in this way. I read it to you in translation—'Mo Tze taught the people how to cultivate land. He appointed Xie as the Minister for Education, whose duty was to teach the people human relationships. Love between father and son, one; two, duty between ruler and subject; three, distinction between husband and wife; four, precedence of the old over the young; and five, faith between friends.' Father and son, ruler and subject, husband and wife, old over young, faith between friends. In other words, the family is absolutely the fundamental unit in society. From family, to extended family, to clan, to nation.
    In the West, with the tendency of modern government taking over more and more the functions of caring for the young and caring for the old, and in fact, caring for everybody—the unemployed, the disabled and so on—the family is becoming irrelevant. So much so that half the children born in some American societies are born out of wedlock. They are living together but they don't feel there is any need yet to make a commitment to each other. But they have committed to the next generation . . .

These are themes Lee has explored again and again. On one occasion when I interviewed Lee I asked him directly whether Chinese values had been important to Singapore's success. His response was equally direct: 'Without them we could not have done it. No amount of exhortation, laws or coercion could have done it. There have to be those cultural underpinnings in the people: a desire to be educated, to acquire knowledge, to be useful.'

The notion of the family as central to the functioning of a decent civil society and also as a metaphor for the political arrangements of that society is thus at the heart of Lee's conception of Asian values. Many Western politicians have at times conceived of the state as a giant version of the family. It is a favourite political metaphor. But for Lee, and for many Confucians, it is more than a metaphor—it is a genuine operating principle, it is the underlying structure not only of society but of the state, of politics. It corresponds in some respects to the traditional Western notion of the natural law, that there is a natural, basic order in human affairs which state arrangements should seek to reflect. The state should do this by reinforcing those relationships in social life, such as by welfare and other economic measures that support rather than undermine the authority of the family. But this pattern should also provide a basic design for the state itself. In Lee's case he argues that the relationship between citizen and government is something like that between son and father. This model certainly implies a hefty dose of submission to legitimate authority.

At both levels it's important not to overstate things or to forget the limits which even Lee applies to his neo-Confucianism. In Singapore you are certainly allowed to live an unconventional life, but the state won't subsidise it. Instead the state will subsidise the social arrangements it thinks are most beneficial for society. Moreover, Confucianism, even neo-Confucianism, is not a mandate for a ruinous, oppressive or irresponsible government. Lee has also often praised the salutary effect which Singapore's clean elections have on the Government. If the Government really lost legitimacy with the people they could throw it out.

But it is in social affairs that Western commentators frequently berate Singapore for being, allegedly, harsh and repressive.

Yet this is unfair. It is much more really that Singapore has decided to use welfare policy and Budgetary resources to reinforce the type of society it wants to be, rather than subsidise lifestyle challenges to that society. Whereas much of Western welfare is designed to help ameliorate the conditions of the dysfunctional, much of Singapore's substantial income redistribution efforts are directed towards reinforcing the 'functional', providing incentives for people to be functional. This happens in a myriad of ways. It is easier and cheaper for a married couple to get finance to buy a home than it is for cohabiting unmarrieds or independent singles. Health benefits are stronger for families than for individuals. The Housing Development Board has built tens of thousands of apartments which provide a good, decent standard of accommodation. They are designed and meant for a traditional family unit and individuals practising alternative lifestyles have difficulty obtaining such apartments. There are financial penalties attached to being a single mother.

This may seem harsh in particular cases but it is hard to argue that it has been broadly unsuccessful. However, it brings us to another fascinating conundrum in the Asian values debate. Lee's Confucian vision is not so radically different from the vision of traditional Christian politicians in the West, especially, say, the Christian Democrats in Western Europe. They too see a basic moral order in human affairs governed to a substantial degree by the place individuals occupy in the web of normal human relationships—father, son, wife, mother, daughter, ruler, subject. Even under a democratic model this basic idea is not necessarily lost. Nor are all these notions as anachronistic as the notion of the divine right of kings. I can remember at my Catholic primary school being taught that all legitimate authority, the authority of the teacher over his students, the authority of the government through laws over its citizens, was a reflection of God's authority.

One question then is whether Lee's vision of Asian (or, as he prefers to call it, Confucian) values is really Asian and essentially non-Western, or merely more traditional than currently fashionable notions in today's Western societies. While this is not the most important question about Asian values, it is worth some exploration.

In an interview with the American journal *Foreign Affairs*, in 1994, an interview which became something of an icon in the Asian values debate, Lee had good things and bad things to say about America. He admired its historic achievements, and socially he admired the easy, democratic way in which Americans of diverse backgrounds could relate to each other. But he had some telling criticisms to make as well:

> As a total system I find parts of it totally unacceptable: guns, drugs, violent crime, vagrancy, unbecoming behaviour in public— in sum the breakdown of civil society . . . The liberal intellectual tradition that developed after World War II claimed that human beings have arrived at this perfect state where everybody would be better off if they were allowed to do their own thing and flourish. It has not worked out and I doubt if it will.

A similar view of America, and the West more generally, was put by Lee's successor, Goh Chok Tong, in his National Day speech of 21 August 1994. He drew a stark contrast between what he regarded as the solid virtues of Singapore and the decadence of the West. The speech is worth quoting at a little length:

> Singaporeans today enjoy full employment and high economic growth, and low divorce, illegitimacy and crime rates. You may think decline is unimaginable. But societies can go wrong quickly. US and British societies have changed profoundly in the last 30 years. Up to the early 60s they were disciplined, conservative, with the family very much the pillar of their societies. Since then both the US and Britain have seen a sharp rise in broken families, teenage mothers, illegitimate children, juvenile delinquency, vandalism and violent crime. In Britain one in three children is born to unmarried mothers. The same is true for the US . . .
>
> We [in Singapore] intend to reinforce the strength of the family. The government will channel rights and benefits and privileges through the head of the family so that he can enforce the obligations and responsibilities of family members. We will frame legislation and administrative rules toward this objective . . .
>
> Western liberals, foreign media and human rights groups also want Singapore to be like their societies and some Singaporeans mindlessly dance to their tune. See what happened to President

Gorbachev because he was beguiled by their praise. Deng Xiaoping received their condemnation. But look at China today and see what has happened to the Soviet Union. Imploded! We must think for ourselves and decide what is good for Singapore. Above all we must stay away from policies which have brought a plague of social and economic problems to the US and Britain.

Goh was explicit and detailed about his government's determination to support the traditional family unit economically. His government was determined to encourage the Confucian vision of the family. Elderly parents, for example, would have avenues by which to seek to legally compel their adult children to provide financial support for them in old age, if such were necessary. Similarly, the system would contain some bias in favour of adult children who wanted to buy units near to where their parents were living. Medical insurance would go to a family through the male head of the family, increasing and reinforcing the male head's authority within the family. There was to be a range of mild financial penalties for single mothers, among them that single mothers would not be allowed to purchase Housing Development Board units directly from the HDB, because to do so would suggest that the Board, as a government agency responsible for considerable wealth distribution, promoted or at least approved of single parenthood. Single parents would be restricted to buying HDB units on the resale market.

Goh also attacked the effect that some manifestations of popular consumer culture were having on the attitude of the young to their elders. He said:

Recently the *Straits Times* carried an advertisement showing a boy saying 'Come on, Dad, if you can play golf five times a week I can have Sustagen once a day'. I found the language, the way the boy speaks, most objectionable. Why put an American boy's way of speaking into a Singaporean boy's mouth? Do your children really speak to you like that these days? These advertisements will encourage children to be insolent to their parents. Many American children call their fathers by their first names and treat them with casual familiarity. We must not unthinkingly drift into attitudes and manners which undermine the traditional politeness and deference Asian children have for their parents and elders. It will destroy the way our children have grown up, respectful and polite to their elders.

Now, where do these combined views of Lee and Goh take us in the question of how much of the Singapore school's view of Asian values is really exclusively Asian and definitively un-Western or even anti-Western, as opposed to merely traditional? As I say, I think this is in some ways the least important question but it is worth answering. Despite Singaporean leaders' locating the expression of Asian values in their society as falling within a distinctly Confucian tradition, everything they extol as Asian values is also prominent in the Western tradition. But this is not to make the slightest criticism of Singaporean leaders on this score. Many Western leaders believe they are espousing universal values; at other times they believe that Western values are universal values.

When the equation is framed in this way—that Western values are universal values—it naturally annoys many Asians. But if you asked people from most Western societies whether they put a high value on family loyalty, devotion to education, thrift, diligence and so on you would get overwhelmingly positive answers. Indeed, Lee's Asian values bear a strong resemblance to Weber's Protestant work ethic. Goh even makes the point that the US or Britain of 30 or 40 years ago was a family-centred, conservative, hardworking society, which he seems able to admire pretty much without equivocation.

Even the more distinctively Singaporean touches such as the strong support for a patriarchal view of the family, and a strongly conservative and authority-centred view of the family's internal dynamics and place within society, are very similar to the types of arguments that social conservatives in Western societies make all the time. Indeed, if the authorship of columns got mixed up in a magazine and much that Lee said about America in the early 1990s was attributed to neo-conservatives such as William Bennett or Norman Podhoretz or Irving Kristol, most readers would not notice anything greatly amiss.

None of this is to suggest for a second that the idea of Asian values is not valid. It is perfectly legitimate for leaders to find the source of good values within their own traditions. If Asian leaders feel a cultural, economic and strategic commonality is emerging among their nations, or that they would like to encourage such a commonality, it is not in the least improper for them to look to Asian traditions, as opposed to Western traditions.

It is a semantic dead end to argue that Asian values are not exclusively Asian. If they're not, so what? Many Western critics of Asian values are happy to talk of Western values, or sometimes American values, when they are really describing universal values as expressed in their particular Western tradition. Often you get the feeling that Western opinion leaders who comment on Asian values just don't like having Asians talk back to them.

Nonetheless, having accommodated all that intellectually, we ought not be detained by it for very long. The more important question is a positive one: what ends are the proponents of Asian values seeking and how successful are they in seeking them?

The idea of the West can be important intellectually here simply because as well as learning positive lessons from the West, from standard accounting practices to the benefits of an independent judiciary, shrewd Asian leaders want to learn the negative lessons of the West. In a sense the Asian values debate is framed in this way: how can we become fully modern and affluent economies while avoiding some of the obvious social problems which have beset Western societies in recent decades? Or, to put it another way: how can we retain something (especially the feeling of community and the coherence of family structures) of our indigenous traditions as we experience the full effects of rapid modernisation and Western consumerism?

Even in this ideological context, Asian values are not a negative rejection of the West, but an attempt to find the best human way forward for societies hurtling through the processes of modernisation.

This reality is perhaps best expressed by Kishore Mahbubani in his striking essay, *Can Asians Think?*, which formed the lead essay in his book by the same name published in Singapore in 1998. In a passage referred to in the Introduction, which we need to look at more closely here, Mahbubani argues:

> It is vital for Western minds to understand that the efforts by Asians to rediscover Asian values are not only or even primarily a search for political values. Instead they represent a complex set of

motives and aspirations in Asian minds: a desire to reconnect
with their historical past after this connection had been ruptured
both by colonialism and the subsequent domination of the globe
by a Western Weltanschauung; an effort to find the right balance
in bringing up their young so that they are open to the new
technologically interconnected global universe and yet rooted in
and conscious of the cultures of their ancestors; an effort to
define their own personal, social and national identities in a way
that enhances their sense of self-esteem in a world in which their
immediate ancestors had subconsciously accepted the fact that
they were lesser beings in a Western universe. In short, the
reassertion of Asian values in the 1990s represents a complex
process of regeneration and rediscovery that is an inevitable
aspect of the rebirth of societies.

A reassertion of pride, an effort to find the right balance in
bringing up the young—these are wholly worthy, indeed necessary,
projects for Asian national leaderships and it is a testament to
the often unconscious and misplaced assumption of superiority,
the intellectual complacency, among so many Western commentators that they find this process unsettling or even illegitimate.

Of course, since the Lee interview with *Foreign Affairs* and Goh's
National Day speech, both given in 1994, the reality of the social
problems they described in the United States in particular has
changed. Teenage pregnancies, crime and especially unemployment have fallen rapidly in the US. A paradox here is that this
has come about partly through that nation's adopting what might
be regarded as aspects of Asian values—cutting back its welfare
system, making the family more self-reliant, launching a full-scale
rhetorical campaign across government and political leadership
in favour of family values.

I asked Lee Kuan Yew in 1998 whether the continued strong
growth in the American economy had caused him to change his
mind about America, in terms of the highly critical views he
expressed in the *Foreign Affairs* interview. He replied: 'We're
talking about two different things here—the economy and the
social culture. The American economy has been booming because
of innovative technology and the entrepreneurship of people at
the top of society. The social problems of America are with the

people at the lower end of society—an unsatisfactory education system and a welfare dependency that have created a large underclass with many drug addicts. There is great buoyancy after seven or eight years of economic growth at two-and-a-half to three-and-a-half per cent, but the long-term problems of this growing underclass have still to be resolved.'

More importantly, perhaps, most of East Asia was plunged into a terrible economic crisis beginning with the collapse of the Thai baht in 1997. The most superficial and silliest Western reaction to this crisis was to think that the whole Asian values debate was invalidated, as if the way in which vibrant, dynamic societies decide to define themselves suddenly loses significance because of an economic reversal.

In Singapore, where so much thinking about Asian values takes place, the reaction was, naturally, utterly different. George Yeo is the recognised leader of Singapore's younger generation of politicians. He is a smart, courteous, engaging, direct and at times intellectually prodigious politician and I have been fortunate to have many discussions with him on these issues over a number of years. In the course of a long discussion in his sky-scraping office in the Port of Singapore Authority's building he told me that the economic crisis, far from eroding Asian values, would in many ways intensify and reinforce them.

'At a time like this, human beings go back to the basics. They often become more religious. Family, frugality, hard work become more important. This [economic crisis] is not going to change the way Asian parents bring up their children. Some may have luxuriated in new wealth, or made light of marriages breaking up—that will all be thrown out. In Singapore now no one complains about the government being frugal, squirrelling reserves, not taking liberties with ourselves.'

He also argued, entirely plausibly, that the economic crisis did not mean that in the long term the global shift of power towards East Asia would be reversed. 'If we take a longer term perspective, Asia is in an organic growth phase. This has its roots in the Chinese revolution and the Meiji Restoration in Japan. In the last 20 years there has been incredible economic growth in a short period of time. It's as if the whole of the 19th century in America and Europe were to be compressed into two decades.

'Booms and busts, crony capitalism, the rise and fall of robber barons are all part of that organic growth. This is not a cataclysmic event, it's a punctuation in Asian growth. It may take a few years, even ten years, to get new institutions in place. The original [economic] projections may be out ten years but this is not a reversal. Look at the history of crony capitalism in New York or Chicago. How long did that take to change?

'Look at Jakarta, Seoul, Kuala Lumpur, Bangkok. The assets are real. The people are educated, the buildings and bridges are there. Of course, the assets will have to change hands, as it were. But this is not a major upheaval like a war.'

Lee Kuan Yew, too, argued persuasively that everything that was good, and justly admired, in East Asian societies before the economic crisis had hardly disappeared, or become unadmirable, in the wake of the crisis. He told me that the economic crisis had not discredited the Asian values debate: 'No, it was the debasement of Confucianist values that aggravated the crisis: corruption, cronyism and nepotism. I prefer to talk about 'Confucianist' not 'Asian' values, because Asia's values vary from culture to culture. Confucianist values of East Asia disapprove of the use of public office to benefit one's friends and relatives. Temporarily it [the economic crisis] has thrown everybody off balance. It will take a couple of years for everyone to sort out his position. The basic virtues have not disappeared—hard work, the willingness to learn, high savings rates, high investment and welcoming of foreign investment. Growth will resume, but the price of restructuring must be paid.'

The crisis suggested that the most obvious reforms needed, Yeo told me, are in financial institutions. Financial institutions in any society reflect deeper power relativities and these will be painful to shift.

Yeo also reflected on the danger of a fault line re-emerging in South East Asia between ethnic Malays, who form the overwhelming majority of the population in Indonesia and Malaysia, and ethnic Chinese. Yeo's take on all this was, as is always the case with him, deeply historical. The reversal commencing in 1997 was the first of its intensity that the ethnic Malays of Indonesia and Malaysia have experienced since they became free marketeers. For the Chinese, business reversals much worse than this are part of the tribal memory. Moreover, many Asian businesses—from the chaebol in South Korea, the bumiputra businesses in Malaysia and the pribumi businesses in Indonesia—have been very dependent on governments. The ethnic Chinese, even when they benefit from government licensing arrangements, or even more direct government patronage, rarely trust governments. A mentor in government today can expropriate your assets tomorrow. The Chinese business instinct is always to hedge, to diversify, not only with money, but with children—to send one to Canada, one to the United States and another to Australia. As a result of all these factors the ethnic Chinese businesses may have been better placed to survive the downturn in Asia than other businesses were.

The one way in which Asian values might be seriously challenged by the economic downturn, Yeo argued, was in the need to provide institutionally competing centres of civic power, to structurally divide civic power in order to provide essential checks and balances.

'The idea of structured power, which really began with the separation of church and state in the West, the separation of spiritual and temporal power, is really an idea alien to the Asian mind,' Yeo said. 'On the other hand, you have got Singapore, Hong Kong and Taiwan. We've responded effectively without discarding our Asianness. Partly because we were colonised for so long, a certain amalgam has come about which allows us to use Western accounting methods but continue to raise our children as Asians.'

Undeniably, the Asian economic crisis has resulted in an increased quotient of humility in South East Asian leaders' pronouncements. Humility is generally admirable but this is not necessarily a wholly good thing in this case. Asia's interests, indeed the genuinely enlightened interests also of the West in Asia, are not served by either a resentful or a fatalistic South East Asia whose people feel that they are not masters of their own destiny. As the Malaysian intellectual, Noordin Sopiee, has observed, the absolute lack of power corrupts absolutely.

Nonetheless, excess humility is to be distinguished from the genuine searching pragmatism that has characterised the region's leadership. In a magazine interview in 1998 Lee Kuan Yew made his normal defence of Asian values, referring to thrift, diligence, family cohesion etc, and argued that they contributed to good economic performance, as they surely do. Yet he was prepared to acknowledge the weaknesses in the Confucian inheritance as well:

> There are certain weaknesses in Confucianism. From time to time in the history of China, whenever there was weak government, Confucianism led to nepotism and favouritism . . . Unfortunately, quite a few of the countries that have been growing fast have this incestuous system where banks are owned by conglomerates and lend money to another section in the group without proper feasibility studies.

What is this but the voice of a searching, pragmatic mind, looking at history honestly and trying to find the right answers for today? The intellectual flexibility of leaders like Lee Kuan Yew is too little appreciated in the West. Again Noordin Sopiee is apt: 'There is one thing about which we are doctrinaire, and that is our pragmatism.'

Another question is how honestly Singapore implements the Asian values it espouses. The answer is: pretty honestly. Of course, there are plenty of things wrong with Singapore. That is the nature of human existence in the fallen state of man.

But despite the Chinese dominance of Singapore, for example, it is undoubtedly a city-state of opportunity for its ethnic minority citizens. Raj is a young and very bright civil servant. He tells his story over a steaming curry at a restaurant at Boat Quays.

'I was born in Singapore and have always considered myself Singaporean, although I am of Tamil background and my parents were born in India. But I have never experienced any discrimination in the civil service because of my racial background, or in Singapore society generally. I am a Singaporean just like everyone else here. I am also a Hindu and go to the Hindu temple. I have friends who are Chinese and friends who are Malay. I think all the races in Singapore realise that we have to get along here, that we have no home other than Singapore.

'But Singapore also offers us opportunity. My father came from India and succeeded in Singapore. He has sometimes thought of going back to India to retire, but when he visits India he realises he wouldn't want to live there now, wouldn't want to give up the life in Singapore—all the friends and family here now, the higher standard of living, the higher standard of cleanliness, the lack of crime—to exchange that for India. So instead he goes back for holidays.

'I and my wife have bought an apartment here. I have everything in Singapore I could possibly want. We travel internationally for holidays. The chance for career advancement is good. I'm happy here and proud to be Singaporean.'

Of course, Raj's account is just one view. It is possible for a writer to find Singaporeans who are profoundly unhappy with the place. But to regard Singapore overall as anything other than a magnificent success is really to determine not to let facts interfere with prejudice. And its success, as its leaders remind us, must be chalked up at least in part to Asian values. They are good values and they have produced a good society. It is a bit different from Los Angeles or Sydney, but surely in this world diversity is no crime. And in occasionally offering a rhetorical and intellectual challenge to some of the assumptions of Western liberalism, and certainly to the assumptions of Western superiority, Singapore has been a vital ingredient, a tangy spice, a rich chilli, in the great human discourse of civilisations and values, of the pursuit of the good life. We are all a little richer for Singapore's bold self-confidence.

5

MALAYSIA:
THE FRONT-LINE STATE

IF YOU STAND AT the top of Pitt Street in downtown Georgetown, Penang, you stand athwart the intersection of three of the world's great civilisations. Penang is a small, bustling island off the northwest coast of the Malay peninsula. To the west is India, and the teeming multitudes of the subcontinent. To the north is China, the oldest civilisation extant, and the largest. And to the south is the vast Malay world. Modern Malaysia is a result of this intersection. Its population is a composition of the three civilisations—more than 60 per cent of its people are ethnic Malays or belong to the indigenous races of East Malaysia, something less than 30 per cent are Chinese and a little under 10 per cent are Indian.

Pitt Street itself embodies this diversity. Amidst the rumbling traffic and elegant traces of colonial architecture are two big mosques, two Chinese clan houses (where ancestors are worshipped), a Buddhist temple, a Hindu temple, and just a few blocks away a magnificent Sikh *gurdwhara*. If ever a nation was itself going to suffer the 'clash of civilisations', to be torn apart by ethnic and communal hostilities, it is Malaysia. And indeed in the late 1960s it did experience murderous race riots in which hundreds of Chinese were killed. As a majority Muslim state it satisfies every criterion of Western paranoia—ethnic division, Islamic predominance and a developing economy. Yet for 30 years, through good times and bad, through the oil shock of the 1970s, the recession of the mid-80s, the political upheaval of the late 80s, the rapid social change associated with the boom years of fast economic growth during most of the 90s and then the most recent savage regional economic downturn of the late 90s, Malaysians have kept the racial calm. Peace among the races, an accommodation at least if not a profound harmony, has been secured.

This is no mean achievement anywhere. For a developing nation making the transition out of poverty and buffeted by the cruelties of market mood swings and radical capital flows, it is worth more recognition internationally than it usually gets.

For an outsider like me, Malaysia's racial mixture and cultural diversity are its most delightful aspect. It is not diverse in the same sense as the United States—you don't have the experience of finding people in substantial numbers from all over the globe in Malaysia. You don't have the experience, as you do in the US, of running into Armenians in North Hollywood, Vietnamese in San Jose, Poles in Milwaukee, Ethiopians in New York. Malaysia doesn't set out to be a universal nation in the way the US does. But even so, its diversity has a quality which is lacking in the US. In most situations in the US, the affluent visitor will find himself in a basically white environment most of the time. In Malaysia, in virtually every social setting, you find yourself dealing with Malays, Chinese and Indians simultaneously. This is an unusual diversity in South East Asia, too. Thus while the vast archipelago of Indonesia is in an absolute sense more ethnically and linguistically diverse than Malaysia, Malaysia often feels more diverse because of the ubiquity of the three races.

In so far as the West has a view of Malaysia it tends to be defined by the nation's high-profile prime minister of such long standing, Mahathir Mohamad. Mahathir's caustic lectures to the West and his determination never to be trod on or told what to do by outsiders deserve attention. But Malaysia is much more than Mahathir. The man who had been his deputy for so long and who was jailed by Mahathir, Anwar Ibrahim, was a balancing voice to Mahathir's. Anwar's profile in the South East Asian region was especially strong.

It is beyond the scope of this book to explore fully the criminal charges brought against Anwar, some of which were still proceeding through the courts at the time of writing. Nor will I examine at length the struggle for power between Mahathir and Anwar.

Instead the contribution of both men to the Asian values debate is examined. On racial issues the two men have mostly been as one. Not the least of the ways in which Mahathir has been misunderstood and misrepresented in the West is that his role in racial reconciliation is never adverted to. Admittedly, the situation is a little too complex for the ready stereotypes with which we like to categorise people. Is Mahathir a racial conservative or a racial liberal?

He started out as a Malay 'ultra'. His 1969 book, *The Malay Dilemma*, was a cri de coeur of Malay dispossession and a determination to reassert Malay pride and control. Yet Mahathir developed as almost an avuncular and unifying figure within Malaysia, ever willing to deliver stern lectures to his countrymen, but looked to as a protector not only by Malays but by ethnic minority groups, in much the same way that these groups once looked to Malaysia's first prime minister, the aristocratic and paternal Tunku Abdul Rahman. Anwar Ibrahim started out as an 'ultra' too, but he was concerned more with the assertion for Malaysia of an overtly Islamic identity rather than Malayness as such. In truth the two are profoundly intertwined, for in Malaysia it is assumed that all Malays should be Muslims, and ethnic issues are often subsumed in religious issues. But on religion, as on race, Mahathir and Anwar have in recent years both been apostles of moderation. When they fell out, it was not over issues of race.

Not long before the outbreak of the regional economic crisis in 1997 I asked Anwar what he thought of race relations in contemporary Malaysia. He argued then that Malaysia's economic success in the 1970s, 80s and 90s, especially the creation of a Malay business class, had resulted in a profound change in race relations. In particular he thought the growing Malay self-confidence generally had resulted in the evolution of a more relaxed racial atmosphere: 'It has improved tremendously. Growth and prosperity have contributed to easing tensions. There is less feeling of insecurity among the races, particularly the Malays, because their economic achievement is considerable. Race relations have entered a new phase. Cultural and religious differences are now seen in a new light. It is considered a strength rather than a source of conflict. This reflects the maturing process in race relations.'

For a self-consciously Islamic leader like Anwar to hail Malaysia's racial and religious diversity as a positive strength is itself a sign of how far Malaysia has travelled. But that interview, one of many I have conducted with the urbane, softly spoken, always relaxed former deputy prime minister, was in the easy days before the 1997 economic crisis. In 1998 I asked him the same question in the very different context of economic stress. It was at the time of the holiest Muslim feast, Idul Fitri, in January. That year the feast fell at the same time as Chinese New Year, the most important celebration in the calendar for the Chinese. The atmosphere in Malaysia at the time was not one of racial tension but of a determined official, and apparently popular, effort to promote interracial good feeling. The Chinese New Year greeting—*Gong Xie Fa Chui*—was everywhere amalgamated with the Muslim celebratory *Selamat Hari Raya* to form *Gong Xie Raya*. Restaurants and hotels across the country featured Malay and Chinese figures, dressed in elaborate traditional costume, in joint celebration.

Anwar was making the most of this happy conjunction: 'This is a great experience for us. All analysts, including those in the media, seem to assume economic difficulties will incite racial disharmony. We have not seen any signs of that in Malaysia.'

The official campaign was at times a bit corny. Typical was a widely screened community service television advertisement of the time. The scene opens on a Chinese teenager. He looks a typical overachieving Chinese 'nerd', head bowed over his books, deep into complex mathematical problems. He is disturbed by a series of noises, the last a lively Hindi song from an unknown radio. He stumbles out of his studious lair, blinking his eyes in the unfamiliar sunlight. Has he been studying all night? He stumbles around in search of the source of the noise, enacting a few slapstick falls and misadventures on the way. Finally he knocks at a door nearby and it is opened by a Malay girl of ravishing beauty, whose eyes sparkle and who smiles beatifically upon him.

The Chinese student is invited into an Edenic garden full of exotic tropical fruits. The Malay girl entices him to try one, which he finds a little bitter but perseveres with anyway (though how a Chinese living in Malaysia could be unfamiliar with its fruit is unknowable). Meanwhile, in the background a famous ethnically Punjabi Malaysian singer, who has converted to Islam, is crooning, in Hindi, a love song about 'the first time I ever saw you'.

This advertisement is almost terminal schmaltz but the interesting, perhaps even important, thing about it is its official promotion of interracial friendship. In this case the advertisement even seems to be promoting interracial romance. Interracial marriage is quite common in Malaysia, but I have never before seen it officially promoted. This commercial was in its way a powerful symbol of government and corporate determination to keep race relations civil.

In a globalising economy ethnic diversity is a comparative advantage and it is smart and true of Malaysia's leaders to stress this aspect. Penang is the perfect example. Penang State consists of the small island and a little strip on the mainland linked by one of the longest causeways in the world. It is Malaysia's only majority Chinese State, although the ethnic scales are balanced somewhat by the predominantly Malay population in the mainland part of Penang.

I went to see Penang's chief minister, Dr Koh Tsu Koon, the only ethnic Chinese long-term chief minister of any Malaysian State, in an inevitably antiseptic conference room in the ultra-modern Penang Development Corporation office tower on the southern end of Penang island, near the airport. Dr Koh leads the predominantly Chinese Gerakan party but is in coalition with the United Malays National Organisation (UMNO), the dominant political party in Malaysia, which spearheads the Barisan coalition, which governs nationally.

For much of the 1990s Penang had an annual economic growth rate of 12 per cent, making it, with southern China, one of the fastest growing regional economies in the world. The Japanese management guru, Kenichi Ohmae, nominated it in his book *The End of the Nation State* as the very model of an effective internationalist city, inviting the global economy and taking full advantage of location, cost, infrastructure and human resources.

'Penang is a microcosm of South East Asia,' Dr Koh told me. 'People have come to see our multicultural and multiracial aspect as an economic asset. Malaysians can easily move into China, India, Indonesia. They are used to dealing with complex, intercultural situations.' Koh is particularly proud of those multinationals that have located their sales and marketing or customer service regional headquarters in Penang, in order to take advantage of the diverse linguistic skills of its inhabitants. If a customer rings from India, China, Indonesia or virtually anywhere in the region they can find an operator who speaks their language.

For Koh, his ethnicity does not compromise his civic loyalty: 'I'm first and foremost a Malaysian. We're very fortunate to inherit the major religions and cultures of the world without losing our own particular cultural heritage. You are no less culturally a Malay, or a Chinese, while still being Malaysian. We all have the chance to accept, appreciate and adopt the good aspects of other cultures. Our diversity is a big virtue, a big asset, which if we didn't manage it well could be a big liability, it could lead to friction. There is a greater sense of confidence in every ethnic group. There is less feeling of threat or insecurity. The late 60s and 70s were very divisive. Now it's more natural for people to interact, to appreciate each other's cultural forms and religious beliefs.'

Koh's fellow Penangite, Anwar Ibrahim, contributed to this by being the first national Malay leader to use a brush to write Chinese characters, an important gesture of cultural appreciation of the Chinese. Anwar would quote the Koran in Arabic and the Analects of Confucius in Chinese.

Like many Malaysians, Koh does not think Western societies are necessarily in a position to lecture Malaysia: 'On my first trip to Sydney in 1980, on my first day there, a group of white kids in a car stopped and shouted at me: Go home!'

Of course, Koh is a chief minister, so he is obliged to be polite. Some others are more sceptical. I had long admired the novels of K. S. Maniam, Malaysia's most renowned English language novelist. Of Tamil background himself, Maniam has often drawn on his own background to depict the traditional Tamil existence in Malaysia of life on a rubber plantation. His works are understated but densely poetic and allusive. They sometimes have a dreamlike quality. They are among the most beautiful works in English in the 20th century. His stories often deal with racial issues, or at least have a consciousness of race as a strong background.

I sought him out in a quiet, old-fashioned bar on the edge of Chinatown in Kuala Lumpur. A small, gentle man, his dark face deeply lined, his hair and moustache flecked with white, Maniam loves his country but that day at least was full of melancholy reflection: 'There's a race race rather than a race riot these days. I can smash someone's face or more likely make them lose face. After World War II the races were separated geographically. When you come to the 1990s you still get the idea of different locations, but locations defined in a different way, sort of like computer locations. It's a sense of separate *mental* spaces—the separate physical spaces have substantially eroded. But mental spaces are harder to break down. It's easier to enter a Chinese area than a Chinese mental space. And the media is always telling each race what it should be.'

Maniam also attributed much of the racial calm to economic growth, but his warning was dire: 'If economic growth stops, it will be horrendous.'

Maniam is somewhat depressed about the prospects for his own Indian community in Malaysia. As Koh pointed out, the Indian Malaysian community has a peculiar structure. It has a strong professional class, a narrow middle class and a huge working class inherited from the days when Indians were over-whelmingly rubber tappers working on the plantations. The Indian politicians have insisted on preserving Tamil language schools, often within or on the edge of plantations. But while Indians are justly proud of their cultural heritage, Tamil is a language which gets them nowhere economically. Moreover, pre-serving the Tamil schools, while useful for Indian politicians in that it preserves their support base, tends to ghettoise the Indians, narrowing their horizons and limiting their opportuni-ties. Urban Indian friends of mine in Malaysia refuse to send their children to Tamil schools for this reason, preferring the national Malay or even the Chinese schools. Overall, Indians remain the most marginalised of the major ethnic groups in Malaysia.

Much less marginalised, but still placed in a slightly equivocal position, are Malaysia's many Eurasians. I talked to one, Anne, a young writer with a British father and a Chinese mother, in her small Kuala Lumpur townhouse. A typical middle-class Malaysian house—downstairs for eating, entertaining and work, upstairs for sleeping, with a car space out front—it is the kind of suburban accommodation that is common throughout Malaysia and a testament to the embourgeoisement of Malaysian life. Anne is an attractive young woman; she looks relaxed in slacks and a smock and, like most Malaysians at home, is sensibly barefooted. She is full of energy, full of smiles. Anne is interesting for many reasons, not least because she has chosen to live in Malaysia, to be Malaysian, although she had the opportunity to live in England and indeed looks European.

She was born in Sabah, in East Malaysia, and educated partly in Penang and partly in England. Her early years were spent in Malaysia, but then from age 11 to 20 she lived in England, returning to Malaysia for holidays. 'When I came back I thought I'd have to speak Bahasa [Malay] fluently to get a job. About three years later I had to decide whether I wanted to be in Asia or in Europe, in KL or London.

'I guess I'm a sunshine kinda gal,' she says jokingly of her decision to choose Malaysia—but then adds: 'I'd rather deal with the problems of a developing country than a country that seems overdeveloped. There are opportunities here, it's up to you to make something of them. The Malaysian point of view fascinated me. I wanted to be part of the action.

'There is a drive to modernise here. But there's also this concern that we remain ourselves, that we don't lose our Asian values. There's a tension there in accepting the paradox—how do you modernise but maintain values, such as the family, which are important? For women the question is how do you reconcile the freedom you get [from economic development] with the place you have in the family. Women friends of mine who are Muslim are very liberal, but they pray regularly each day and have an inner spirituality.'

Anne was conscious of her unusual racial status while she was growing up: 'I'm from Sabah where there's a lot more intermarriage, not the automatic Chinese, Malay and Indian division. With economic development there is a multiracial middle class. But there are also multiracist stereotypes—that the Malay government workers are slow, that the Chinese would sell their mothers, that Indians are low achievers.

'My school in Penang was truly multiracial and multireligious but there were all kinds of intricate hierarchies among the Eurasians. For example, if your father was *mat salleh* [white] rather than your mother, that was one point more, and if your father was American that was half a point less than if he was English.

'From my non-Eurasian cousins there is one of two reactions. Either they imagine that you think you're so great, such a big deal, because you're *mat salleh*, or they have a kind of awe, a great interest in you.' Anne has had plenty of incongruous racial experiences. When she went shopping with her mother as a child, people often assumed she was with her *amah*, that her mother was the family servant. Similarly, in a small traffic accident she is assumed to be a foreigner, and the locals are astonished when she speaks Bahasa and the Chinese dialect Hakka. But for all that, she loves Malaysia and bounces her own energy off the swirling social energy, the social-hybrid vigour, around her.

Ivy sees another side of Malaysia's multiracial life. She runs a women's shelter in Kuala Lumpur for battered wives and it is there, after having promised faithfully never to disclose its precise location, that I meet her. There is a locked gate, high walls and strong physical security. There are lots of little kids running around, mainly Indian, like Ivy; they are all as cute as can be, very shy, not used to *mat sallehs* [white people]. My heart melts—how can anyone abuse these kids?

The way Ivy sees it, spousal abuse is a terrible problem in Malaysia. It's most often associated with the Indian community, and with alcohol, but Ivy's work has shown her that it cuts across all races and all classes.

She discusses racial issues in a complex and nuanced fashion, recognising the advances that have been made but also the limitations, frankly discussing the special privileges Malays get which other races do not. But there is one comment Ivy makes that strikes me very strongly: 'When I walk down the street in Western countries, in New York or Sydney, I'm acutely aware that I'm brown. When I walk the streets here I don't feel that I'm Indian all the time. As a kid I was told not to go to the Malay *kampungs* [villages] or I might get beaten up. Now I never hear anything like that. This country provided enough plates of rice for my father, a Sri Lankan immigrant, for him to give his family opportunities. I'm a great optimist about Bangsa Malaysia.'

Bangsa Malaysia literally means 'Malaysian nationality' and is intended to connote a diminished emphasis on ethnicity and a heightened emphasis on the unity of Malaysian citizenship.

Ivy would like to see greater progress in the status of women in Malaysia. She points out that it is not just Islam, but most other religions too, that afford women an inferior place in the social hierarchy. Economic progress has helped Malaysian women in achieving some economic independence but it has also led to great dislocation as women have migrated from rural to urban areas in search of work, often as a result becoming cut off from the support network of the extended family.

These of course are problems familiar in many developing countries. Part of Malaysia's uniqueness lies in the way these problems are blended with its predominantly Islamic identity. The West has a cockeyed view of Islam. More Muslims live in India than in any country in the Middle East. More Muslims live in Indonesia than in any other country in the world. The world's vision of the typical Muslim ought thus to be, say, of a Javanese woman, yet it is almost invariably of an Iranian mullah. Malaysia is one of the most economically developed of all Muslim societies. And it has to confront the challenge of building a decent compact with its large (nearly 40 per cent) non-Muslim minorities.

The Western media tends to demonise Islam, especially by an exaggeration of what it labels Islamic terrorism. There are just as many examples of insane and destructive behaviour carried out by nominal Christians, in Kosovo or Northern Ireland or Latin America, or by nominal Confucians, in Tibet or Tiananmen Square, or by nominal atheists—the Khmer Rouge, the North Korean communists—as there are of such behaviour from nominal Muslims. One problem in Western analysis of Islam is that in Islamic societies actions tend to be carried out in an Islamic idiom even when these actions cannot in any meaningful way be attributed to Islamic teaching or even serious Islamic organisation. When someone like Branch Davidians leader David Koresh of Waco fame embarks on lunatic paramilitary civil disobedience, which results in appalling death and destruction, we write him off as just an American nut who got out of control. But if Koresh had linked his nuttiness in any way to Islam, or worse, actually called himself a Muslim, the world would have been filled to saturation with learned articles denouncing the threat of the new international Islamic menace.

It is even more absurd that Malaysia should be caught up in these Western stereotypes, because the Islam practised in Malaysia is overwhelmingly tolerant, sensible and socially beneficial. Even when it does seem to constrain civil liberties it is more in the essentially trivial category of such things as banning participation by Malay women in beauty contests rather than the imposition of onerous constraints on the society as a whole. And Malaysia is such a diverse, sophisticated society that even limited moves such as these become hotly contested and are often reversed.

More importantly, the Western media, in its generally one-dimensional rendition of Dr Mahathir, misses one of the most complex, subtle and important dynamics at work in any Islamic society: his attempt to harness the traditional moral virtues of Islam—thrift, honesty, family fidelity, obedience, abstemiousness, communal solidarity—with the traditional Chinese and Japanese ingredients of East Asian economic success. This was particularly embodied in Mahathir's 'Look East' policy in which he urged his countrymen to emulate Japan. This in itself was a strong assertion of Asian values, the very idea that a developing country could look to an Asian society for inspiration rather than always to a Western society. The Japanese development model has been shown to have its flaws and its limitations, but it served Japan well for 40 years and it served Malaysia well for at least two decades.

The larger reality was that Mahathir was trying to reconcile Islam with the modern world. There is a vigorous debate about how to adapt Islam to the needs of modern life and the modern economy. This is of course a clumsy outsider's way of expressing a complex intellectual process. One might just as well say the attempt is being made to adapt modern life to the needs of Islam. But the important, the essential, point is that the attempt is being made with basic goodwill towards both Islam and the modern world. The two are not seen as antithetical. Of course, not everything practised under the guise of 'modernity' needs to be accepted, and Mahathir's robust rejection of the bits of Western modernity he doesn't like earn him the most publicity in the West, but there is no feeling that Islam and the modern world are at war. Rather there is an attempt to see what an authentic application of Islamic ethics to the realities, the good and the not so good, might produce.

Malaysia's endeavour here is of global importance. If Malaysia succeeds in becoming a fully developed nation it will not only demonstrate the viability of multiethnic, multireligious societies but may offer a new vision of how an Islamic society can reconcile Islam and economic modernisation. The exciting aspect of Mahathir's endeavours is that he tried to use Islam as a constructive force for modernisation, rather than succumbing to the Western stereotype of Islam as a force for feudalism or at least antique Arab chauvinism. This remains just as true despite Mahathir's harshly critical statements concerning Western hedge fund managers and the United States, in connection with the Asian economic crisis. Mahathir was most certainly not rejecting modernity in those statements, he was blaming hedge funds and criticising US policy.

None of this means that there are no difficult Islamic issues to manage in Malaysia. All my Malaysian friends acknowledge that there has been an Islamic resurgence over the last 20 years. Rehman Rashid, in his marvellous book, *Malaysian Journey*, describes how the success of the Ayatollah Khomeini in overthrowing the Shah of Iran initially produced a burst of support and applause among Malaysians, especially students. But now the Islamic societies in the Middle East are recognised in Malaysia as basically unsuccessful, certainly not models Malaysia should follow. Yet Malaysia is still more consciously Islamic than it was 20 years ago. Malay friends in the civil service tell me that 20 years ago, during the Muslim fasting month of Ramadan, most Malay civil servants still ate lunch. Now virtually no one does, certainly not in public.

I asked Anwar Ibrahim about the Islamic resurgence in Malaysia. 'We do not see religiosity, be it Islamic, Buddhist, Confucian or Christian, as a threat,' he said. 'What we are against is extremism and intolerance, particularly if it has a violent tendency. The resurgence of religiosity is a global tendency and not confined to Islam. It is something we should view positively because it gives a sense of fulfilment beyond materialistic pursuits and strengthens the moral fabric of society and the family.'

Indeed, Anwar has argued that the role, the respect, given to organised religion is one of the essential Asian values, and distinguishes East Asian societies from the West. This is a difficult argument to sustain for Japan, China or even Korea, but in different ways it does apply to South East Asia and even to South Asia. In taking religion seriously, Asian societies actually resemble the way the West was for most of its existence. It is only recently that mass atheism has come to be a hallmark of advanced Western liberalism, and Anwar has identified this as the source of some of the social malaise to be found in many Western societies.

As for his own society, he told me: 'The problem is with militancy. The solution is to promote tolerance and a universal perspective among religions. In Malaysia we certainly view Islam as a modernising force. Islam promotes rational thinking and orderliness. The role of Islam's critical values such as justice, respect of human dignity, the rule of law—these are crucial in the formation of a modern nation state and a democratic and multicultural community.'

Both Anwar and Mahathir have been trenchant opponents of Islamic fundamentalism, though both have problems with the term itself. One reason for opposing fundamentalism is its incompatibility with the modern economy. When the Islamic fundamentalist Parti Islam SeMalaysia (PAS) won control of the State government in Kelantan it decreed that women could not work at night. As a result, factories in Kelantan were effectively limited to one shift per day. Some of them closed and Kelantan lost outside investment to other States.

Of course, Mahathir and Anwar have made in-principle arguments against fundamentalism as well as pragmatic arguments against it. But the vision of development is also important to the vision of the good life, meaning a moral and fully rounded human life, which both Mahathir and Anwar have promoted for Malaysia.

In an important speech to the UMNO General Assembly in September 1997, Mahathir directly linked economic development to religious dignity: 'To really redeem the dignity of race and religion, our progress must at least be on a par with those said to be advanced in this world, those respected, even feared, by all, including Muslims and Islamic countries.'

In this same speech, which caused something of a sensation in Malaysia at the time, Mahathir also made the case, which he has made so many times, for a moderate and tolerant Islam:

> I realise that what I am saying will not make many people comfortable, including UMNO members. But we are facing a problem of increasing intolerance to anyone who does not give priority to the form and shape of Islam . . . In several other Muslim countries, the fanatic groups are prepared to kill people of the same faith because they want to seize power to implement their opinion. In Malaysia, groups like these have already reached a level of slandering and denying the 'Muslimness' of others. If left like this we will also become like certain Muslim countries which are already weak and oppressed by foreign powers. We have to defend the true Islamic teachings before tragedy befalls us.
>
> The reason they [other Muslims] are proud of Malaysia is not that we have exhibited the kind of Islam which is extreme but that we practise moderation in Islam. Malaysian Muslims have successfully dealt with the problem of ruling a multiethnic and religious population . . . Although from the beginning there were attempts to split the Malays through religion, this attempt failed. The majority of Malays had a moderate attitude as is required in Islam and not an extreme attitude that is condemned in Islam.

This side of Mahathir, it is fair to say, gets far too little international recognition. The leaders of Islamic fundamentalist groups such as PAS are locked in an endless struggle with the moderates and the modernisers for the soul of the majority Malays. Having spoken at length with PAS leaders I find them, by international standards, a pretty moderate sort of Islamic fundamentalist. Their critique of modern Western society is the same as would be made by any conservative religious person of virtually any faith. They even make a reasonable case for the role religious values should have in crafting state laws. Although for many Islamic thinkers the intertwining of state law and religious law is very intimate, while in the West we pride ourselves on the separation of church and state, the truth is that most societies have some profound historical connection between law and religion; they just strike a different balance. Most Western laws have their origin in some Christian ethical concern, or even, distantly, in natural law theory, an explicitly Christian idea.

That is not to support the PAS agenda of implementing Islamic law much more rigorously and pervasively in Malaysia (most Malaysians clearly don't want it) but simply to recognise that even religious fundamentalists occupy more a different point along a continuum than a different solar system.

A spokesman for PAS, at the end of a long discussion, made one especially revealing comment: 'Among Muslims the understanding and commitment [to their religion] is increasing much better than before. But foreign influence and the influence of non-Muslims is also increasing. In the past non-Muslims never interfered in these matters but now they talk much more and we can't say openly what we think.'

The point which perhaps PAS does not like to acknowledge is that non-Muslims are right to participate in the national discussion about how to give expression to Islamic values, because although in Malaysia specifically Islamic laws governing such areas as marriage, divorce and custody of children, or observance of fasting laws and a ban on alcohol, apply only to Muslims, they indicate the nature of the relationship between the state and the individual citizen and non-Muslims have a huge and legitimate stake in the definition of that relationship.

Nonetheless, it is worth pointing out that PAS spokesmen generally do say that while they would like to implement Islamic law if they gained political power, they would not force its observance on non-Muslims. As my PAS interlocutor put it: 'Of course, non-Muslims might have a wrong idea of Islam and be frightened, but this is not realistic. Chinese and Indians are Malaysian citizens—we cannot expect them to follow our religion.'

I spent an afternoon in a suburban Kuala Lumpur coffee shop with a very different group of Islamic thinkers. Sisters In Islam was formed in 1988. It sprang from the concern of a handful of women about the status of women in Islam. The group's spokeswoman, a feisty, unveiled, highly articulate, middle-aged academic, Norani, told the story: 'Sisters In Islam came about because we were concerned that Islam had so often been used by men to promote bad practices. We began with a concern about the implementation of Islamic family law. Very often men are saying things like "Islam gives men the right to beat their wives", or "Wives must be obedient to their husbands".

'Some of us women went back to the primary source of Islam, to read the Koran. Everything we believe in concerning the rights of women was validated in the Koran. It's all there in the Koran. It didn't come about just with Western feminism. Islam was regarded as a very liberating religion 1400 years ago. It gave women lots of rights. We had never heard these rights in our religion before but they are explicit in the verses of the Koran. This was so exhilarating and a wonderful experience for us.

'But the professional literature, the literature about the Koran, had been written by men. Men read the verse on polygamy and interpret it as a universal right to have up to four wives. Women read the same verse and see the injunction that if you can't treat them all justly you should marry only one. Polygamy is allowed in Malaysia. In some States you need the first wife's permission but if you are having trouble you can just go across the border to another State (where the religious courts always rule in the man's favour) and marry there. .

'Many women have been very happy to hear themselves reaffirmed. You don't just cower into silence because some men say it's all just Western feminism and you're not allowed to say it.'

Sisters In Islam believe that lack of education in Islamic matters for Islamic women has been fundamental in denying women power: 'There is this exclusive group of men who, because of their training and their ability to speak Arabic, can say what it is to be a woman. We've had informal links with women's groups in the Middle East and many have taken the same route as Sisters In Islam—they've gone back to the Koran and worked within the religious framework. There's nothing radical or revolutionary about it although the traditional Ulama [religious teachers] view it as such.'

Nonetheless, the Sisters recognise that in Malaysia they are dealing with a relatively liberal environment: 'There's not much cultural excess baggage associated with Islam in Malaysia. Malaysia's Islamic tradition was never like the Middle East. Men and women participate in the public sphere here. We never had *purdah* or segregation. That's all new and most of it is from the Middle East influence.'

The wearing of the veil, of a *tudong*—the traditional Muslim head-dress—is much more common now than it was 20 years ago among Muslim women, though it is still very far from universal. Norani commented: 'Veiling is part of the Islamic resurgence. There's a new definition of what it means to be a Muslim woman. Part of the motivation for the return to veiling and similar practices doesn't actually come from Islam. It's part of the need to create a distinctive, post-independence cultural identity. You use women as symbols of your culture. Veiling should be a matter of choice. It's up to you if you want to do it and that's fine, but you can't impose it on someone else.

'But people are ignorant. They do as they're told. We began our work because we asked the question, "How can Islam be so unjust to us?" We found it's not unjust after all. We do not want to give up our Islamic life, our Islamic identity. Malaysia has traditions of equality. It was once a rural society and women worked with men in the fields.'

I heard views similar to Norani's from Marina Mahathir, the prime minister's daughter. Marina is a phenomenon in Malaysia and ought to be better known in the West. Her 40th birthday party, in 1997, was a rollicking event. It could not have been held for the daughter of any other South East Asian leader. It was a surprise party, held in Chow Kit, Kuala Lumpur's notorious red-light district and was organised partly by the city's transsexual community. Streets were blocked off and guests included prostitutes and drug addicts. There were 500 people, countless balloons, stilt-walkers, professional dancers—as Marina herself put it, 'all the marginalised communities'. The party was held primarily to thank Marina for her work on AIDS.

At 40, a single parent (she later remarried), feminist, social liberal and chairperson of her country's AIDS council, Marina was both an unusual Malaysian and something of an icon for social progressives. She is a celebrity in Malaysia, a kind of radical democratic princess, perhaps the most liberal, feminist and frank mainstream voice in her society. She is also at times hugely controversial. Yet she also legitimately reflects the diversity of Malaysia. She pushes the boundaries but is in no sense a negative critic operating from outside the mainstream.

I talked to her at length in her modest, unairconditioned office in the back of an old but lovingly renovated Chinese shop house in downtown Kuala Lumpur. She said: 'I think Malaysia likes to think of itself as a conservative society but all kinds of things go on that aren't conservative; even Western societies would be shocked. The bureaucrats are much more conservative than the people.'

She recalled giving a talk to a group of women in a highly conservative area of rural east coast Malaysia, where PAS is strong. Many of the women wore *tudongs*. She didn't know how the talk was going over and whether the women would discuss issues of sexual health frankly. She was surprised by their open-ness and their determination to get the facts: 'The first question was on oral sex, whether it could cause an infection.'

Marina Mahathir's story tells us a lot about modern Malaysia. Dr Mahathir was not prime minister during her childhood and she grew up in a happy and relatively normal household. (She would later describe her family as one of the 'most kissy-huggy' families she knows.) When she was about 16, Marina was sent by her father to California for a long stay with family friends. 'I think he regrets it now,' Marina recalled. 'As a 16-year-old it created a profound impression on me, on who I am.' She went to England for her A-levels and studied international relations at Sussex University. She broke into journalism in a modest way in Fleet Street and came back to Malaysia in 1980, where she worked on women's magazines and in public relations. She married a Frenchman who worked in the hotel industry and they had a daughter, Ineza. She lived with him in Japan for a year or two but the couple later divorced. Marina has custody of their daughter. This highly internationalised life is representative of thousands and thousands of modern younger Malays.

'My multiracial marriage was not an issue for my family or friends,' she said. 'If the outsider converts [Marina's husband converted to Islam on their marriage] it's no issue at all. I have two cousins, one engaged to an American and one to an Irishman. That's no problem.'

Although she is much more socially liberal than her father she has a loving relationship with him and greatly admires his historic achievements in Malaysia. Nonetheless, not only the Western press but the South East Asian media as well find her fascinating. 'In Singapore and Indonesia there's so much interest; I'm such an oddity in those countries. In Indonesia they look at me and say, "How can you possibly be like that?"'

In the book, *In Liberal Doses*, a collection of her newspaper columns, Marina frequently attacks the country's religious authorities. She was particularly vexed by the beauty contest case, in which some Malay women were briefly arrested for participating in a contest. The incident led to some of Marina's most trenchant pieces. In one she wrote:

> On the scale of horrendous ways to exploit women, beauty contests rank pretty low [in importance] . . . what worries me most of all is this, what next? What constitutes indecency in Muslim women? Not covering our heads? Wearing skirts? Short sleeves? Will there be men patrolling swimming pools and admonishing women for wearing swim suits? Who will be targetted next? Models? Singers? Actresses? TV announcers? Sportswomen? Female public figures such as politicians? Will it end when women retreat into the home, never to emerge again? . . .
>
> Otherwise we are out there to tempt weak, sex-crazed men. Can all these weak men please identify themselves so we can avoid them? . . . Compared to incest, child abuse, wife battering, drug abuse and corruption, whether you are dressed right or wrong according to somebody's arbitrary values should rank pretty low on the scale of the concerns of our times. By the way, has anyone in the State ever issued a fatwa on corruption?

By South East Asian standards Malaysia has a pretty wide range of permissible opinion but those lines are a very direct, in-your-face rejection of hardline religious interpretations.

Like Ivy's, Marina's views are shaped in part by the realities that she deals with day by day: 'People's attitudes to AIDS are changing, but not nearly fast enough. I deal a lot with desk jockeys who have no idea about the problems people really face. You learn from having to rescue people from villages and the little cruelties they face. You have to be empowered to take action and you're very unempowered when you're sick. If society would do the education work first it might not have some of these other problems.'

Overall, Marina remains optimistic about Islam in her country: 'I think we've always had a pretty tolerant brand of Islam in Malaysia. There are those who want it to be more strict but it always seems to be directed against women. I thank God we have a multiracial society because we always have a basis of comparison. Our domestic violence law was held up for years because it was said to be anti-Islam. Does that mean non-Islamic men cannot beat their wives but Islamic men can? Ultimately my father had to insist that it was passed.'

Norani, from Sisters In Islam, acknowledges that one of the biggest factors that progressive Muslim women have had going for them has been Prime Minister Mahathir's personal liberalism and leadership on religious issues. How, then, does he come to have such a definitively negative image in the West?

Partly, of course, it's his style. He talks back. He's crotchety. He's abrasive. He's verbally confrontational. But when you boil most of the rhetoric down, Mahathir has two basic complaints about the West, and both are reasonable, or at least not baseless, even if from a Western point of view they are often overstated. One is that the West is socially decadent. The other is that the Western powers bully and coerce smaller, less powerful nations like Malaysia. Even in his frequent jousts with the Western media Mahathir is often motivated by the disparity in power between an institution like, say, the New York Times and the Malaysian Government. The New York Times can affect the investment levels that flow into Malaysia; the Malaysian Government cannot materially affect the New York Times, nor more broadly the economic health of the United States. Moreover, it's important to realise that Mahathir doesn't take much coercive action against the Western press. He merely argues with it.

Western journalists who deny the power, and therefore the responsibility, of their own position are being disingenuous at best. And surely it's better to have an outspoken South East Asian leader who argues with the Western media rather than one who censors or excludes it. Malaysia is totally open to foreign journalists and Mahathir himself remarkably accessible. Even if he declines to give a particular foreign journalist a one-on-one interview it is very easy to find out when his frequent press conferences are being held, to go along, sit down the front and ask the most provocative questions you like. Indeed, certain Western journalists often do this. Mahathir is infinitely more accessible to Western journalists than an American president, or even an Australian prime minister, is to a Malaysian journalist.

All the same, sometimes Mahathir's rhetoric is excessive and even damaging to Malaysia. Fitting into such a category are the convoluted remarks in which he appeared to suggest that it was at least a possibility that some of the currency speculators who, so he had it, played a role in bringing down the value of the Malaysian ringgit may have been motivated by their being Jewish and therefore hostile to a Muslim nation's success. Mahathir's actual remarks were ambiguous and he backed away from them as soon as they were uttered. Nonetheless, they were hurtful to Jews and counterproductive to both Mahathir's and Malaysia's cause.

Sometimes, too, his rhetoric, while containing seeds of reasonable complaint against Western arrogance, is itself needlessly over the top. Calling the American currency trader George Soros 'a moron', while obviously plainly inaccurate, is also gratuitous and pointless. Similarly he seems sometimes to attribute a conspiratorial malice to unseen Western powers which is either unfair or grossly overdrawn. This was particularly in evidence in his response to the East Asian economic crisis. In an address in Hong Kong in late 1997 Mahathir said:

> I don't know about the average man in the street but quite a few people who are in the media and in control of the big money seem to want to see these South East Asian countries and, in particular, Malaysia stop trying to catch up with their superiors and to know their place. If they don't they just have to be made to do so and these people have the means and the wherewithal to force their will on these upstarts. There may be no conspiracy as such but it is quite obvious that a few at least, media as well as fund managers, have their own agenda which they are determined to carry out.

And on other occasions he accused Western powers of wanting to make Malaysia an economic colony.

Without endorsing Mahathir's view, it must be said there is something in it, in that a lot of the Western media comment on East Asia's travails was filled with an appalling and often badly informed Schadenfreude. This was particularly true of American commentary and could lead to a resurgence of anti-Americanism in the region. And many Western media and political commentators instantly and wrongly attributed East Asia's economic problems to a lack of total Western-style democracy, so that issues of corporate governance and financial system weakness were intertwined with issues of political ideology.

But overall the conspiracy interpretation of the great financial crisis doesn't hold up. It presumes a degree of coordination and precise planning, on the part of a vast array of players, that is simply not credible. Western hedge funds *were* part of the problem—they were too unregulated and were irresponsible. Mainstream Western authorities recognised this eventually. But the hedge funds were not the only people selling Asian currencies; numerous Asians were doing so themselves. The failure of many Asian banks and corporations to hedge in advance their American dollar debts was hardly attributable to a Western conspiracy. Absolutely no one predicted the crisis in anything like its full dimensions—how could anyone possibly have been controlling it?

Nonetheless, Mahathir's willingness to 'talk back' to the Western powers is one of the attractive features of his personality, though in the wrong context it can be hazardous. There is also the question of how much it is motivated by domestic concerns. This should not be overstated. Mahathir has not needed to wage an anti-Western verbal war to secure his position. But he has been the master of the theatre of Malaysian politics. Lacking significant domestic opposition, at least for most of the last decade until Anwar's jailing, he has at times used bouts of anti-Westernism to unify Malaysian politics, and perhaps even to help mould an internal transethnic single identity for his state, partly defining it in contrast to the West.

Somewhat like the Thai leader, Chuan Leekpai, Mahathir has seen Asian values as a positive force that would help the region come back from the economic crisis. In an interview in 1998 he remarked: 'Asian values have their good and bad points. But Asian stoicism, diligence, family loyalty, community orientation, respect for authority, law and order and orthodoxy—these are the strong values which pulled Asians through the years of foreign oppression and helped rebuild their societies. These same values will stand them in good stead in striving for recovery from the present and future turmoil inflicted upon them.

'Are Asian values bad as compared to Western values? History provides the answer. The two world wars and the dropping of the atom bombs on Asian cities, the holocaust, the killings of Bosnians—these were not perpetuated by Asians. [And] currency trading is not an Asian invention.'

In recent years Mahathir and Anwar, though at least publicly never absolutely directly at odds before Anwar's arrest, presented the Malaysian world view in very different tones of voice. This was never more evident than in the response of the two men to the regional economic crisis. I spent January and part of February of 1998 travelling around Malaysia, mainly enjoying myself, but I did interview both Mahathir and Anwar, coincidentally on the same day. The crisis, then six months old, totally dominated the nation and the leaders' conversation. As usual, their response was a study in contrasts.

Anwar saw the crisis as offering the region a great and historic opportunity. It would end crony capitalism and in the long run lead to reformed and more soundly based modern economies, he told me. 'It will lead to a new Asia which will be more confident and more mature, and liberal and democratic. The great lesson we have learnt, which is actually a transformation and a revolution in itself, is that it has called for greater transparency, greater accountability, for greater democracy. Now people assess what the markets say, what people perceive, whether awards and grants are given to your party supporters or to friends and family. These are now openly debated, without exception.'

But he added an important rider: 'At the same time, having learned the lessons of this turmoil, we recognise that Asian identity, Asian solidarity and Asian values are not only important but will be more pronounced than ever.'

Anwar was thus formulating a complex and multilayered response, designed to perform several tasks—to deal with the inescapable reality of the economic crisis, but to seek to energise the crisis for constructive reform while remaining faithful to the region's core values.

Mahathir, who has certainly pushed the envelope of reform on countless occasions himself, was more lugubrious, seeing starkly the downside of the crisis not only in economic terms but in terms of loss of South East Asia's bargaining power and political strength vis-a-vis Western powers. He told me: 'If you consider that democratically elected leaders can be displaced by outside powers there must be some loss of independence. Even if they are not democratically elected, if people have lost the power to choose their own leaders, by whatever means, then there must be a loss of power.' Mahathir was being unusually elliptical that day but I assume he was referring to the political pressure that the International Monetary Fund, and the money markets generally, brought to bear, which effectively resulted in changes of government in Thailand, South Korea and later Indonesia. I asked him whether this would lead to regional resentment against the influence of outside powers. He replied: 'People dare not speak out now, but privately, of course, they have voiced a lot of stiff resentment.' Later Mahathir would himself speak more strongly on these themes.

Mahathir is always softly spoken in interviews. In one-on-one meetings he is solicitous, deeply courteous and answers questions slowly and quietly. In that interview he told me he was literally afraid to speak out, following savage international market reactions to his earlier harsh criticisms of the international currency trading system (he had blamed currency traders for the collapse of regional currencies): 'It's been said I've now toned down my criticisms. That is basically out of fear. It is no longer safe to speak out and give your views. If you say the wrong thing you will be brutally punished by having your currency devalued. We lack the freedom of speech now. It has been pointed out that there is a very close relation to opinions expressed or deeds done with the devaluation of currencies. The currency is devalued, jobs are lost, people suffer. It's a very heavy punishment on the whole nation. No leader, I think, would want to say things which allow punishment, not on him personally, but on his people.'

At the time I was astonished to hear these words from the man I had come to regard as the most consistently forthright and outspoken statesman in Asia. The great paradox of Mahathir has always been that, while he championed Asian values, his personal rhetorical style, his style of leadership, was so Western, so upfront, so dialectical. That day, in a further irony almost too intricate to unravel, the power of the Western financial markets seemed to have forced on him an uncharacteristic Asian reticence. Of course, he would later recover full rhetorical self-confidence.

Again Mahathir had at least half a general point. It was acceptable for a Western economist like David Hale, or even the chairman of the US Federal Reserve, Alan Greenspan, to draw attention to the shortcomings of the international money markets, but it was, for a time in 1998 anyway, not acceptable for a South East Asian leader to do so—because the markets would interpret that as a retreat from pro-market reform and punish the currency accordingly.

For his part, Anwar tried to bridge this contradiction by offering an interpretation of the crisis which accepted plenty of home-grown blame, but also gently drew attention to the power of outside forces and the unsatisfactory nature of totally unregulated currency trading and short-term capital flows. Anwar said: 'The pace of liberalisation in the region had been so fast that I don't think we had the infrastructure for a free-market operation in place. The general public, except for a very few, have no comprehension about how a free market operates, or how the stock market operates. Secondly, of course, there's the issue that has been much discussed—the inherent weaknesses within the particular systems. You have a modern banking system but directed by those in power [as to where] to lend, as in Korea, and prior to that the Thai problem. There was the question of overlending to the property sector, a lack of prudence on the part of the banks because of political connections, and a failure of supervision. Then of course there was stock market corruption, nepotism and cronyism, which are all related.

'My reservation about that criticism is that it assumes the Western system is quite free from these excesses. Accepting all these facts, we cannot deny the role of the currency traders and short-term speculators who manipulate the market. If it was incorrect for [regional] governments to allow these excesses I think similarly it's unacceptable for the international system to condone the excesses of these manipulators and speculators.

There was thus a perfectly respectable Malaysian case that the international currency markets needed some reform. However, it was for a time a dangerous case for South East Asian leaders to make. Both Mahathir and Anwar were disappointed at the unforthcoming nature of the US response to the crisis and at Japan's lack of action.

Mahathir's most radical actions, of course, were jailing Anwar and imposing currency controls. Outsiders probably overemphasise the ideological content of the struggle between Mahathir and Anwar. The specific charges laid against Anwar are obviously only part of the story. Partly it was a struggle between two very tough and determined politicians. Partly it was a generational struggle. Partly it had to do with longstanding factional struggles in UMNO. And partly it was ideological.

Imposing currency controls was also a radical step, but one that had been suggested, after all, by the Western economist-guru, Paul Krugman. It may or may not have been good policy; it certainly was not unreasonable policy. It was an assertive attempt by the Malaysian Government to regain control of its economy. And the totally uncontrolled, extremely volatile flows of very short-term capital were widely recognised as a problem that merited serious policy attention.

Mahathir's most famous clash with a representative of American power came at the Asia-Pacific Economic Cooperation forum leaders' meeting in Kuala Lumpur in November 1998. At the last moment Bill Clinton had cancelled and his vice-president, Al Gore, had gone instead. At a speech in front of Mahathir preceding the APEC Business Summit dinner, Gore made what might be considered a scandalous intervention in Malaysian politics. Part of his speech was a standard American call for democracy. He said, inter alia: 'And so we continue to hear calls for democracy, calls for *doi moi*, people's power, *reformasi*. We hear them today—right here, right now—among the brave people of Malaysia.'

This was a speech of bizarre, almost surreal, oddity and

obnoxiousness. For a start, *Doi Moi* is the official slogan of the Vietnamese Communist Party. Since when has anybody accused the Vietnamese Communist Party of being interested in democracy? Is the Vietnamese Communist Party, a thoroughly Stalinist outfit, to be equated with Cory Aquino's People Power revolution in the Philippines in 1986? *Reformasi* is indeed a word that various groups use, both in Malaysia and in Indonesia, but Gore's using it in this way virtually equated Malaysia with Indonesia. In the context, this was grotesque. Elections in Indonesia under Suharto had been almost wholly farcical. No one could describe them as fair. In Malaysia, even the Opposition describes the elections as clean. To equate Malaysia with Indonesia in terms of *reformasi*, as Gore's speech tended to do, was both inaccurate and unfair.

The whole performance was abysmal, and emblematic of the Clinton administration's general hamfistedness and perpetual concern to get a good TV grab at home no matter what havoc it might cause in US foreign policy. Gore's gauche intervention could only be contrasted with the sotto voce performance that Clinton had given a few months earlier on his visit to China, cooing and billing to the Chinese Communist Party leaders. Why so sweet in Beijing and so strident in Kuala Lumpur? Did Malaysia really deserve this? Gore also conveyed an air of pompous superiority in turning up to the dinner and delivering his insult, only to leave without waiting for the meal. Making such an inappropriate and bad-mannered intervention on behalf of Mahathir's political opponents could only reinforce every negative thing about the West that any Malaysian had ever thought. Indeed, the Malaysian Opposition felt that Gore's intervention seriously damaged their cause.

One of Malaysia's leading intellectuals, Dr Noordin Sopiee, the head of the Institute for Strategic and International Studies, an urbane internationalist and an immensely sophisticated man, took out a full-page advertisement in the Malaysian *New Straits Times* in response to Gore's speech. Its text read:

As a Malaysian, I am fed up of stupid, ignorant, 'kurang ajar' [a Malay expression meaning extremely ill-mannered] idiots insulting my country.

Mr Gore should not only have left the meeting room immediately after insulting us. He should have got on the plane and left the country, and he should not come back until he has learnt some manners.

I am not a politician. I do not want to play politics. I am not anti-American. For these very strong words, I certainly apologise to my many, many American friends who are also very embarrassed.

I do not even know if other Malaysians feel the same way. But enough is enough.

Noordin Sopiee. A citizen of Malaysia.

Noordin's sentiments were understandable, if harshly expressed. But the whole incident, which at its root was Gore's fault, can only add to the serious misperceptions that Americans and Malaysians tend to have of each other. Must it always be thus?

Asian values, Western nightmares.

6

CHINA AND THE
CONFUCIUS THEME PARK

IN CHINA IT'S VERY often the slogans that give you the clue.
Not that you ever believe the slogans exactly, but they always
tell you something. In 1985 I worked in Beijing as a newspaper
correspondent. I remember one day wandering down one of
Beijing's countless *hutongs*, or little alleyways, which form an
intricate latticework across vast swaths of the city, when, peering
obtrusively into someone's living-room (which was in any event
open to the street), I saw a painted slogan on the wall.

My interpreter translated it. The sign said: 'Marry late, have
one child, support the four modernisations!'

Although in subsequent years I frequently visited cities of
greater China—Hong Kong, Taipei, Kaoshiung etc—I did not
return to mainland China until 1997. In that visit the first slogan
I saw was above the entrance way to the Hard Rock Cafe next
door to my hotel. It said: 'No Drugs or Nuclear Weapons
Allowed.'

Of course, neither slogan is really convincing as ideology; they
convince more as a sign of a desire to suck up. But what a
difference in the politically correct a decade makes! To have lived
in Beijing as a correspondent in 1985 and not to have returned
until 1997 is like visiting two separate planets. Or perhaps it's
like visiting a city you remember from a past life, say 1000 years
earlier. Traces of the old city remain but a new city has been
built on top of it.

In China it is not the little things that strike you but the big
things, like the giant freeway from the airport, the enormous new

buildings everywhere, the volume of traffic, including countless thousands of taxis. In 1985 there weren't independent taxis. A foreigner could rent a car with driver for a single journey, or for an allotted period of time, from the big hotels, but you couldn't easily hail a taxi in the street. If you were going anywhere out of the way, you made the car wait and you didn't pay the driver until you got home. Foreigners in Beijing were either wealthy, in which case they had cars and drivers, or poor, in which case they rode bicycles. Now there are cabs everywhere.

Naturally, the changes involve much more than just cabs. Beijing today has become much like any other anarchic, raucous Asian city, development belting along helter-skelter, with touts and hucksters everywhere, night markets and international brand signs, neon lights and, above Beijing Railway Station, even a giant television screen showing soap opera to the masses.

That now is normal enough. What was really odd was the Beijing of 1985, with its puritanism and its stark, Stalinist buildings, its order, its floods of bicycles dominating the broad streets, the drabness of people's clothes. While I've often enough felt nostalgic for the Cold War—its moral purpose and the solidarity it brought—I never thought I'd ever feel nostalgia for any aspect of a communist society. Undoubtedly the Beijing of today is a vastly better place than the Beijing of 1985. And yet, and yet . . .

There were elements of the old order that were not wholly unattractive—perhaps just the security of the old work units, the giant compounds that would house, clothe, feed, educate and otherwise look after their employees. Of course, they massively restricted the inhabitants' freedom as well, deciding when they could have children, when they could marry, how and where and, often, with whom they could live. But they did provide an identity and a sense of security, and in the unbelievable turbulence that has swirled through China in the 20th century (and in centuries past) very often security was what a great many people chiefly craved.

I took a look in 1997 at some of Beijing's icons, to see if they had changed from 1985. Walking down Chang'an Avenue, the Avenue of Eternal Peace—and what might be described as Beijing's main drag—I am struck by three great changes. One is the affluence and colour in people's dress, with not a Mao suit in sight. Another is the proliferation of modern buildings, many with Asian-international brand names—Lucky Gold Star, Lotte, New Otani, Samsung. And the China World Trade Centre looks exactly like its namesake in Taipei. Indeed, the whole city looks like Taipei, without quite the intensity of traffic—yet—that you find in the capital of the renegade province.

The third thing that strikes me on Chang'an Avenue is the beggars. People suffering terrible deformities, others with disturbingly passive, perhaps drugged, children. The pathos is real enough and the line of beggars seems to stretch endlessly. They were not there in 1985. Yet the city overall must be ten times, twenty times, as affluent as it was then. So why so many beggars? Is it a sign of the growing gap between rich and poor, or of the dislocation of some state-owned enterprises? Or were the poor always there but kept out of sight in formerly tightly controlled Beijing? Certainly there were beggars, and often enough starvation, in other parts of China. The fact that they are now on the streets of Beijing is probably really a sign of greater normality, and fractionally less control by the state authorities.

I stroll down to Liulichang, the antique art and book centre of Beijing. I used to visit this district in 1985, drawn as much by the serenity, the sense of scholarly calm, as anything. Now it's chaos. Traffic, tourists, shopkeepers shouting, everybody giving voice, bargaining, offering deals. And, everywhere, American Express signs.

I pass by the Confucian Heritage Restaurant but it is closed. Inside the staff have divided themselves between two tables and are furiously playing cards. It was while I was in China in 1985 that Confucius was rehabilitated. After the revolution that brought the communists to power in 1949, Confucius fell out of favour. But he really came in for the chop during the Cultural Revolution, the decade of Mao Zedong madness and brutish iconoclasm that swept China from 1966.

During the Cultural Revolution there was a movement to 'criticise Confucius and criticise Lin Biao'. Lin Biao had been a defence minister and was once close to Mao. But like so many during the Cultural Revolution he was accused of wanting to restore capitalism and fell into disgrace. Confucius at the same time was accused of having wanted to restore slavery and thus, in some bizarre fashion, Confucius and Lin Biao were linked. This often happens in China. Some old figure is linked to a contemporary figure in a complex ideological campaign. Sometimes the linking is not too explicit and thus the criticism of the one can be a heavily veiled criticism of the other.

In any event, by 1985 the Confucius derided as feudal was forgotten and the party instead focused on the progressive Confucius, the man who emphasised education and human enrichment, as well as conservative values such as filial piety. In retrospect, the 1985 rehabilitation can be seen as a decisive moment, a turning point in the history of the Chinese Communist Party. Once, in the service of a modern, invented, and Western-originated universalist ideology (communism), the party was going to destroy the feudal elements of Chinese society and history. Then, when they effectively abandoned Marxism, what could take its place but nationalism and something the Sinologist, Bill Jenner, has called 'the tyranny of history'. Now there is a Confucian Heritage Restaurant and in due course, no doubt, there will be Confucius theme parks dotted all over China. From brutal iconoclasm to conventional authoritarianism to crass commercialisation—thus we witness the three stages of communism.

I once asked Pierre Ryckmans, the great Belgian Sinologist, who under his pen-name Simon Leys has published a new translation of the *Analects of Confucius*, what he thought of the 1985 rehabilitation. He remarked that he thought it was quite a dangerous development for Confucius. And indeed, the much traduced sage of Chinese history has at times been used to justify all manner of Asian authoritarianism.

But for anyone remotely interested in Chinese culture and history, and in the influence of the great Chinese stream of humanity on the world, it is worth making some serious acquaintance with Confucius. Ryckmans's translation of the Analects allows a non-Chinese-speaking Western audience to do that really for the first time.

The Analects has to be considered the most influential book in the history of the human race, a highly disconcerting view for Westerners who have been brought up, even unconsciously, to assume that the classics of the Western canon have no equal in terms of influence or beauty. Yet the Analects, spoken by the Chinese sage 2500 years ago and written down and put together by his disciples, has had a bigger impact on a greater segment of the human race over a longer time than any other book. Ryckmans's translation (published in the US by Routledge) gives us non-Chinese speakers an opportunity, at an altogether new level of literary quality and human sympathy, to make the acquaintance of the living Confucius.

The Confucius we meet is completely unlike the Confucius of popular imagination. How do you think of Confucius—as an ethereal, frail scholar locked up forever with his books, barely speaking except to utter periodic, profound aphorisms? Something like an upmarket version of the blind monk in *Kung Fu*, addressing everyone as 'Grasshopper' and dispensing enigmatic advice to all?

Instead, what we meet in the Analects is a complete man, vigorous and active in the enjoyment of life, an archer, a charioteer, a man who undertook arduous and adventurous journeys, a man who conceived of his public career as primarily that of a political administrator and reformer, who sought, unsuccessfully, state power to give effect to his ideas for good government.

We also meet a man whose philosophy was profoundly humanist and, in its way and for its time, revolutionary. One of Confucius's central ideas was that to become a gentleman it was necessary to possess certain moral qualities, that moral improvement was the purpose of education and that moral education was the hallmark of the gentleman. This was indeed revolutionary because it democratised the status of the gentleman, it opened up this status to anybody prepared to devote themselves to education. It thus fatally undermined the idea of an hereditary aristocracy. China's system of an all-powerful civil service selected on the basis of competitive public examination open to all, which derived from Confucius's ideas, was the most liberal system of government in operation anywhere in the world until modern times.

How, then, have Confucius and his teachings come to be seen as a justification for East Asian authoritarianism, not least by some within East Asian governments? As Ryckmans demonstrates, this is partly through the selective quotation of passages in the Analects which emphasise obedience—of child to parent, of citizen to ruler. But throughout the Analects there is encouragement for legitimate dissent. One disciple asks the Master how best to serve the prince. Confucius replies that he must tell the prince the truth, even if it offends him. Similarly, a strikingly universalist view of human nature comes through. Confucius declares that, while it is possible to rob an army of its commander-in-chief, it is impossible to deprive even the humblest man of his free will.

Nonetheless, the effect of centuries of rulers' invoking Confucius in support of obedience was to make the sage unpopular with democratic and revolutionary Chinese movements in the early part of the 20th century. Yet, as Ryckmans points out, the influence of Confucian concepts was so pervasive that it provided the unconscious psychological substructure even of Maoism, ostensibly the most revolutionary of creeds. Thus the Maoist re-education camps were a reflection, albeit a grotesquely distorted reflection, of the Confucian view that all faults can be rectified by moral education.

One of the most intoxicating and delightful revelations of the Analects is Confucius's view of the central importance of language to politics and life. As Ryckmans rightly points out, this is an insight shared by figures as diverse as Orwell and Chesterton. It is frequently the discovery to be made at the 'bloody crossroads', as Lionel Trilling called them, where literature and politics intersect. Get the language right and almost everything else follows. Get the language wrong and it is almost impossible to get anything else right. Without the right language, as Orwell argued, it is impossible even to think thoughts which correspond with reality. When Confucius is asked what would be the first thing he would do if he were to be given state power, he replies: 'It would certainly be to rectify the names.'

This statement is used by Ryckmans as the occasion for a marvellously provocative textual note. Ryckmans's interpretive notes form almost another book as fascinating in its way as the Analects themselves. Ryckmans argues that in the Confucian view the socio-political order is completely dependent on a 'correct definition of each individual's function, identity, duties, privileges and responsibilities'. Ryckmans asserts further that the teaching is as relevant today as when Confucius formulated it, that much of the 'moral chaos' of our own time, with its 'infantile adults, precociously criminal children, androgynous individuals, homo-sexual families, despotic leaders, asocial citizens, incestuous fathers . . .', is a reflection of a drift into confusion, especially about the obligations and roles attached to particular stations of life—father, mother, teacher etc. Even sexual differentiation, Ryckmans argues, has become confused. This is of course Ryckmans's own extrapolation from Confucius, but, reading the Analects overall, it is a perfectly reasonable extrapolation and serves to underline the importance of the harmony between individual, family and society in Confucius's view.

The striking contemporary relevance that Ryckmans—and, I would think, the average Western reader—easily finds in the Analects comes in part from a singular advantage that non-Chinese people have in reading the work. It is our only advantage but it is an important one. The Western reader comes to the Analects fresh, without the vast accretion of meaning and asso-ciation that the Analects, as the pre-eminent classic of Chinese civilisation, holds for every Chinese. It is similar perhaps to the joy a Chinese might experience in reading Shakespeare, or the Bible, for the first time. But of course to achieve such pleasure in the reading of a foreign classic one must either master the foreign language or benefit from the services of a translator who is at the same time a writer, literary stylist and thinker of the highest order. In approaching Ryckmans's Confucius we are fortunate to have such services at our disposal.

Like all classics, the Analects have the capacity to grow through interpretation and history. Yet for the Western reader what strikes one is the extraordinary sense of modernity about the work. No single book is a better introduction to the Chinese mind.

I ponder these notions as I walk away from the Confucian Heritage Restaurant, across from Liulichang and the antique shops, to the long, crowded market-street of Dazhalan. Every-thing seems to be for sale here: clothes, trinkets, appliances. There is an exceptionally grimy cinema showing what appear to be kung fu slash-and-chop epics. There is a video parlour with kids crowded in, pouring their money into slot machines and games of every variety. In pre-communist times Dazhalan used to be the centre of the red-light district and there is still an air of slightly disordered raffishness about it. But it is no longer a red-light district.

Yet the sex industry is much in evidence in Beijing. Outside my hotel that night a female pimp approaches, not to sell herself but to tell me that if I come to her dance club, just five minutes away by taxi, I can choose any girl I like for US$100. Barely a hundred metres from my hotel is a small pub, with an admirably direct sign, 'Drinking Establishment', on its wall. Inside, the arrival of an unaccompanied male causes half a dozen heavily made-up young women in black miniskirts to leap to attention. There is nothing particularly strange about this. All big cities have their sex industry. But Beijing used to be so prim and proper, so puritanical. Now it's just like everywhere else. When I lived there in the mid-1980s there was almost no nightlife after 8.00 pm, apart from the exclusively Western and stultifyingly dull disco in one or two big hotels (which were off-limits to most Chinese anyway lest we foreigners pollute them with our wicked ideas). Now in Beijing the nightlife doesn't get going until 11.00 pm, rocks on all night and is overwhelmingly patronised by locals.

Back on Chang'an Avenue I call by the Beijing Hotel. It used to be the one, big, international hotel, government-owned and with a relentless atmosphere of Stalinism in its architecture and deportment. Its vast foyer was the most cosmopolitan place in Beijing. African students (always a persecuted and fascinating community) used to mix with Eastern Bloc diplomats, American exchange scholars would strike up affairs with European business-men, and so on. The hotel also ran one of the most Stalinist Sichuan restaurants in China open to foreigners. If you hadn't placed your order by about 6.30 pm you could forget about a meal. The waiters took aggressive indifference to its extreme ideological endpoint, an almost sublime solipsism suffusing them as they ruthlessly avoided the glance and gesture of hungry customers.

But truly there has been a cultural revolution in the Chinese approach to the service industry. Now the Yiyuan Garden Restaurant drips with smiling attendants, has been refurbished to within an inch of its life, and oozes luxury and opulence. Once it was like the dining-room in an unruly Victorian boarding school with particularly unsympathetic prefects; now it could be a posh Chinese restaurant in any five star hotel in the world.

The hotel foyer, alas, is a cosmopolitan meeting place no more. Instead, like much else in Beijing, it has been ruthlessly commercialised and knick-knack, souvenir and convenience stores line both sides.

The commercialisation proceeds with gusto. The underwear store has distinctly lascivious photographs of exclusively Western women in the briefest of briefs. Gone are the days when the authorities cancelled the broadcast of a Tina Turner concert (and replaced it with a program on Soong poetry) because it was too raunchy. But I note one touch of the old Beijing. In the substantial art store, filled with replicas of traditional Chinese art, is a single, huge portrait of Lenin, awaiting the arrival of the last True Believer.

Not far down the street, opposite Tiananmen Square, which this day looks busy but peaceful, with no sign of the events of 1989, I wander into the Forbidden City, the palace complex where for hundreds of years Chinese emperors lived and reigned. Here surely at least, I think, nothing will have changed. It is of course down to the merest good fortune that the Red Guards didn't smash up the Forbidden City during the Cultural Revolution. But here still is the vast complex of halls and residences and traditional buildings, the vast and symmetrical designs exerting a certain druglike influence over the senses. It is both bare and opulent; certainly it is imposing.

In the centre of the Forbidden City I walk up the steps to the Hall of Great Harmony, the tallest and largest of the palace buildings. And here, at the very heart of Chinese civilisation, what do I see? On the board explaining the building's history and structure, a prominent sign: 'Brought to you by American Express.' This, truly, is the new China.

The old Beijing does lurk here and there. In 1985 I used to spend almost every evening, dressed in a white suit, propping up the bar and inhaling beer and peanuts at Charlie's Saloon in the

Jianguo Hotel, feeling like Sydney Greenstreet in a Humphrey Bogart movie and listening to a beautiful Filipino guitar and vocal combination. To my astonishment, Charlie's is still there and still has a Filipino band.

But now Beijing's hordes of yuppies swarm to discos across the city. One night at JJ Disco Square I watched Beijing's beautiful people—young men in suits, many others in bomber jackets (the informal uniform at that time in the computer industry), young women favouring short pants despite the freezing spring weather—bopping and jiving to the loudest music I have ever heard. This was disco mania, without any recognisably Chinese characteristics.

Of course, while Chinese yuppies may party hard, they also take the business of making the money needed for partying very seriously. In 1985 the non-state commercial sector was small and its participants sometimes had difficulty finding marriage partners because people feared they would be arrested in the next mass purge. Now the private sector, making up a substantial majority of the Chinese economy, is the hippest place to be. One famous private company is the User's Friend Software Company, which specialises in creating software in the Chinese language and compatible with Chinese financial systems.

Wang Wenjing, its owner-manager, is in his early 30s and wears a windjacket over an open-neck shirt. A small, round-faced man, he positively looks like (in the best and most flattering sense) a computer nerd. But this computer nerd has in fewer than ten years taken his company, which he founded alone with borrowed capital, to a position where it supplies 40 per cent of the Chinese market for its product, employs 350 people, has 20 branches throughout China and a turnover measured in tens of millions of dollars.

'I don't think of myself as a pioneer,' he tells me, 'though this is one of the earliest private companies in China. At the time there was no precedent, but China had a law which allowed private companies. I didn't think I was taking any risk at the time because I thought this line of business must have a bright future.'

In mentioning risk Wang is presumably talking of commercial risk, but in fact he took an enormous political risk. He bet his life on the belief that the party would not go back on its economic reform program, that he would never be denounced as a 'capitalist roader'. Now he praises the Chinese Government's efforts to protect intellectual property rights. His software has frequently been pirated by other Chinese operators.

In 1985 people were still hedging their bets about the future much more. In that year I interviewed a senior figure at the Marxism-Leninism-Mao Zedong Thought Institute, who explained to me where Mao had gone wrong in the early 1950s. Indeed, it seemed as if Mao had hardly had any Mao thoughts after the early 1950s. He also explained to me that the party would never retreat from reform, never again have mass campaigns and purges. At the end of the interview, however, he asked me not to use his name in print. Having talked about Mao in that fashion, he feared his words might be used against him in the next mass campaign or purge (which he had just told me could never happen). He was right to be cautious. I subsequently heard he was purged after the Tiananmen Square massacre of 1989. In 1985 China was full of such contradictions. Now, while contradictions abound, they interfere with normal life far less.

The state-owned sector is still huge, and its reform the most vexed issue in China, but the private sector is growing so rapidly it is leaving the state sector in its wake. And the visual impressions of Beijing, as of many Chinese cities, are overwhelmingly of a raucous private economy and society. The neon lights and discos, the giant TV screens, the crass commercialism and the computer software companies can all be seen as part of what Chinese just naturally do when the government isn't treading on their necks. For all the crassness, for most people life is far better than it was a decade ago. But if this is socialism with Chinese characteristics, it also looks a lot like capitalism with Chinese characteristics.

The maintenance of the Chineseness in those characteristics is bound to be one of the great challenges for China in the early decades of the 21st century. For much of the Chinese leadership today, their ideology seems to have been reduced to three precepts: economic growth, Chinese nationalism and Chinese power. Balancing those three involves some happy synergies—economic growth produces more Chinese power—but also some difficult contradictions: Chinese nationalism, if it means policies hostile to the market, may be the enemy of economic growth. Similarly, economic globalism inevitably breaks down elements of cultural nationalism. Or, the exercise of Chinese power, if it is of a military kind, can damage economic growth if it makes other countries reluctant to trade and invest in China. Managing the three imperatives—growth, power and nationalism—is a complex task for the leadership. Mostly, the interests of maximising Chinese power and economic growth combine to defeat the more extreme manifestations of Chinese nationalism, when these are in conflict, and produce generally pragmatic policies.

But Chinese nationalism is destined to be one of the great forces in the 21st century. The death of Marxism-Leninism as any meaningful ideology has left a vacuum in mainland Chinese life which is tending to be filled by a crass materialism, the re-emergence of all kinds of folk superstitions, for some the reawakening of interest in conventional religion, and for many the recrudescence of Chinese nationalism.

In recent years the Chinese Government has increasingly tried to make its claim of ownership of Chinese nationalism an exclusive claim, especially, as Sinologist Geremie Barme argues, to emphasise 'strengthening its hold on cultural nationalism'. But it is exceptionally difficult to determine how deeply this cultural nationalism really runs in China. The recrudescence of nationalism is not a phenomenon afflicting only the aged leadership of the Politburo and likely to pass away when they join the Great Helmsman in the Sky. My experience of Chinese officials is that the younger and more internationally switched-on they are the more nationalistic they tend to be.

But it is difficult to know how widespread this is across China. The Chinese don't do opinion polls, or if they do they don't tell us about them.

There are several factors that could lead to an exaggerated conclusion about Chinese nationalism. For one, in a period of leadership transition traditional Communist Party dogma tends to be emphasised. In foreign policy this means, particularly, making the resumption of control over Taiwan a priority. After all, Mao Zedong, inherently a much more ideological leader than any of today's Chinese leaders, could, from his greater leadership security, talk airily to Richard Nixon about Beijing's being relaxed about not resuming control of Taiwan for another 100 years. Today's more insecure leadership is sometimes forced to make it a priority.

Then again, nationalism may be partly a response to constant Western criticism over human rights, trade practices, weapons proliferation and the rest. Nationalism is a normal reaction to criticism anywhere, especially among the Chinese with their inbuilt sense of historic grievance against the West.

On the other hand, there are other possibilities. One of the most intriguing is that the Chinese leadership may be using an exaggerated estimation of nationalistic sentiment as a point of leverage in both domestic and international politics, to silence domestic critics and to subdue international critics who may be cowed into a fear of provoking a nationalist backlash in China.

Nonetheless, Chinese nationalism is clearly on the rise to some extent. In Beijing I raised these issues with Pan Yue, the then vice deputy-general of the National Administrative Bureau of State-Owned Assets. Pan is a real mover and shaker in Beijing. His father-in-law was a senior military figure on the Politburo and his own position put him at the centre of the debate over reform of China's state-owned enterprises. A charming and cosmopolitan man, Pan is regarded as a neo-conservative because of his views about the centrality of Chinese culture. His prescription for China's future bears this out: 'China fell back behind the West 200 years ago. In the past 100 years the world powers have been on top of China in political and economic respects in order to block China, to pressure China, to take away the property of China. In the 21st century the centre of the world economy will move from the Atlantic to the Pacific and Chinese culture will dominate the Asia-Pacific region. Chinese culture dominates in Hong Kong, Taiwan, Macau and Singapore. Even Japan and Korea are long influenced by traditional Chinese culture. This allows the countries of the region to communicate well. In the past Western culture has had a big impact on China, especially Chinese youth. Now many Chinese youth go abroad to study but come back to find their own roots and traditional culture. The two cultures are not against each other. We don't reject Western culture, we can make use of it.'

It is possible of course to find much more extreme versions of Pan's views throughout China. Interestingly, when I commented on them in Singapore there was some unhappiness, for while Singaporean officials recognise the role of Chinese culture in Singapore's success they are fastidious in distinguishing cultural Chineseness from political Chineseness. Elsewhere through South East Asia, especially where ethnic Chinese minorities have had difficult times, there is great sensitivity to the idea of Sinicisation of the region.

Occasionally there are popular manifestations of Chinese nationalism which give a hint of what lies below. In 1996 a right-wing Japanese group put up a small structure on one of the disputed Daioyou islands in the East China Sea. Both Japan and China claim these islands. The Japanese action sparked immediate anti-Japanese protests in Hong Kong and Taiwan. The pan-Chinese nationalistic reaction in Hong Kong was very strong and some Japanese residents there reportedly held fears for their safety.

The reaction in mainland China was equally enlightening. At first happy with this outbreak of pan-Chinese nationalism, Beijing then refused permission for anti-Japanese protests in Shanghai and elsewhere in the country. In a peculiar way this is one of the most telling signs that Chinese nationalism may indeed be very powerful. Patriotic demonstrations in China's past have sometimes spun out of control and become anti-government demonstrations. Beijing may well have felt that nationalism might have become a powerful enough spark, just as sentiment against corruption had become in Tiananmen Square in 1989, to lead to something that would be difficult, or at least messy, to control.

The taming and controlling of nationalism will be an important factor in China's future political evolution, just as controlling political Islam is a perennial challenge for Indonesia's leaders.

Much Western thinking, especially at the popular level, about China's political evolution is severely limited by the Western tendency towards binary, dialectical, either/or formulations. Either China will embrace human rights and democracy and become just like, say, Taiwan writ large, or it will continue as a darkly authoritarian regime which suppresses human rights and is an enemy of human freedom.

Both alternatives represent fairly extreme and unlikely

positions along a continuum of possibilities for China's future. Most continuums are in fact bell-shaped curves, with the extremes at either end much less likely to occur than some result in the middle. Perhaps the most likely, and certainly the most hopeful, scenario is for China's political development to unfold along recognisable East Asian authoritarian lines. Hopefully, over time, it will become soft authoritarianism.

Part of the problem in Western and especially American reactions to China comes from the classically American confusion of democracy and human rights. They are related concepts, obviously, but they are not the same thing, and the American habit, even at the highest level, of speaking of them as though they were is an obstacle to good policy on China, policy which would actually encourage the expansion of human rights.

The distinction between democracy and human rights is fundamental. Democracy does not always lead to respect for human rights. It mostly does, but not always. Hitler, after all, was voted into power, albeit with a minority of votes. The southern states of the United States were all democracies when they denied basic civil rights, even effectively the franchise, to their black populations right up until the 1960s. The majority sometimes does vote to persecute the minority. Similarly, non-democratic states do not always abuse basic human rights. Perhaps the best example of that is Hong Kong itself. In all its history it has never been a democracy, yet for several decades it has certainly observed its citizens' basic human rights. The British never felt they had to introduce democracy in order to secure human rights while they were ruling in Hong Kong.

No outsider really has the right to demand of China that it become a democracy. In any event, the demand it impractical. You may as well ask the wind not to blow or the clouds not to rain. But outsiders, and Chinese for that matter, do have the right to ask the Chinese Government to observe its citizens' most basic human rights. Again, the doctrine of much of the Western human rights lobby—that all human rights are equally important—is analytically ridiculous and gets in the way of a sensible discussion. The right to life is more important than the right to organise a trade union. The right to choose whom you marry is more important than the right to free political expression. The right to freedom from arbitrary arrest is far more important than the right to total freedom of speech.

Numerous East Asian societies have developed a basic civic compact between people and government that goes something like this: citizens are free to do anything they like, except for the things that are banned, chief among which is serious political opposition to the government. Citizens can seek their fortunes, marry whom they wish, practise the religion of their choice, read most books, watch most television, listen to most music, emigrate, educate their children how they wish, cultivate their gardens, and so on, so long as they do not attack the government. In return the government provides physical security and an environment that fosters economic growth.

Economic growth, in the globalised information age, inevitably leads to citizens' enjoying greater political space. That is not to say that economic growth necessarily leads to democracy, though it often does. But there is no need to make such a claim, a more ambitious claim, for the political benefits of economic growth still to be recognised as vast. The reforms in China over the last 20 years have massively increased the amount of freedom that Chinese people enjoy. But just as obviously the reforms have not led to the creation of a democracy. Nor are they likely to, although the experiments with giving a degree of choice at village-level elections are a positive and hopeful, if modest, sign. But if the reforms were ever abandoned, the cost in freedom (not to mention the cost in wealth) would be enormous. Thus anyone interested in supporting Chinese freedom, rights and welfare will support the reforms.

The Indonesian political scientist, Arief Budiman, has argued that there are three ways in which democratic space can open up in an authoritarian society. One is licensed democracy, where a government allows its citizens greater freedom of expression; another is democracy arising from a clash between different elements of the governing elite; and the third is popular democracy arising from the growth of a civic society. While Indonesia has had advances and reverses in all three types in the last decade or so, China has had occasional small bursts of the first, very little of the second and almost none of the third. It seems that any Chinese Government that is effective enough to be in power at all will likely be effective enough to maintain, in effect, a monopoly of power. The Chinese Government has shown us that it intends to remain authoritarian.

In the very long term greater real democracy may be possible. In the most thoroughly private, off the record, late night, *in vino veritas* discussions senior Chinese sometimes drop the idea that full democracy is not the superior system for China. They simply make the point that it is totally impracticable in a nation of 1.2 billion people, one with no tradition of democracy and which is still very poor and has, overall, very low education levels. But implicit in this argument is a recognition of the long-term legitimacy of democracy and the very long-term possibility that it could, eventually, gradually, come even to China.

In the nearer term there are also prospects for opening up greater democratic space short of full democracy. A Chinese Government that feels secure and is pursuing foreign investment and economic growth may well decide to license a little bit of democracy. This is what happened to some extent under Hu Yaobang and Zhao Ziyang, two former secretaries of the Chinese Communist Party and at different stages designated successors to Deng Xiaoping, who were successively stripped of their positions. Neither of these men was a liberal democrat in the Western sense. They believed in the monopoly of political power that the Communist Party enjoyed. But they wanted to loosen up a bit.

Yet even if China remains fully authoritarian, and this is the very hardest bit for many Western human rights activists to grasp, the range of autonomous space available to hundreds of millions of Chinese citizens is vastly increased simply by the operations of economic growth. If as a Chinese you go abroad for business or study you cannot fail to learn the political realities of other countries. If you can afford a television set and live in an area that picks up Hong Kong TV, or if you have a good radio, you will hear much of the outside world. Then there is the insidious and subversive influence of fax machines, photocopiers and, worst of all, e-mail. These technologies are beyond the control of repressive governments that seek economic growth. They do not necessarily threaten the survival of such regimes, they do not necessarily presage democracy, but they do result in much greater knowledge, communication and freedom.

China has already had a lot of the easy economic growth that it is going to enjoy. It will now become harder for it to sustain very high rates of growth. This makes the reform of unprofitable state-owned enterprises all the more urgent. It also makes the development of a reliable framework of commercial law more urgent. By the end of the 1990s the state-owned sector was down to around one-third of the Chinese economy and the private sector was growing very rapidly. But there has been a great debate among ruling circles in China about how much of the state-owned sector the state needs to hang on to in order to maintain control of strategic industries. Moreover, probably 200 million people or more were either grossly underemployed in the state sector or simply unemployed altogether. The prospect of sending tens of millions of workers into unemployment has naturally been extremely unattractive. But the state-owned sector is also a vast and continuing drain on the country's ramshackle banking system, and the blurred lines between state and private enterprises are a fertile ground for corruption. The reforms in ownership of state enterprises announced in 1997, which involved selling shares in many of the enterprises, were clouded by uncertainty about how much real financial discipline the new structures of ownership would impose. Would the enterprises still get preferential credit treatment? Would they be allowed to go belly up if they could not pay their way?

The emergence of a reliable system of commercial law in China would bring enormous political benefit, and increased freedom, to many Chinese. The reform of the unprofitable state-owned enterprises, which in many ways have been above the law, would at least make possible the more general development of reliable, society-wide legal frameworks. Thus are economic and political reform intimately linked.

Political reform is also intimately linked to the somewhat paranoid world-view that Chinese leaders hold, or at least seem to hold. I sought some deeper understanding of the Chinese world-view on the campus of Beijing University, in a day-long discussion with four eminent Chinese scholars in the field of international relations, and in a formal interview with Yang Jiechi, at the time China's assistant foreign minister.

The campus of Beijing University is one of the most beautiful sites in what is still a fairly drab, grimy and polluted city, notwithstanding its greatly spruced-up centre. The campus is set amid spacious and lovingly tended traditional gardens, the buildings are serene and quiet and, on the day I visit, a small lake shimmers in the unseasonally warm spring sun. Go through a spacious courtyard and you reach the university's international relations department. Here you are received in an elegant meeting room, you sit on a plush sofa and steaming Chinese tea is brought to your elbow. All the courtesies are observed and the experience is wholly gracious.

But the message, in its way, is unnervingly uncompromising. The same is true at the Chinese foreign ministry. These discussions, and countless others, offer a sense of the shape of the official, collective outlook of China's leadership. Although there is much talk of China's devotion to the cause of peace, at the same time there is a disquieting element to the view from Beijing. For it is a view based to a distressing degree on a sense of grievance, again exhibiting the 'tyranny of history'. An encounter with a Chinese official often includes a lengthy disquisition on the wrongs that China has suffered at the hands of Western colonial powers, and frequently ends with the words: 'And in all that time China did nothing wrong.'

Of course, the officials are right to say that China was long humiliated and oppressed, but it is striking, and disturbing the extent to which Chinese officials seem to think that this should be relevant to policy considerations today—even as they claim that China should be considered a great power.

Two other elements of the Chinese world-view stand out: the centrality of the United States; and the centrality of the Taiwan issue.

At our meeting, Assistant Minister Yang offered a brief review of Sino–US relations: 'In mid-1995 the US made the decision to allow [Taiwan president] Lee Teng-hui to visit the US. At the beginning of 1996 the US sent two aircraft carriers to the Taiwan Straits to show off its military might. This caused unprecedented tensions in the relationship. The Chinese Government made repeated and solemn representations to the US on this. As a result the US came to appreciate the seriousness of the Taiwan issue. The US side reaffirmed its commitment to a one-China policy. We oppose Taiwan independence and Taiwan's participation in international organisations such as the United Nations, which is composed of governments. The US also said it would engage in a policy of constructive engagement with China.'

Yang said that the summit between China's President Jiang Zemin and America's President Bill Clinton had improved relations but Beijing was still waiting for more concrete actions. This formulation embodies a central point of the Beijing world-view. The way the dialogue is constructed with the Chinese, the foreigner is always expected to make some significant policy gesture, to take some specific action, merely to earn China's goodwill so that subsequent negotiations can take place in an atmosphere of amity. This may not be an Asian value but it is certainly a Chinese value.

Yang put criticisms of China down to the erroneous 'China threat' view held by, in the Chinese view, many mistaken Western commentators. There were pluses and minuses in the US relationship, Yang said, but the 'core issue' was Taiwan, with Lee Teng-hui 'continuing to work rampantly towards independence'. Beijing's view of the Taiwan issue is highly ideological—not just that Taiwan should rightfully be part of China but that China is justified in taking any action it likes, including military action, to resume control of Taiwan and that no one else has any right to 'interfere'. And any official contact between another country, such as Australia or Canada, and Taiwan is regarded as 'interference'. There is a droll irony to this view, given that one of the first and biggest billboards one sees on emerging from Beijing Airport is for ACER Computer Company, one of Taiwan's best known corporations.

But the official Chinese view is even more ideological than this. An associate professor at Beijing University told me that most nations supported China when it fired live missiles across the Taiwan Strait in 1996 in an unsuccessful attempt to intimidate Taiwanese voters during their presidential election. I found this an extraordinary assertion because I couldn't recall a single country that had supported China publicly during this confrontation. Of course, most countries were too intimidated to publicly support the American intervention either, but virtually everyone was dismayed by the Chinese action, which also had the surely unplanned effect of regalvanising the Japanese in their commitment to the American alliance.

I put it to the professor that there had been no sign of public international support for China. Ah, he replied sagaciously, many countries at the time expressed their support of the one-China policy and to do so at that time meant they were really supporting China's actions. Given that the US, which sent the carriers to constrain and oppose China, and Australia, which publicly backed the US action, both also formally support a one-China policy, this seemed literally a nonsense argument. But it is official Chinese doctrine nonetheless.

Beijing has shown itself to be a classically Leninist regime. As it demonstrated in Tiananmen Square in 1989, and once again in the Taiwan Strait in 1996, it views the world through the prism of power. It is extremely comfortable in the use of power, sometimes too comfortable, such that it can miscalculate how much real power it has, and the changing nature of power itself.

But it has a deep appreciation of the extent of American power. One of the most widely and deeply debated questions in American intelligence analysis of China is the question of whether China has decided that it wants America out of Asia as a military power. At a formal level, China's official position is that it opposes the stationing of any nation's troops on foreign soil. Therefore, officially, it is opposed to the American forward deployment in the region.

But for a long time during the Cold War China was happy to have America constraining the Soviet Union. Then, too, China was happy that the American security guarantee meant that Japan would not become a major strategic military power. Despite the disparity in size between China and Japan, China knows, as well as anyone, that Japan could become a ferocious strategic competitor. And more generally the Chinese were also open to the argument that the American military presence in the region promoted overall stability, which was in China's interests as much as anyone else's.

On the other hand, China suffered a major reverse in the Taiwan Strait crisis of 1996. It had to back down when the Americans sent their aircraft carriers. China is almost light years away from matching America's truly awesome military power. Nobody of course wants a military conflict but if there were to be one between China and the US there is no doubt that China would lose. Thus the American military presence is a severe constraint on the exercise of Chinese power, especially regarding Taiwan, which has become a litmus test of nationalist political correctness among the Chinese leadership. Every morning when the leaders of the People's Liberation Army wake up they confront the daunting magnitude of the American Seventh Fleet. For leaders deeply attuned to calibrating power, and to the psychological as well as physical deployment of power, this is highly disagreeable. Similarly, the redefinition of the US–Japan alliance, such that it became an alliance for the region rather than just a guarantee of Japanese security, and the suggestion that the alliance could even be brought into play in a crisis involving Taiwan, were deeply distressing to the Chinese.

As one droll and very senior American Pentagon official put it to me, he told the Chinese that there was a simple way to get the best out of the American forward deployment in East Asia. They liked the fact that the American presence constrained Japanese strategic redevelopment; they didn't like the fact that it constrained Beijing with regard to Taiwan. Therefore, he'd told them, don't have crises with Taiwan—and the bit of the US presence you don't like won't come into play. Sound advice, but I'm not sure it was best appreciated in Beijing.

While it is clear that there is much that Beijing doesn't like about the American military presence in East Asia, it is not clear if it has a long-term strategy to rid the region of that presence. Given the disparity in Chinese and American power, the only possible strategy Beijing could have is a political strategy. A view, admittedly highly contested, has developed within the American intelligence community that Beijing has had such a strategy. This view has been based in part on Beijing's active involvement in multilateral security forums, such as the ASEAN Regional Forum, combined with a campaign by Beijing to render continuing US military alliances in the region too politically costly to maintain. Certainly any such strategy would explain the bizarre Chinese press campaign that has run intermittently against the US–Australia alliance as well as the US–Japan alliance. One can understand, even if not agree with, Beijing's complaining about the Japan alliance, but to regard Australia, a nation of 19 million people, as a strategic threat is ridiculous. Yet in August 1996 the *People's Daily* described the US alliances with Japan and Australia as 'two crab-claws' aimed at China and reflecting 'the Cold War–style thinking of some brains'.

One way in which China and its many friends in the West have been highly effective in political strategy is in framing the debate on China policy, especially in the United States, as a simple one between containment and engagement. Containment was the policy the US and its allies used to stop Soviet expansionism during the Cold War. Yet in truth no one of any standing in the 1990s was proposing a policy of containment against China. Even Richard Bernstein and Ross Munro, authors of the hawkish *The Coming Conflict With China*, did not propose a consistent policy of containment of China but rather a maintenance of the status quo, with strong American support for Japan and Taiwan. They advocated, where possible, cooperation with China.

Their book was primarily an examination of some worst-case thinking about future Chinese assertiveness. It would be bizarre if there were not such a book in the US, if only to provide an alternative to the hundreds of best-case assumption books positing uninterrupted Chinese economic growth and strategic benevolence.

Numerous Western officials have privately expressed surprise at how much the Chinese approve whenever a Western politician declares himself to be in favour of engagement with China, not containment. But the reason is obvious. The more China gets the international debate framed in the fashion of this simple dichotomy the more it succeeds in limiting the range of legitimate response to Chinese actions. Anything that any Western politician does or says that is critical of China can thus be ruled out of order as an expression of containment.

Yet the paradox is that engagement will only really work if there is a concomitant willingness to resist China when it does the wrong thing internationally and to criticise it, in proportionate terms, when it abuses its own citizens.

Every rational person in the world wants to engage China

rather than contain it. Everyone wants China to emerge as a prosperous, peaceful country that abides by the rules of the international system. If the US were remotely trying to contain China it wouldn't have allowed US$50 billion trade deficits to emerge between it and China. If that is containment many countries in the world would like to be contained. So the debate should never be framed as containment versus engagement because that formulation renders clear thinking about China all but impossible.

Nicholas Kristof and Sheryl WuDunn, in their impressive *China Wakes*, list four main areas of conflict between the US and China: human rights; nuclear weapons and missile technology proliferation; China's trade surplus with the US; and Taiwan. The US is hardly blameless in its China policy. Indeed, the first Clinton presidential term exhibited grotesque incompetence in China policy. Even the second Clinton administration, though better than the first, was marked by inconsistency, reversals, wild mood swings. It was difficult to discern a coherent China policy. But neither is China blameless in these four areas and criticism of China, especially in South East Asia, should be considered no more illegitimate than is criticism of the US.

The Chinese Government directly influences the destiny of a vast river of human life. The Chinese universe, however, is much greater than anything the government can encompass. It is a civilisation of immense continuity and antiquity, an attitude of mind, a culture, even politically much much more than just the narrow range of views to be found in the Politburo. Like everyone who has ever lived in China, whose senses have been ravished by the sensuality of Chinese cooking, by the tonal cadences of Chinese speech, by the beauty of traditional Chinese calligraphy or the intimate humanity of its traditional architecture, a part of me feels forever in exile when I am not there. Luckily for the likes of me, though, there are Chinas aplenty beyond China.

You rarely hear much from Chinese officials about Asian values as such, unless the officials are scoring points against the Americans in South East Asia. But from countless Chinese you do hear endlessly about *Chinese* values, about the value of Chineseness. The challenge, the richness, the texture of Chinese culture are an inestimable blessing to mankind. They represent one of the great reservoirs of human achievement and human reflection, of humanity itself. The encounter with China, the search for its wisdom, its artistic and literary inheritance, the sheer scale of the Chinese experience, make it a crucially formative element in what we know of the human condition. Like America, China is a universal for mankind. No one is wholly untouched by it. The exposure of the entire globe to Chinese influences, diverse and multitudinous, will grow in decades to come. So too will Chinese exposure to the West. It could be a deeply fruitful liaison.

Then again . . .

7

CAPITALIST CHARACTERISTICS: HONG KONG IN THE CHINESE UNIVERSE

How Chinese is Hong Kong?
And just how Chinese are Hong Kong's values?

Foolish questions? But Hong Kong can and does regularly make fools of wise men. And while Hong Kongers would overwhelmingly describe themselves as Chinese, and now of course they live under Chinese sovereignty, it is a very different sort of Chineseness from that which you would find in Beijing or Sichuan or Harbin. The city it's most often compared with is not on the Chinese mainland at all. People often talk of Hong Kong as having the energy, the buzz, the pace of New York. And the skylines are not all that dissimilar.

But first let's take a look at Hong Kong. Literally a look.

Come with me on a helicopter ride above Hong Kong. We start at a helipad by the harbour, next to the strange, wing-tipped building that hosted the ceremony in which Britain handed over sovereignty to China on 30 June 1997. Helicopters are exhilarating and today is no exception. A graceful sweep across the island and then we cross the harbour to Kowloon. The scale of construction when we undertake this flight in mid-1997 is staggering. Seemingly countless high-rise buildings reach up into the air like perfectly formed stalagmites. We fly past a forlorn Vietnamese refugee camp and later over the construction site of Hong Kong's vast new airport. The guide tells me it is the biggest engineering project in the world, involving huge tracts of reclaimed land, bridges linking one island to another, public transport and road systems.

Out into the New Territories and Hong Kong's little known farming fields and green hills. You forget how much greenery there is in Hong Kong, out beyond the city. The Scottish helicopter pilot says the sight reminds him of home. We fly further, to the border of mainland China. Even after the reversion to mainland Chinese sovereignty this border is still intact. We fly along the river that forms the border itself, surveying the mainland city of Shenzhen. Designed as a buffer zone (or decompression chamber) between Hong Kong and the mainland, Shenzhen is astonishing from the air, again because of the sheer scale of the development. It is massive. Indeed from the helicopter it looks just like Hong Kong. Can ever a border have been so tightly policed which keeps apart two cities so seemingly similar? Colleagues tell me that the border police who keep the area under surveillance at night look across the border through their field glasses and telescopes and spy karaoke bars and heavy drinking sessions and nightclubs and discos on the other side, which is certainly a far cry from the old Berlin Wall or the border between South Korea and North Korea.

But the similarity from the air begs the question. As Hong Kong and China integrate will China come to look more like Hong Kong, as in Shenzhen, or will Hong Kong come to look more like China? Who is going to transform whom?

China's capitalist surge has unleashed vast entrepreneurial energy similar to that of Hong Kong. But there's a difference. China's capitalism is still a wild west capitalism. Corruption is rife and people connections—*guanxi*—are more important than laws. Hong Kong, on the other hand, is a success in large measure because it is a business entity run under a Western legal system embodying the dependable rule of law, the free flow of commercial information and an independent judiciary.

As the years roll by, how will the integration with China change all this? What parts, if any, of Hong Kong's modern life are incompatible with Chinese values?

It comes back to the question: How Chinese is Hong Kong? Is there such a thing as a separate culture of Hong Kong? Globalisation means that many people will face in their own lives and in their own families these questions of culture, loyalty and civic identity. What about the Australian executive who lives in

Hong Kong, and has done for decades, has his Hong Kong-schooled son at an American university, takes most of his holidays in South East Asia, has married a Hong Kong Chinese wife, but still maintains his Australian passport and thinks of himself as an Australian? Equally, what about the Hong Kong executive who has a Canadian passport, works in Hong Kong, but has his children at school in Vancouver, where they live in a house that he owns, sometimes by themselves, sometimes with their mother who spends about half the year in Vancouver, half in Hong Kong and seemingly another half in aeroplanes? How Chinese is this Hong Kong family?

China can be a nebulous concept at times. Singaporean leaders such as Lee Kuan Yew talk about the importance of Chinese values to their island nation's success. But they certainly have no desire to become part of the Chinese nation. Instead they distinguish between China as a cultural identity and China as a political identity. Hong Kongers sometimes make a similar distinction. But whereas Singaporeans will tell you that they embrace the culture but reject the political entity, some Hong Kongers will virtually tell you the opposite—they accept the reality of Chinese political sovereignty but feel uncomfortable about the cultural implications.

Hong Kong is also the only place in the world I've struck where large numbers of people will say, proudly, that their primary cultural loyalty is to business. This is worth pondering for a second. The Western mind, while certainly capable of any amount of avarice, tends to distinguish between business and life, except for those we dub 'workaholics'. The Chinese seem to have almost a genetic attachment to business and making money, and their prodigious work effort often, it seems to me, derives in part from not drawing a line between that part of life which is work and that part of life which is just life. In other words, many of the joys of leisure—creativity, intellectual stimulation, the attainment of pleasure, the enjoyment of the company of one's family, the refinement of one's soul—for many Chinese can be found in business.

James Tien, a Liberal Party legislator and, when I meet him, chairman of the Hong Kong Chamber of Commerce, is a case in point. A fit-looking, elegantly appointed, supremely confident man, he receives me in his spacious, panelled office, with its magnificent views of Hong Kong Harbour, and sips medicinally hot water as he speaks.

'People in Hong Kong are concerned about making money,' he says. 'Why aren't they concerned about other things? There are two reasons. Under British rule we never had democracy. The Queen appointed governors and they were all honourable people, certainly not corrupt. Also they conducted a lot of consultation with the community. People thought they didn't need to have the vote in order to have influence on the government. Democracy is a means to the good life and we already have the good life. The other thing is that Hong Kong is such a small city-state. A lot of countries that talk about human rights have either a racial problem or a religious problem. Hong Kong is 98 per cent Chinese and the other 2 per cent have an even better lifestyle than the Chinese. Nobody here cares what anybody's religion is.'

In Hong Kong's elections for its legislative council, voting has generally been very low, with around a 40 per cent turnout of eligible voters. James Tien offers an explanation: 'The mentality of voting, of citizens' obligations, is not really there. When you have voting day, people are busy going to the races or playing mah-jong. Rightly or wrongly the only thing Hong Kong people are concerned with is money. All six million people you could make that point about. I couldn't really say whether we're lacking something in life because of that. Most people don't go to church or a Buddhist temple or anything. But on the other hand our crime rate is very low. If you're willing to work you'll always get a job. Every country has its own problems. I feel safer in Hong Kong than in New York. People here are not destitute.'

Tien's own story is typical enough of Hong Kong. He was born in Shanghai and came to the colony as a small child. His father arrived without a cent and made a fortune in the garment industry. Tien went to college in the United States, holds a British passport (or at least did at the time of our interview), but says: 'In my heart I feel I am Chinese.'

He emphasises that the success of China's economic reforms has greatly changed the attitude of Hong Kong people to China and to their own Chineseness. Mainland cities like Shenzhen, while still not as comfortable, prosperous or free as Hong Kong, don't represent such a grim future any more. But it is perhaps at that level of practicality, rather than through an intimate attachment to classical Chinese civilisation, that many people think of themselves as Chinese.

Of course, Tien's view is just one and is hotly contested by many other Hong Kongers. But it is an influential and widespread view in Hong Kong. One man who violently disagrees with the proposition that Hong Kong people care only about making money is Martin Lee, the leader of Hong Kong's Democrats Party. I have interviewed Lee many times. He is perhaps the most famous Hong Konger. An eminent barrister, he has been a great irritant to Beijing and is possibly Hong Kong's most widely known democracy campaigner. He has an immense following in the United States and in many Hong Kong Chinese communities around the world. He also consistently wins such democratic elections as have been held in Hong Kong.

In his relatively modest though busy barrister's chambers I ask him whether Hong Kong people really do have deep civic aspirations. In answer he walks across his office and picks up a large photograph of a million people marching in Hong Kong to protest against the Tiananmen Square massacre of 1989. He says: 'It was plain insulting for the leaders in China to say, as they did in the early days, that after reunification horses will continue to run and you can continue to go to dance parties, as if gambling and sex were all that Hong Kong people wanted. But what could our people do? The general feeling was one of hopelessness. Most people came here because they fled communism, or their parents did.'

As the differing interpretations of Lee and Tien remind us, identity and culture are heavily contested items in Hong Kong, as they are in most societies. They remind us too that the much discussed 'clash of cultures', while nonsense as a predictive principle of history, normally occurs within cultures rather than between cultures.

Will there be a clash of cultures between Hong Kong and China? Perhaps one reason for optimism that there *won't* be such a clash comes from the degree of economic integration that the two societies had achieved long before China resumed sovereignty over Hong Kong. That integration has forged a larger region, southern China, which in itself has become Asia's fifth tiger and for much of the 1990s the fastest growing economy in the world.

I saw it all at work in Locky Chu's factory.

The moulds for the Batmobile toy cars to be sold with one of the *Batman* movies were being designed and manufactured in a scruffy 14-storey factory building in Chai Wan on Hong Kong island. The factory owner, Locky Chu, held one up with pride. Only the moulds were being made in Hong Kong itself. The actual toys were to be mass produced by a joint venture company, partly owned by Chu, in mainland China. This division of labour—design in Hong Kong, manufacture in mainland China— is typical of the Hong Kong economy.

In many ways Chu, 43 when I met him, the founder and major shareholder in APAC Industrial Co Ltd, is the classic Hong Kong success story. Born in Macau of mainland Chinese parents, he learned the trade of mould-making as a young man. His father, while happy to equip him with a trade, was nonetheless keen for him to go into the family restaurant business. Instead he went to Hong Kong to practise his trade. In typical Hong Kong fashion he lived with a cousin who owned a Chinese medicine shop, sleeping on the floor of the shop on a foldaway bed. For ten years he worked for another company, attending Hong Kong Polytechnic at night, and saved HK$300 000 (less than US$50 000) as his start-up capital.

He began making moulds and dies but soon, with subcontractors, branched into making the finished products, mainly appliances and toys. Now his Hong Kong operation has an annual turnover of about HK$10 million and his mainland manufacturing outfits, the joint venture, have a turnover of about HK$300 million.

But here's the rub. His Hong Kong operation is actually not profitable, because wage costs are too high. It actually makes a loss. So why does he keep it going?

'We maintain it because it supports our operation in China,' Chu says. 'Without this operation in Hong Kong the operation in China would not work. So this industry can survive a bit longer. Many people ask, Why not move your whole industry to mainland China? Mould and die is the key to this industry. It is certainly much cheaper in China—land is cheap, labour is cheap and the labour supply is infinite. If you want to you can hire 1000 people in a week.

'But in Japan, in Germany and the US they have mould and die shops. It's the key. If the moulds are bad, the business is disastrous. You need quality control, quality assurance and quick reaction time. Research and development, mould design, production planning are all here in Hong Kong. Production is only one part of the process. After production, we still have a lot to do—marketing, shipping, quality control, after-sales service.

'So the front part and end part of the business stay in Hong Kong.'

Hong Kong's experience is similar to that of numerous Asian cities which function as high-tech organisational and service centres for vast low-wage hinterlands—cities like Singapore, Penang and even, to some extent, Bangkok. It also represents one version of the future of the globalised economy, heightened and compressed no doubt, but representative nonetheless. For example, Chu's design computers in Hong Kong are all linked to the computers in his plants in mainland China. His mainland operations are near Shenzhen, only a few hours drive from his downtown Hong Kong headquarters. But, in principle, there is no overwhelming reason why they couldn't be anywhere in the world.

Except at the very highest of the high-tech end, manufacturing can no longer really expect to be profitable in Hong Kong over the long term. Chu's experience is emblematic. His unprofitable Hong Kong plant employs 85 people, his profitable mainland joint ventures employ about 3500.

To hear Chu tell it, Hong Kong may be starting to lose its motivational edge: 'In my day everybody tried to develop their own business. Nowadays the entrepreneurial spirit has declined a bit. Welfare is too generous. There is too much protection from the government. Young people rely on protection from the government rather than doing hard jobs themselves. They like to spend money rather than having the motivation to save.'

Is this Westernisation or just affluence? At the level of affluence Hong Kong has achieved, comparable to or a bit higher than that in most Western nations, such slackening of the extreme economic drive is surely inevitable.

Much has been made, and rightly so, of Hong Kong's economic value to China. But China is also extremely economically valuable to Hong Kong. China is Hong Kong's biggest trade partner, representing in 1996 some 35 per cent of Hong Kong's trade value. Two-way trade was then worth more than US$100 billion. China is not only Hong Kong's biggest trade partner but also the biggest destination of its foreign investment, as indeed Hong Kong is the biggest investor in China. By 1995 Hong Kong provided two-thirds of the total realised foreign investment in China. In Guangdong province some 42 000 enterprises have some Hong Kong participation and around four million Chinese in Guangdong work for Hong Kong enterprises. Similarly, a vast amount of mainland Chinese money has flowed into Hong Kong.

Of course, all such statistics can contain an element of exaggeration because of the mainland's opaque business practices and because some mainland businesses send their money out to Hong Kong and bring it back into the mainland so it can gain the favourable treatment meted out to foreign investors. Nonetheless, the underlying reality is huge.

The cycle in Hong Kong's economic development is fascinating. Before the 1950s it was an entrepôt economy. Then, in the 1950s and 1960s, manufacturing developed strongly. Now manufacturing is effectively winding down and entrepôt trade has again become hugely important as, of course, has services trade. Indeed, services now account for something like 80 per cent of GDP. China's training needs alone will provide vast ongoing demand for Hong Kong. In 1997, estimates were that Shanghai alone needed 50 000 qualified accountants but had only 10 000.

Hong Kong is also providing a potential model for China's future in business practice. Tam Wing-pong, when I meet him Hong Kong's deputy secretary for trade and industry, believes this role will grow in importance. 'We provide an important test case for China to observe,' he says. 'Business people from Hong Kong brought to China not only entrepreneurialism but also modern practices of business management. Look at the securities market. In the early 90s when China reactivated their markets they had learned a lot from the Hong Kong market. Some

Chinese state-owned enterprises also sought listing on the Hong Kong Stock Exchange but had to fulfil stringent Hong Kong rules for listing. So listing on the Hong Kong exchange serves Chinese companies in two ways. It helps them raise capital but they are also forced to revamp their accounting practices. They have to redo all their books and methods of organisation. This is one of the best ways to help them move from a planned economy.'

So there is no doubt that China and Hong Kong have been of huge benefit to each other, each one being a key to the other's stellar economic performance during the past decade or so. As Tam explains: 'That's why Hong Kong has been so active in campaigning for the US to give permanent Most Favoured Nation trading status to China. Not because we are China's mouthpiece but because it is in Hong Kong's interests. It's nothing to do with the sovereignty issue. Any problem between China and the US would have a huge impact on Hong Kong.'

But there is of course divergence as well as convergence. One of the countless ironies of Hong Kong just before the handover was Governor Chris Patten's deciding to introduce modest health and welfare initiatives, which resulted in the marvellous phenomenon of a Tory British politician being accused by the Chinese Government of dangerous socialism. Similarly, Hong Kong's new chief executive, Tung Chee Hwa, is a proponent of interventionist industry policy, which would certainly be a break with Hong Kong's laissez-faire past.

Locky Chu tells me he is thinking of selling his extremely valuable downtown premises for housing and moving out to Hong Kong's New Territories, still in Hong Kong but near to the border with the mainland. One would imagine that this, too, is a transitional phase in an ultimate total shift to the mainland.

But for this integration to proceed smoothly China will need to respect, perhaps even more than Hong Kong's political freedoms, the freedom of commercial information and commercial practice. The case of Jimmy Lai, which came up shortly before the resumption of Chinese sovereignty, is instructive. Lai is a businessman who wrote a magazine article which referred to China's then premier, Li Peng, as a 'turtle's egg', an extremely insulting term in Chinese. Subsequently his business interests on the mainland suffered, as was perhaps to be expected. But Lai also runs a

profitable magazine group, Next, in Hong Kong. He tried to float
Next but the banks declined to underwrite him. He claimed that
this was because of political pressure. The banks denied that their
motivation was political. It is impossible for an outsider to unravel
the commercial from the political in a dispute such as this. But
the case does throw up the concern of some Hong Kongers for
commercial freedom, as do press reports of market analysts coming
under pressure for writing unfavourably about mainland companies—the so-called 'red chips'. If mainland business practices, such
as bribery, corruption, politicisation of commercial information,
or discrimination against those politically out of favour, infiltrate
Hong Kong, it will lose at least some of its international commercial attractiveness. It will also lose an important feature of its way
of life.

Shortly before the resumption of Chinese sovereignty over
Hong Kong I went to the governor's mansion to ask Chris Patten
about these issues. The *feng-shui* of the mansion is all wrong, so
the locals say, although the residence certainly looked fine to me.
Stately, grand, spacious—whatever else you might say about British
colonialism (and you might say a great deal) they left behind some
magnificent buildings. Patten was in good form that day, a little
harassed perhaps, with all the last-minute media attention. The
BBC's Jonathan Dimbleby lurked on the balcony, waiting to make
his final instalment of the TV documentary, *The Last Governor*.

Anyway, the feng-shui of the governor's house is said to be not
good. Feng-shui is the Chinese superstition concerning house
directions, window and door placements and the rest. According
to this superstition the way you align your doors and windows
can suck all the energy out of the house, or incline the money to
move through it too quickly, or do a hundred other things, all of
them having a great effect on your chances of prosperity and
happiness. Feng-shui has become a powerful influence in the global
economy. Even in San Francisco, Vancouver or Sydney it can be
difficult to sell a house with the number four, which is traditionally
unlucky in Chinese. The ideological vacuum in Chinese life has
led to a great revival in folk superstitions, traditional remedies,
rituals and customs of all kinds. The vacuum comes from the death
of communism in China and the dimming of hopes about democracy as a civic creed in Hong Kong.

In any event, feng-shui is said to be behind the reluctance of Patten's successor, chief executive C. H. Tung, to live in the governor's mansion. The old building used to have good feng-shui but then skyscrapers sprang up, blocking its view of the harbour. Some of the skyscrapers have sharp edges pointing towards Government House, a big no-no in feng-shui terms. This is blamed by some locals for all of Patten's troubles with the Chinese.

On the day I see him I ask Patten about the Jimmy Lai case, which was important not so much in itself but as a potential harbinger of things to come. Patten's response is cautious, yet pointed: 'I cannot comment in great detail on a specific case. There may be commercial arguments of which I am not aware. In a rather more general way, if political correctness becomes a guiding principle in Hong Kong's market place, it will help to ensure that Hong Kong's progress to a status as the London or Manhattan or Frankfurt of East Asia is set back. I don't think there's any conceivable doubt about that. If people think that investment analysts are going to be less honest about a mainland company than they would be about a local company, if people think that the market is going to freeze out a player who is unpopular in China, if people start to feel that in order to do business here you've got to get on the right side of a Chinese firm that may have *guanxi* in China—if those things happen, then "one country, two systems" starts to look pretty tattered.'

Martin Lee, again, is more pessimistic when I put the same questions to him. He says: 'Anybody doing business in China requires timely, accurate information on China. You don't get this in China, you do get it in Hong Kong. We have a free media when it comes to economic matters. But this black hand which is interfering in our political freedoms is interfering in business freedoms now. That is something I forecast all along. Many businessmen have been put into jail in China simply because their contracts went sour, even though they were in the right. They will arrest a businessman or his wife or child as a hostage.'

Most business figures do not agree with Lee or Patten at all. Henry Tang, a pro-business Liberal Party member of Tung's executive council, is dismissive of these concerns: '*Next* is a tabloid magazine, based on scandals, with a list of lawsuits as long as my arm. Hong Kong people have always been very judicious investors. Hong Kong people would not put politics before business. And if one or two investment analysts do withhold information, others won't. The importance of maintaining ourselves as an open society where information flows freely is fundamental. Personally, I believe it will be business as usual [under Chinese sovereignty]. That doesn't mean we won't change anything. Hong Kong is a dynamic and evolving society. We are very open. Western ideas, among others, are coming in very fast.'

Allen Lee, the leader of the Liberal Party and an important politician in Hong Kong, tells me quite flatly and convincingly that Hong Kong's future success is intimately tied up with and dependent on China's future success. In his cramped basement office Lee, who exudes great energy, makes his arguments in staccato jabs: 'Look at our economic performance. Investment booming. Property prices booming. The business circle is very confident about the future, especially China's future. We've put US$60 billion into China. Hong Kong is China's biggest foreign investor. We are investing in manufacturing and infrastructure in China. So business people are very confident; politicians are a bit sceptical.'

Since then, of course, Hong Kong suffered in the great regional recession the second half of 1997, but that meltdown had nothing to do with Hong Kong being connected to China. The fact that at the time of the handover of sovereignty the Hong Kong business community was so confident reflects well on both Hong Kong and China. And Hong Kong's subsequent problems did not come primarily from China.

No one had a bad word for Hong Kong's new chief executive, C. H. Tung. Martin Lee described him as a man of integrity and Chris Patten gave me the following assessment: 'He's a respected businessman with very good links internationally. He's well known in the shipping business. He certainly has my best wishes and the whole community wants him to do well.'

But it may be that Tung's longest term challenge will be one few were predicting. Businessmen don't have a very good record at switching to politics, especially if they are making the switch at a very high level, as Tung has done. This is because the skills of a politician are different from those of a businessman. Business-men tend to lose their tempers under sustained hostile questioning; they are not used to coping with relentless media scrutiny; they haven't had the practice in avoiding political traps when speaking off the cuff; they often lack broad policy expertise. Yet, watching Tung doing interviews on CNN and in the local media around the time of the handover, his media training was obvious, if recent. He had quickly, so it seemed to me, learnt a good many of the tricks of the trade. I thought it would be fascinating to watch how Tung developed in the job. Would he become more and more a politician, campaigning, cajoling and convincing, or would he retreat into the role of haughty and distant mandarin?

In a sense, it could be expected that Tung's development would mirror Hong Kong's development—whether Hong Kong became more democratic, as China had promised, or less so. The Chinese criticised Patten heavily for his democratic experiment of enlarging the franchise for the Legislative Council and increasing the number of seats directly elected. Yet the Chinese themselves have promised eventually to implement full-scale democracy in Hong Kong, save only that certain matters, such as defence, foreign affairs and security, will be run from Beijing. Hong Kong's Democrats, on the other hand, argue that Patten did not go far enough early enough—that if a wholly democratic administration had been set up, early, in Hong Kong, then Hong Kong's own leaders could have negoti-ated their future more effectively with Beijing. They may or may not have got a better deal but at least they would have been running their side of the negotiations themselves.

Patten is an amiable and articulate fellow but the international media portrayal of him as a great democratic champion standing up against the wicked Chinese was a bit hard to take. This is not a criticism of Patten himself particularly; more one of Britain's historical role, and historical failure, at least politically, in Hong Kong. For the first 140 years of their rule the British showed virtually no interest in democracy in Hong Kong. Their excuses now for why they did not act then are lame. Better established democratic institutions would have been harder to disturb and there is no reason to suppose that the Hong Kong people would have done a worse job running their own affairs, or negotiating with Beijing, than the British did.

Similarly, the idea frequently put in much of the Western media that the Chinese have behaved with consistent villainy towards Hong Kong is just wrong. The Chinese are not beyond criticism and have at times been pedantic and heavyhanded. But, taking the widest view, it has to be acknowledged that a large part of Hong Kong's success in the 1980s and 1990s has occurred as a result of deliberate Beijing policy. In other words, Beijing has wanted, as an act of policy, Hong Kong to develop the way it has. This is one of the least remarked but most substantially based reasons for cautious long-term optimism about Chinese sovereignty in Hong Kong.

According to Martin Lee, China's late paramount leader Deng Xiaoping once said that if there is a good system even evil men cannot do evil. But if there is an evil system, even good men cannot do good. Lee uses that proposition to justify his pessimism. Yet it seems to fly in the face of much East Asian experience over the last 40 years. All kinds of odd systems have produced good results; some very well designed, or at least highly democratic, systems have produced poor results. Rather it seems that human ingenuity and free will can contrive good or bad results in almost any system, which is of course no reason not to try to make the system itself better.

One of the features of Hong Kong in some danger of being lost amidst the economic and political preoccupations of these times is its role as a kind of mediating cultural point between Asia and the West. Hong Kong is probably the Asian city most intimately known to the largest number of Westerners. Not only have hundreds of thousands of Westerners—primarily Americans, Australians, Canadians and Brits—lived there at one stage or another, but Hong Kong and its interaction with the West have generated icons of popular culture which have entranced many in the West. The Fragrant Harbour, Wan Chai, *The World Of Suzie Wong*, Nathan Road, Kowloon, the Star Ferry, the Peak, novels by Robert Elegant, John Le Carré and many other Westerners, have established Hong Kong in the Western mind in a way perhaps unique among Asian cities.

Yet if there is one development devoutly to be wished from Chinese resumption of sovereignty in Hong Kong it is that Hong Kong should be increasingly interpreted to us culturally through

Hong Kong's own voices. Interpretation in this way has happened in Asia much more than it has in the West. Hong Kong has the biggest and most vibrant film industry of any society its size and its films are popular throughout Asia and among Chinese communities around the world. Some of its movie stars, such as Jackie Chan, and a number of its pop stars have become immensely famous throughout Asia.

But for Western audiences most of their romanticised and stereotyped knowledge of Hong Kong comes from Western sources, generally expatriates who have lived temporarily in Hong Kong or perhaps visited briefly. There was a rush of expat novels around the time of the handover of sovereignty. Most expat novels of Hong Kong are pretty much rubbish, although there are honourable exceptions and even some of the rubbishy ones are entertaining. The famous Paul Theroux reproduced most of the key stereotypes in his novel of the handover, *Kowloon Tong*. This was a pretty silly novel on the whole, but still a great deal funnier than most of its critics allowed. In it the odious American character, Hoyt, describes his vision of Hong Kong's future under Chinese sovereignty. There will be, he says, increased crime and corruption including police corruption, an increase in prostitution, child labour and 'pitiful' wages. Hoyt concludes this recitation with the comment: 'All bargains. It'll be beautiful.' This comment was silly because it appeared to be the reverse of what happened. Wages went up as reunification approached. And certainly after reunification there was no slackening of regulation concerning child labour.

But more generally, Theroux's entertaining novel reinforces a whole raft of stereotypes: the ineffectual (and inevitably sexually odd) Brit, the crude American, the brutal and corrupt mainland Chinese army officer, the sexually alluring Asian beauty selling sex for money. There are sympathetic Hong Kong characters in the novel as well, but it deals primarily in stereotypes. Of course, examples of such types certainly exist. Otherwise they would not have become stereotypes. But too much Western thinking about Hong Kong is trapped in highly inadequate caricatures.

While expat novels written or set in Hong Kong are mostly rubbish, it is worth trying the novels of Hong Kong writers instead. Timothy Mo's *The Monkey King* is worthy of Jane Austen in its minute description of family politics, in a family outwardly unremarkable but made vivid and unforgettable by Mo's depiction of them. It also achieves the extraordinary feat of rendering Chinese speech patterns in English. If you are not going to learn to speak Chinese this is one of the most intimate and useful encounters you can have with the language.

Beyond the glitter of the city, grim sites began to appear around Hong Kong as it struggled to cope with the prolonged aftermath of the Vietnam War. In any society, of course, good and bad coexist, and in Hong Kong the refugee camps were certainly bad.

In 1986, on the first of many journeys through the refugee camps in South East Asia, I visited Hei Ling Chau, about an hour's journey from Hong Kong. A dozen European aid workers took the ferry with me to the island, whose desolate isolation made it perfect for concentration camp purposes. Previous Hong Kong administrations had thought so as well. Before it became a refugee camp it was a leper colony.

A four-wheel-drive vehicle met the ferry to take us up a long, thin road which snaked and coiled around a small mountain, until, near the island's peak, it reached the wire fences, the guards, and the bleakness of the camp itself. Hei Ling Chau was run by the Corrective Services Department and its inmates were treated much like criminals, their lives spent cooped up inside a wire enclosure the size of a couple of football fields.

That day some 1900 Vietnamese were eking out an increasingly hopeless existence. From mid-1982 Hong Kong had confined all new Vietnamese refugees in closed camps, where visits were allowed only by relatives or officials, and inmates were allowed no freedom to come or go. Instead they waited, many for year after desolate year, in the hope of resettlement.

Over the years many, perhaps one and a half million, were resettled in different countries of the world. I have met Vietnamese refugees everywhere from Israel to Central America to Germany, though the majority of course went to the United States. But the delay, and the gratuitous cruelties along the way, are a poor advertisement for international humanitarianism. Nonetheless, the fact that so many were resettled ultimately speaks well of America, and the other major resettlement countries such as

Australia, Canada and France, in living up to at least some of the responsibilities inherent in alliance or, in France's case, former colonial possession.

At an international conference in Geneva in 1979 the broad shape of the refugee program was worked out. The countries of the Association of South East Asian Nations and Hong Kong agreed to offer first asylum to the refugees—to allow them at least a safe landfall and to allow the United Nations High Commissioner for Refugees to set up temporary camps to house the refugees in the countries concerned. In exchange, the United States led an international effort to ensure that the refugees were resettled into third countries. The first-asylum countries were assured that they would not be left with a large residual population of refugees who could not be resettled.

Eventually, there is little doubt, some people left Vietnam who did not fear special persecution on the basis of race, religious or political belief or membership of a political group; that is, people who were not genuine political refugees. But in the early years the overwhelming majority certainly were genuine refugees and even right to the end some people were leaving with very well-grounded fears of persecution.

No one really expected the Indo-Chinese refugee outflow to continue over so long a period, but then very few really predicted just how oppressive and brutal the communist regimes of Indochina would be. The fact, that, a decade after the fall of Saigon in 1975, 30 000 Vietnamese were still prepared each year to brave the dangers of the sea and the depredations of pirates to seek a most uncertain landfall was a tribute to the failure of the Hanoi Government at all levels.

As the refugees continued to come, the conditions, especially in Hong Kong's notorious camps, became worse and worse. Certainly the conditions in Hei Ling Chau were primitive. Fourteen bare huts, each the size of a small church hall, a minimal administrative block, a tiny clinic and a playing field made up the facilities. Two huts were for meals, two for the school and ten were living quarters, each housing about 180 people. In the living quarters people slept two to a bunk, with three levels of bunks, one atop the other. Privacy was non-existent.

The Hong Kong administration had been niggardly and

reluctant to allow any improvement. It took years for the barest schooling facilities to be set up. It is almost impossible to describe the bleakness of the camp. It was a lunar landscape—barren, windswept and empty of any ornamentation, save the people. Walking around the camp at first I was overcome by an immense depression of the spirit. What had these people done to deserve this? They were our friends, weren't they, our allies? Is this how we redeemed our historic promises, promises we had written in blood, the blood of the refugees and the blood of our own soldiers?

But then the children came swarming around. A stranger, any stranger, was both a big sensation and a tiny ray of hope. The kids, extraordinarily deprived in terms of educational experiences, or even any normal socialisation, were nonetheless radiant in the innocence and exuberance of early childhood—before they learnt, before they had any idea, just what a crummy hand life had dealt them. And with that fragile resilience of all kids, that resilience that tears you up inside and makes you want to do anything you can to protect it because you know just how fragile it really is, they were cheerful—smiling, laughing and running everywhere. Sometimes in life something strikes you very simply—this is just *unfair*.

Sister Christine, a Vietnamese nun from the Sisters of the Good Shepherd, described the countless problems the refugees faced, the exquisite and gratuitous agonies the authorities put them through. For example, many refugee families were split up in their flight. The men often went out first, sometimes to avoid compulsory military service in Cambodia; the women followed later. A husband and wife, even if they were lucky enough to both end up in Hong Kong, could easily end up in different camps. But the Hong Kong authorities were deeply suspicious of any kind of family reunification across camps. The families could only reunite if they all went to a closed camp. But some of the men at the open camps had outside jobs. Naturally a refugee family needs all the money it can get. So the husband would stay in the open camp unable to care for his wife and children in the closed camp, unable to provide them any protection from the violence endemic in all such situations.

'One of the worst problems is the idleness,' Sister Christine told me. 'Men especially lose their role and their identity. Some men go crazy over the years. The longer they stay in a closed camp, the worse is the culture shock when they ultimately get out and are perhaps resettled somewhere. Only recently we had a suicide. He was a very proud person, a very kind man. He had been rejected by the United States again and just couldn't stand it any more.'

Two years later, in 1988, I went back to Hong Kong's camps and found the conditions if anything worse still. Sham Shui Po for one was a ghastly place; another, Sun Yick, more so. Yet even these were reputedly not the worst of the Hong Kong camps. Some were completely closed to outsiders, and I was not allowed to visit them.

As the Hong Kong administration made conditions ever nastier, in an attempt to discourage any more refugees from coming, the level of violence, crime and bitter factionalism within the camps increased. The authorities then used this violence to blacken further the reputation of the refugees, to make sure that public sympathy never went their way. The fact that Hong Kong, one of Asia's richest societies, treated the Vietnamese in this way is infinitely to the discredit of the British authorities who ran the place all through this period.

Yet, amidst its headlong materialism and even selfishness, Hong Kong is capable of great unorganised kindness to strangers. And ordinary middle-class Chinese Hong Kongers, professionals and semi-professionals, neither business nor political elite, tend to have the same range of concerns as middle-class folk in most Western societies—lifestyle, health, environmentalism, gender equity, family values, how to keep teenagers on the straight and narrow, and all the rest. It might be said, though, that these concerns have perhaps not been as prominent in Hong Kong's public life as they have been in the public life of similarly middle-class societies.

Of course, just becoming a middle-class society is a triumph for Hong Kong, and not just an economic triumph. Many of the immigrants and refugees who flooded there throughout the years thought of it as a temporary place, a way station on the road to some more distant and secure home. Short-termism was thus abundant in civic life even if not in personal life in Hong Kong. And while Hong Kong's success must be credited primarily to the effort and ingenuity of its own people, Deng Xiaoping's conception of 'one country, two systems' contributed mightily to enlarging the idea of modern Hong Kong as a permanent society, a permanent place, a home even for generations.

Hong Kong's irrepressible energy and its record of success against the odds make it not only disheartening but probably dumb to bet against it in the long term. It is still a triumph of hope over experience, of industry over circumstance, of determination over limitation. As the most Western of Chinese cities it will continue to play an important mediating role between China and the West, between Asia and the West, and that role will be more than just a financial one.

8

TAIWAN'S MODERNIST
REBUTTAL

ARE MINISKIRTS AN EXPRESSION of Chinese values? To wander around the five star hotels, flash restaurants, countless wedding dress shops, cafes and even traditional tea houses of Taipei is to be confronted with one of the countless paradoxes of Chinese life. There seems to be an unwritten law that every Taiwanese woman under the age of 30, and plenty of them over it, wears her skirt at least eight inches above the knee. Young Taiwanese women in the fashionable parts of the capital dress like Chinese versions of the cast of the American soap, *Melrose Place*. The young men look pretty flash too, but they favour dark suits.

Yet Taiwan is the purest version of a truly modern Chinese society we have. Taiwan is the only self-governing Chinese democracy in the world. In May 1996, in an inauguration ceremony in front of 50 000 people, its president, Lee Teng-hui, took office as the first directly elected national leader in 5000 years of Chinese history. More than a fifth of mankind is Chinese. If democracy is really unsuitable over the long-term to traditional, Confucian, Chinese values, this is bad news for the world. For the Chinese, not only in mainland China but in Hong Kong and Taiwan, throughout South East Asia and indeed throughout the vast Chinese diaspora across the world, are one of the greatest cultural and financial forces in the globe.

Taiwan is the 'other China', the anti-communist redoubt to which the Nationalist Kuomintang leader, Chiang Kai-shek, fled in 1949. Now this tiny, crowded, polluted, wealthy, uncertain

155

island of 21 million people is a self-described 'beacon' for the whole Chinese people. The way it answers a raft of questions of identity and political orientation will have a profound influence on the destiny not only of its own people but of China itself and the Asia-Pacific region as a whole. Is Taiwan a part of China? Can it be a true democracy? Can it marry rapid development with decent human values and retain its Chinese cultural quality? What of the tension between local Taiwanese culture and the broader Chinese identity? Is modernisation the same thing as Westernisation? What will a Chinese society that is fully modern, wealthy and democratic look like in the 21st century? What principles of social authority come into play if Confucianism withers? How does the Chinese family adapt to the global economy? And finally, can Taiwan pursue its own path without conflict with the mainland?

The new Kuomintang building in downtown Taipei is a grand, splendid, modern affair. I visited it to meet John Hsiao-yen Chang, the secretary-general of the KMT. The KMT's new headquarters had been open for only two days when I was there, yet the building itself had been completed some months before. The mayor of Taipei at the time, however, was a member of the opposition Democratic Progress Party (DPP). He believed the KMT had acquired the building at something below fair market price. So the Taipei City government for some months refused to connect water or electricity, and the KMT, once the mighty ruler of all China, one of the great mass-based political parties of Asian history, was powerless to do anything about it.

I recount this droll little tale to illustrate the remarkable depth and texture of Taiwanese democracy. If there is one aspect of democracy that East Asian societies sometimes have genuine cultural difficulty with, it is the divided nature of authority in a democracy. In most Asian cultures there is, at least as an ideal, a unity to legitimate authority. The notion that there can be divided but legitimate authority, indeed competing and struc-turally clashing authorities, is often seen as alien. Yet checks and balances, countervailing authorities, are the very heart of democracy.

That Taiwan moved with such little cultural fuss from a martial law community in 1987 to such a robust democracy that the KMT couldn't get its electricity and water connected (even if that was taking DPP chutzpah to something of an extreme) is an historical achievement of the first order. That Taiwan also survived the great East Asian financial crisis of 1997 better than any other regional economy gave it an attractive double-edged story to tell—democracy and economic success. By the end of the 1990s its prestige in many ways stood at an all-time high.

Many of its cleverest intellectuals believe its economic resilience was intimately related to its democracy. Politically motivated loans were exposed by the raucous Opposition and the free press. Corruption, while certainly a problem, was limited by media exposure and an at least partly independent judiciary. Democracy bred transparency and transparency discouraged corrupt collusion. But of course for people living in Taiwan it is the flaws in the glass that are perhaps most visible.

Diane Ying is a hard-driving, fast-talking, ultra-modern journalist. When I met her she was the editor of a business magazine, *Common Wealth*. She deals with these issues and their application to Taiwanese business life every day. She is attractively impatient with foreigners who laud Taiwan's achievement of establishing a democracy without, in her words, seeing 'some of the grit in the system'. Her downtown Taipei office, fitted out in soft beiges, elegantly stacked bookshelves, a few chrome surfaces, conference table, computer and CD player, could be in Manhattan or London or Sydney. It is a representative example of an editor's office, a part of the great, transnational culture of the modern communications industry.

Ying gives President Lee Teng-hui substantial credit for institutionalising democracy, but describes Taiwan now as still a 'crippled democracy'. She asserts that corruption, violence and the lack of a completely independent judiciary have seriously impeded the development of a fully functioning democracy in Taiwan. She also articulates a widespread concern, somewhat lost in the endless security worries about the mainland, with social issues.

'We do not pay enough attention to the social infrastructure,' she says. 'Taiwan now has a per capita income of US$12 000 but sewerage coverage of the whole island is only 3 per cent.'

Like many professional Taiwanese I meet she is more concerned with the pragmatic issues of governing Taiwan, rather than the great, historic questions of Chinese identity. 'In the last eight to ten years we have opened up travel to China,' she says. 'Before that you could only learn of China through books and history, you tended to romanticise China. When I finally went there my dreams were shattered—the China of the history books is no more. And then, China is so big, its problems are so huge. The best way we can help China is by making Taiwan a model, a beacon. If we have the dream of saving China and thereby neglect the real problems of Taiwan, that is just day-dreaming. A big difference in people's attitudes depends on whether they have actually had the chance to go to China. They might still have fanciful dreams and think that Taiwan is the equal of China. And that's wrong. We can only compete in quality, not quantity.'

Diane Ying's view is typical of a widespread reassessment which has gone on throughout Taiwanese society. When I first visited Taiwan in the mid-1980s the attitude was very different. In those days almost the obligatory first port of call for a foreign visitor was the magnificent National Palace Museum, which houses the artistic treasures of Chinese culture that the Nationalists moved around China, initially to save them from the Japanese, and then moved to Taiwan to keep them away from the communists. The world has reason to be thankful to Chiang's Kuomintang for this, for who knows what depredations might have been wrought on this priceless collection had it been on the mainland during the mad iconoclasm of the Cultural Revolution in the 1960s and 1970s.

And the collection in the National Palace Museum, only a small portion of which can ever be shown at one time, and most of which nestles deep inside a mountain to keep it safe even in the event of military hostilities, is indeed magnificent. It is in its way one of the great museums in the world, offering a majestic representative collection of the Chinese arts spanning 5000 years. But a museum in the end is just a museum. It is not an adequate symbol for the vibrancy of Taiwan. A living society is something more than a museum. Yet in the mid-1980s this artistic collection was a significant part of Taiwan's claims to political legitimacy. The stress was on Taiwan's role as the guardian of Chinese civilisation, of true Chinese culture. The presence on the island of individuals who could allegedly trace their own ancestry directly to Confucius was also prized.

But Lee Teng-hui is a native Taiwanese, the first such to be Taiwan's president. In response to the demands of democracy he and his government and their legions of officials have had to emphasise the concrete challenges of managing the Taiwanese economy and modern Taiwanese society, rather than the lofty but theoretical task of safeguarding Chinese civilisation. The paradox is that, in confronting the real challenges of Taiwan, they are far more likely to have a lasting influence on mainland China than by engaging in a rhetorical war over legitimacy and political inheritance.

Nonetheless, China certainly remains the shadow over all Taiwanese life. In the run-up to the 1996 Taiwanese presidential election Beijing conducted a furious personal campaign of abuse against Lee Teng-hui, labelling him, among many other epithets, the 'harlot of history'. It conducted live missile firings within a few tens of kilometres of Taipei and Kaoshiung (Taiwan's second biggest city, located in the south of the island). The United States responded by sending two aircraft carrier battle groups to the waters near Taiwan, to protect its security. This was the most powerful naval armada the US had assembled in Asia since the end of the Vietnam War. In an immediate sense, China's bullying was counterproductive. In a four-way electoral contest Lee won 54 per cent of the vote, a landslide victory, more than 20 percentage points better than his nearest rival.

Lee has earnt his place in history. He became president by accident when Chiang Ching-kuo, the son of Chiang Kai-shek, died in office in 1988. Antonio Chang, publisher of *The Journalist* magazine, and a former dissident in the dark days of martial law, shares the judgement with most Taiwanese I meet that Lee deserves high marks for his democratic reforms.

'President Lee did liberate us from the martial law system,' Chang says. 'That is his great contribution. He changed the KMT from an authoritarian party to a chaotic party. His weakness is he doesn't know how to institutionalise the new system. The fact that he became president was only accidental. He was an outsider. He became chairman of a party he never really liked. He was chosen because he was underestimated, like Sadat under Nasser.

It was felt he was clean, he had no independent power base, he was only a scholar. It was thought that he would be easy to control, that he had no ambition. But he outsmarted them all. He spent five or six years consolidating power by playing one faction against another. He used public opinion brilliantly. Any Taiwanese native son would have been popular after 40 years of the mainland Chiang dynasty.'

But while the size of Lee's victory, and the legitimacy of Taiwan's democratic process, strengthened Lee vis-a-vis Beijing, it did not lessen the complexity of dealing effectively with the mainland. Su Chi was vice-chairman of Taiwan's Mainland Affairs Council when I first met him; later he went on to become a minister in the Taiwanese Government and then head of the Government Information Office. He is recognised as one of the most brilliant and articulate of Taiwan's analysts of the mainland and of cross-straits issues. Smart, alert, witty, clever as he is, Su Chi, with the unmistakable American accent in his spoken English, nonetheless comes across slightly as the absentminded professor. On the day I first talk to him he is surprised to learn that he has been quoted on the front page of the *China Post*.

'What did I say?' he asks, as he calls for the newspaper to be brought to him. Certainly he has an answer for everything. Today he explains to me the true meaning of President Lee's offer to go 'on a journey of peace' to the mainland to negotiate the troubles between the 'two Chinas'. Su's explanation is suitably subtle: 'President Lee meant his offer to be something which might induce a breakthrough. He tried to show that his ideals are grounded in Taiwan but not limited to Taiwan.'

Grounded in Taiwan but not limited to Taiwan—what an absolutely beautiful formulation to encompass the new ambivalence, the sense of fluidity but limitation, with which the Taiwanese Government must these days approach the China identity question. They cannot declare formal independence, which many Taiwanese would like, because that would most likely provoke Chinese military action against them and anyway the Americans have told them not to do this, that in such circumstances the American military guarantee would not operate. Similarly they cannot forsake their Chinese cultural heritage, which was central to their state's being for 40 years. Yet they must accommodate their citizens' wish, like that of most citizens in most polities, that their government pay primary attention to the here and now problems of running their own society.

How Beijing should deal with Taiwan is, says Su, a subject of intense debate within leadership circles on the mainland itself. But why is Beijing so uptight about Taiwan? Why not smother it in kindness and pursue a kind of de facto reunification, leaving sovereignty to sort itself out in 50 or 100 years time? Partly the explanation lies in the internal politics of the Chinese leadership and the recrudescence of nationalism in mainland China.

But Taiwan has also done things that have changed the equation. Su outlines these: 'Taiwan has done three significant things in the last decade. First, it has democratised. Second, it has built up cross-straits relations [between China and Taiwan] from near zero to their very substantial level right now. And third, we have built up our international connections. Beijing doesn't like our democratisation because it proves the falseness of their claims that the Chinese don't suit democracy—all this stuff about Asian values, you know, the idea that there's a Chinese way and it's not a democratic way. Also, they don't like our developing international connections. In tandem you had President Lee's visit to Cornell University in 1995 and then our presidential election. Beijing didn't like either of these two processes and they tried to put a stop to them. The only means available to them was military intimidation. Some people in Beijing argue that this is counterproductive. We know the shape of the debate in Beijing but we don't know how it will come out.'

Like many Taiwanese, Su believes Taiwan's experiment with democracy will ultimately have a great effect on China itself. Evidence of this, he claims, is Beijing's intermittent efforts to stop their people hearing about it. 'In mainland China's internal media they don't even use the word "election" when talking about Taiwan. They use a very wordy term which means "how Taiwan chooses its leaders". Also, during and after the election they restricted visits here of scholars who used to come freely. And they restricted mainland journalists from coming here altogether. In March 1996 in five star hotels in Beijing even the

CNN news service was pulled for a week, during our election period.'

Like Diane Ying, Su acknowledges that Taiwanese are moving away from China in psychological terms: 'In the past decade people here have got a lot richer. They travel more—in fact they travel more than the Japanese—and the education level has improved. So people are more comfortable with the values of other countries. The president has talked of blending Western and Chinese values on Taiwan.'

Dr Michael Wu, one of Taiwan's leading academic political analysts, tells me that he thinks the relationship between Taiwan and China will remain tense: 'If it remains tense but stable I will say, "Thank God!" Democratisation in Taiwan right now is a strategy to deal with China. But in the last half century Taiwan has been under heavy exposure to the West, especially America. If we want to influence China, influence the Confucian world, we should educate their young people. If you can educate the top one per cent then China can change.'

Dr Wu, like Pierre Ryckmans, thinks that Confucius has had a rough time from commentators: 'In Confucian thought there can be democracy. The idea that Confucianism equals authoritar-ianism is wrong.' Taiwan's democracy, according to Wu, is just opening up and that is changing the consciousness of its people: 'In the last 40 years of authoritarian Kuomintang rule people were educated into a consciousness of greater China. But politics and education are changing from greater-China consciousness to Taiwan consciousness. That's what worries China. But we should live in reality. We are in Taiwan, not China. In the next 20 to 30 years Taiwan will become a real nation in terms of conscious-ness, culture and so on. We will become a different country, separate from China.'

Su Chi, too, thinks that Confucianism has been far too narrowly interpreted by those who wish to equate it with political authoritarianism: 'People forget how tolerant Chinese civilisation is—and the essence of democracy is tolerance. The Chinese have never had religious warfare, because they are basically tolerant. In Taiwan we've never had class warfare. Politically we are going to be tolerant. This is why Singapore and Taiwan are not as close as before; we differ on questions of values. There are so many different Chinese values, so many different 'isms—Confucianism, Daoism, not just one . . . In China we've had six different capital cities, so the centre of cultural gravity has changed several times. This is something very different between Japan and China. Japan tends to have the feeling of being just one big national family. That's not the feeling among Chinese.'

In Taiwan itself, for the first few decades after the flight of the KMT from the mainland in 1949, there was substantial discrimination in favour of mainlanders and against native Taiwanese, with both sides tending to define the children of mainlanders as mainlanders as well. By the late 1990s, something of the reverse was coming into force. It was chic to be a Taiwanese, to speak Taiwanese and, when speaking Mandarin, to have a pronounced Taiwanese accent. In the 1998 race for mayor of Taipei, the DPP incumbent even rather ludicrously accused his mainland-born KMT opponent of 'putting China first', a charge hotly denied by the KMT man, who won. But the very fact that a charge of 'putting China first', however farfetched, could be a significant negative in Taiwanese politics shows how far, psychologically, Taiwan has travelled away from the mainland.

The issue of Taiwan's independence has traditionally been at the heart of Taiwan's politics. The ruling KMT upholds the status quo, which acknowledges in theory that there is only one China and that Taiwan is part of China. However, it also holds that in practice there are two governments and two political entities. Moreover, it has given up its historic claim to sovereignty over, to being the rightful government of, the whole of China. Had it given up this fantasy much earlier Taiwan may have been able to keep its seat at the United Nations, just as both Germanies were represented at the UN when East and West Germany were separate nations, and just as South Korea and North Korea have traditionally both been represented in international forums.

The KMT's own view on independence and unification have undergone continual, gradual but profound evolution. KMT spokesmen now say that while they are in favour of unification in principle this could never be seriously considered until Beijing had renounced the use of force against Taiwan, and until mainland China itself had become democratic, capitalist and affluent, a set of conditions which seem to suggest unification could be a hot topic of negotiation around the 24th century or so. Indeed KMT spokesmen even resort to one of the oldest clichés of Chinese rhetoric, saying that in Chinese civilisation 100 or 200 years is but the blinking of an eye, and there is no need to rush unification. When a democratic politician commits himself to not doing something for 200 years that is pretty much as solid a commitment as you could get. The KMT's rhetoric on unification is merely the minimum political genuflection, necessary both to its own past and to not causing excessive trouble with Beijing, that it must make while at the same time resolutely opposing unification in terms of real actions. The KMT these days even says its main priority is the maintenance of the status quo, which is independence in everything but name. Given this attitude by the KMT, and the even more staunchly pro-independence attitude of the DPP, it can be seen, as opinion polls readily confirm, that there is virtually no support in Taiwan for unification with China.

Meanwhile the New Party, a right-wing breakaway from the KMT, is one of very few groups that argues for a stronger application of one-China principles. Kuen-Chen Fu, a senior legislator from the New Party, receives me in his cramped office in the Taiwan legislative building, an elegant old structure in downtown Taipei built around a quite beautiful traditional court-yard which is a precious oasis of green in a smoggy city. He tells me that whenever Chinese throughout history have tried to break up greater China it has led to 'bloody civil war', tragedy and eventual reunification. 'To sever the people of Taiwan from China is against the scientific evidence,' says Fu. 'We are all Chinese.'

The New Party candidate came third in the 1996 presidential election and the party's future is uncertain. In truth, it probably came into existence primarily to stop the Democratic Progress Party. The DPP is the traditional opposition party in Taiwan. Its leaders were mostly dissident leaders during the martial law days. Its ranks contain many heroes of the struggle for democracy on Taiwan and it deserves at least as much credit as the Kuomintang for producing the democratic Taiwan of today, even though it has always been in Opposition. Traditionally, however, the DPP favoured formal independence for Taiwan. It did this not only on principle but because the KMT's claims to be part of a greater China were for a long time part of its ideological excuse for not implementing full democracy in Taiwan. After all if the government in Taipei represented all 1.2 billion Chinese, then it would have been inherently unjust, not to say undemocratic, to allow the mere 21 million Chinese who happened to live on Taiwan to choose the whole government. Abandoning the fiction of being the government of the whole of China was thus an essential step towards democracy. Similarly, from the DPP's point of view, democracy could only be realised fully if Taiwanese were accorded internationally, and by its own leaders, the same rights to national self-determination that all other functioning nations enjoy.

This is a substantial and reasonable argument. The problem is that Beijing is utterly determined that it will not allow this argument to triumph. Thus Beijing has repeatedly declared that if Taiwan declares formal independence for itself, Beijing will use military power to resume control of Taiwan. This situation is anomalous, indeed farcical, for Taiwan is already independent in everything but name and has been since 1949. The people who founded the New Party were scared that the nature of democracy was such that if the only options in Taiwanese politics were the KMT and the DPP, then eventually people would get tired of the KMT and one day elect the DPP. They might do this for reasons which had nothing to do with Taiwan's independence but they would have voted for a party demanding full and formal independence. This calculation also always allowed the KMT to argue that a vote for the DPP was dangerous on national security grounds, in that it would enrage Beijing.

However, the DPP itself has worked this out and many of its shrewdest leaders want to abandon a commitment to formal independence for the reality of de facto independence, so that national security concerns do not become a permanent roadblock to the DPP's winning power in Taiwan. Recent Taiwanese politics can be seen as the DPP's manoeuvring to make national identity less of a central issue so that it can concentrate on real national needs. If the DPP is smart it will never again allow itself to go into a presidential election with policies which suggest to Taiwan's conservative and security-conscious electorate that voting DPP is a security risk, and even threatens war with China.

In his inauguration speech Lee said that independence was neither possible nor necessary. Saying it was not possible was a

concession to Beijing; saying it was not necessary was a concession to his own electorate, and its pride in its democratic
achievement.

Voluntary reunification is not taken seriously by anybody.
Vincent Siew, who went on to become prime minister of Taiwan,
once told me that any reunification is likely to be a very long time
off: 'It depends on what the mainland can do to narrow the gap
between the two societies. Economically we [Taiwan] are quite
advanced, politically we are a democracy, socially we are open and
free. Unification can only occur without pain if the gap [with the
mainland] is narrowed. Whether mainland China can continue to
reform towards a market economy and a free society is unclear.'

That there are still one or two authoritarian touches to
Taiwan's political culture, especially in the choreographed mass
rallies and lingering style of the KMT, is undeniable. But the
substance and reality of Taiwanese democracy is also undeniable,
and far more important than the aftertaste of 40 years of at
times brutal authoritarianism.

I-Jen Chiou, when I met him the secretary-general of the DPP,
told me he believes that historically the government has benefited
hugely from the dominance of national security and identity
issues in Taiwanese politics, which is especially heightened whenever there are public disputes with Beijing, as there were during
the 1996 Taiwan presidential elections. He would like Taiwanese
politics to centre on core domestic issues, such as corruption,
which everyone in Taiwan acknowledges is a significant problem,
and social development. Chiou, who like many DPP leaders spent
time in prison in the past for his political beliefs, gives only 'low
credit' to President Lee for Taiwan's democratisation, citing corruption, lack of a fully independent judiciary and political censorship on television as limits to real democracy.

The DPP's electoral fortunes have waxed and waned. Its
candidate did poorly in the presidential election against President
Lee, but this was attributable at least partly to the Taiwanese
people's reaction against Beijing's campaign of intimidation
against Lee. The DPP has never quite established itself as an
alternative party of government although at times it has pulled
off spectacular coups such as winning the much coveted post of
mayor of Taipei, which it subsequently lost.

Chiou argues that the psychological and cultural distance between China and Taiwan is increasing but that the economic distance, because of Taiwan's massive investment in mainland industries, is diminishing. The Taiwanese Government, he says, has reacted to this partly with its 'Look South' policy, which encourages Taiwanese firms to invest in South East Asia instead of China.

Su Chi, for his part, claims that most Taiwanese investment in the mainland is by small firms—the so-called 'army of ants', who tend to be adept at finding ways to survive in politically troubled times.

The structure of Taiwan's economy turned out to be an unpredicted blessing when the regional economic crisis broke out in the late 1990s. Partly because of the failure of government attempts to create giant protected industries in the 1960s—such as a car industry—Taiwan was not burdened with a structure of huge and inefficient conglomerates like the South Korean chaebols. Instead its economy was dominated by small and medium enterprises, or SMEs. In Taiwan, with a population of 21 million, there are 1.3 million individual businesses.

'There are so many presidents and chief executive officers,' says Su Chi, 'because Chinese people like to be their own boss. And the government encouraged the development of SMEs because they thought it would encourage social stability. We learnt this from our failed policies in the mainland [when the KMT ruled all of China], where we lost the masses because they were too poor and the business conglomerates too big. So here we encouraged farmers, for example, to be businessmen. This structure helped us survive the two oil crises and then the financial crisis of 1997—our businesses were so small and so flexible. And small businesses always go for profit whereas big conglomerates go for market share.'

It meant, too, that Taiwanese businesses were financially conservative. They tended to save and invest from their own resources rather than relying excessively on borrowing. Certainly there was relatively little borrowing in foreign currencies, which became such a problem in the other Asian tigers.

The opposition DPP acknowledges this success in its own society but believes that the KMT business arm and its connection with vote-buying practices in the countryside, its resemblance, perhaps, to Japan's Liberal Democratic Party, should be a much bigger issue. Chiou of the DPP thinks that much more of Taiwan's political debate should focus on crime and corruption. He tells me: 'Organised crime is a big and growing problem. Many politicians have connections with gangsters.' He alleges that vote-buying is particularly rife in rural areas and is mostly effected through local gangs of organised criminals. His own experience bears out the problems: 'The situation here is a little similar to the Japanese-style *yakuza* gangs, but it is somewhat worse here. I myself was beaten up in the street, in broad daylight, because I had criticised the activities of the organised criminals. Another legislator was slashed with knives. Police did not find the perpetrators.'

Chiou acknowledges the changes that have taken place in Taiwan, making Taiwan a more normal society concerned with its own needs, but he argues that the government is still lagging behind the social reality. 'Children in our schools are forced to learn a lot about Chinese history and geography but they don't learn enough about Taiwanese history and geography. They learn something unrealistic, so the only reality is popular Western culture. Children learn about the Yangtze River but they've never been there. They don't know about the rivers in Taiwan. All they know about is Coca-Cola and McDonald's.'

Chiou's argument is similar to that which is heard in any derivative society, any society that was once a colony, or might consider itself a stream of a great culture, as Canada or Australia, say, might in relation to the broader Western culture. Nonetheless, you feel that Chiou is bound to win this argument in the long run. The more democratic a society gets the more likely it is to want to celebrate, examine and understand its own experience; to scrutinise and evaluate its own history and literature.

Despite its varying fortunes, the DPP office fairly hums with life. There are dozens of young party workers around, dozens of computer terminals. A poster of the Magna Carta adorns Chiou's wall—an odd inspiration for Asian democracy. Why not something Chinese, or, if not, then perhaps the Gettysburg Address or the American Declaration of Independence? Perhaps it reflects a Chinese preference for evolutionary rather than revolutionary democracy. Perhaps, on the other hand, it's just a poster someone gave him.

Some Taiwanese opinion-makers, particularly the old hardliners from the mainland, are worried about the dilution of Chinese values in Taiwan and the rising influence of Western culture—a complaint heard in many rapidly developing Asian countries—but others are relaxed about it. Ming Chu-Ming, a member of the ruling KMT's central committee, is in the relaxed camp.

'We love China,' she says, 'for history and perhaps for the future. But it's a kind of myth or dream. We have to adjust to reality. Look at Chinese philosophy and tradition—all the family is supposed to live together. But people now commonly accept that small family units can live together, but still you love and respect the older members who may not be living with you. Ever since the world became more high-tech it's become smaller and smaller. Culturally it's become harder to shut your door. I prefer Chinese noodles to hamburgers, my kids prefer French fries. What can I do? Say they're not Chinese? You can't bind your feet any longer.'

Ming is a high-powered woman, educated and brought up in the new Taiwan, a product of the perhaps inadvertently liberating forces of economic growth and globalisation. A bevy of subordinates help her with a clearly overcrowded schedule and a vast list of appointments. She talks rapidly and fondles not one but two mobile phones as we drive across town. Traffic jams are never going to be dead time to someone like Ming. She worries about things like Taiwan's soaring divorce rates but thinks that the mixture of Chinese and Western cultural influences will be an advantage for Taiwan's citizens in dealing with the globalising economy.

She says: 'In Taiwan you can be Confucian, Chinese and modern all at the same time. Sometimes you take your kids to McDonald's, sometimes to grandma's. They're lucky, they've got a choice. The 21st century is going to be an international era. International education will be important to people's success.'

Certainly for a Westerner, to read much modern Taiwanese literature is to traverse themes extremely familiar, given of course a Taiwanese flavour, a Taiwanese ambience. But from popular novels you get the impression that the concerns of the average Taiwanese are not that different from the concerns of the average San Franciscan. There is sense in this, of course. Human culture is fascinating and what separates one national culture from another is particularly fascinating. But the human experience is singularly unified. The human condition is truly universal. What unites us must be 99 per cent of us and what divides us just one per cent. Of course, people are interested in the one per cent.

Much modern Taiwanese literature, like modern literature in most places, is, ostensibly at least, subversive of traditional values, although such literary subversion can also paradoxically and perversely play a role in affirmation, even when the conscious aim is subversion. This is not the case with one hugely popular Taiwanese novel, *The Butcher's Wife*. Written by Li Ang, it recounts in starkly realist terms the long abuse of a wife by her husband, leading to . . .?

You guessed it—the murder of the husband by the wife. It is *The Burning Bed* in postmodern prose. A much more gentle and certainly more beautiful book, *Bound Feet: Stories of Contemporary Taiwan*, by Catherine Dai, explores in fictional form mainly issues of family attachment and duty. At first this seems distinctly Chinese, although many of the background themes of romantic conflicts, career dilemmas and the rest seem familiar enough. But is even the stress on familial obligations so utterly and distinctively Chinese? Isn't it also very much the way most Western societies functioned just a little while ago, the way some still function today? If you substituted Irish names for the Taiwanese names the stories could fit almost perfectly into modern Ireland. The main real cultural difference from most Western societies is that the extended family is still somewhat stronger in the stories in *Bound Feet*. Whether that strength will survive the full experience of modernisation and long-term affluence is an open question, and perhaps what much of the Asian values debate is really all about.

Taiwan is a small country with a high-performing economy. It has an astonishing history, having been thoroughly neglected by mainland China for most of its existence, and periodically colonised by European powers. Japan ruled Taiwan from 1895 to 1945 and set the basis for much of the subsequent economic expansion. And though all the normal evils of colonialism accompanied Japanese rule it was nonetheless a more successful and relatively benign colonisation than most in modern Asia. The Taiwanese are not nearly so hung up about their Japanese experience as are some of their Asian neighbours. Unlike the Koreans, for example, they don't feel it necessary to go round their main cities blowing up remaining Japanese buildings. Instead they rejoice in their colonial architecture and put the grand old buildings to good use. After 1945 Taiwan was formally under Chinese rule. From 1946 to 1949 it underwent a kind of gangster despotism when the KMT carpetbaggers stole everything that wasn't nailed down, and undertook one gruesome massacre in 1947.

From 1949 the beaten Nationalists, having lost the civil war on the mainland to the communists, set up their government-in-exile on Taiwan. This was virtually another period of colonisation, with all kinds of abuses by mainland oligarchs against the native Taiwanese (that is, not Taiwanese aborigines, themselves a depressed minority, but Taiwanese-speaking Chinese born on the island). KMT rule in Taiwan was harshly authoritarian until the 1980s, when political reform really got under way. However, the KMT was certainly effective in land reform and industrialisation, producing decade after decade of rapid economic growth and transforming Taiwan from a subsistence agricultural society with a tiny industrial base into a big, affluent industrial power.

As the Cold War unfolded, Taiwan fell increasingly under direct American influence. For a time much of the anti-communist West paid the Taiwanese Government a good deal of the honorary tribute accruing to the real Government of China. It had a seat at the United Nations, and the United States sometimes affected to see it as the true representative of the Chinese nation. All of this contributed to a distorted international view of Taiwan. Whether it was seen as the true representative of the Chinese people, or whether it was seen as a 'renegade province' in line with Beijing's wishes, it was seen entirely as an element of China.

Yet its history, and the influences that have shaped it, are more complex than this and different in their way from those of any other Chinese society. The role of Japan in Taiwan's history (President Lee is typical of his generation in speaking fluent

Japanese) is different and deeper than in any other Chinese society. The role of America, which was friend, protector, tutor and intimate collaborator for 40 years of the Cold War, is also greater in Taiwan than in any other Chinese society. Tens of thousands of Taiwanese have earned their PhDs at American universities, some coming back to become intellectual, scientific and commercial leaders of Taiwan, others staying in the United States and forming the leadership of an important and powerful American ethnic community and a pivotal part of Taiwan's effective lobbying and influence effort in the US.

Taken altogether this is a distinctive national experience. Taiwan is a unique nation which deserves greater recognition and analysis in its own right *as Taiwan*. It is a big trading and investing power—by the late 1990s the 14th largest trading economy in the world—and it plays a crucial role in North East Asian security. It is at the heart of US–China relations.

Some Taiwanese even believe their society played a decisive role in the collapse of communism. The theory goes like this . . . A crucial factor in the mainland's embracing reform from the late 1970s was shame and outrage at how vastly better Taiwan, ruled by the communists' bitter civil war rivals, was doing in economic terms than China itself and at the obvious total inferiority of the communist economic model. Thus, according to the theory, Taiwan prompted Chinese reform, which in turn led the Soviet Union to extreme frustration about its own sclerotic economic system and a desire to reform for fear of how far China could pull ahead after it started to record very high economic growth rates. And the rest is history. So Taiwan was responsible for the end of the Cold War and for the collapse of communism. This is a pretty contentious theory and assumes far too simple a chain of causation. Yet it is not wholly without merit and illustrates the global relevance of Taiwan.

Now Taiwan is both affluent and a democracy. Its democracy is not perfect but nor is it fake. As Taiwan struggles to secure its independent existence—politically, economically and strategically—it is one of the richest Chinese societies the world has ever known. Certainly it is the most free.

There are few things less attractive than boot-licking dressed up as high principle, yet this is what we mostly get when we hear the world's diplomatic leaders blathering on about a 'one China' policy. The world is timid in confronting China's bluster over Taiwan, its petty, vindictive effort to keep Taiwan diplomatically isolated, to prevent it from joining the United Nations or the International Monetary Fund—bodies which Taiwan is eminently qualified to belong to. Of course, China's constant threats may have contributed to making Taiwan stronger, but they are unattractive and wrong in principle. Taiwan's people are human beings like anyone else. They deserve the right to determine their own future.

Taiwan is the living rebuttal of the notion that democracy is inconsistent with Chinese culture, or with Asian values more generally. Its miniskirts and Mercedes-Benz cars, its raucous discotheques and quiet tea houses, its policy struggles with corruption and competition, its gross pollution and gridlocked roads are all an inevitable part of the encounter with extremely rapid modernisation.

We all have a stake in Taiwan's success, both as a democracy and as an economy. The world very badly needs at least one modern, functioning, successful Chinese democracy. Taipei is a dirty, crowded, polluted, clogged-up city. It is also, in its way, one of the great hopes of mankind.

9

CULTURE, CONSUMERS AND CORRUPTION IN BUDDHIST THAILAND

THE DAY I WENT to visit the then prime minister of Thailand, Chuan Leekpai, the car I was travelling in could not make it to the main entrance of Bangkok's Government House because there were too many protesters outside. It was early 1998. The protesters didn't have any signs and it wasn't clear exactly what action of the government's they were protesting about—perhaps mooted fuel price rises or other parts of the austerity package the International Monetary Fund had imposed as part of the conditions for its financial bailout of Thailand.

Perhaps it was just the generally held and broadly credible notion of democratic electorates everywhere that if things are going wrong the government is more or less to blame, or at least to be held responsible for getting them to go right again.

In early 1998 I hadn't been in Bangkok for a couple of years and several changes were instantly noticeable. First, the notoriously dreadful traffic was clearly not as bad as it had been for most of the 1990s. This was wryly described as the one significant achievement of the Chavalit Yongchaiyudh Government. It had overseen such a staggering economic crisis that no one could afford to drive any more. Bangkok yuppies—'Buppies'—had sold their Mercedes-Benzes in the thousands. Certainly far fewer people were going to the airport for foreign travel.

But there were other changes too. The temper of the democratic debate was different. There seemed, despite the severe economic difficulties of the nation, an expectation that democratic procedures, in form and substance, would be adhered to.

174

Whereas once a crisis of this kind would have led almost inevitably to military intervention, now the strong expectation was that the country would handle its worst economic setback in decades through the regular mechanisms of state afforded by the democratic system.

The other paradoxical change was an almost infinite increase in humility among Thai officials and commentators. Thais are by no means proverbially arrogant but there was a time in the 1980s and early 1990s when the Thai economy was one of the two or three fastest growing economies in the world. This led Thais—policy makers, businessmen and commentators—towards a degree of hubris, as though they had cracked the genetic code for sustained rapid economic growth. Regional analysts became very fond of straight line graphs which showed regional economies, and particularly Thailand, becoming much bigger economies and exercising much greater relative power. The straight line graphs made the fatally mistaken assumption that present trends would continue unabated for 20 or 30 years. It was easy then to project forward to a point at which Thailand would be the seventh largest economy in the world. The problem was that some people started to behave as though that speculation were already the reality. By 1998 speculation had ceased. Reality had returned.

There was another noticeable change too. There were more beggars on the streets.

The economic crisis that began in Thailand in the middle of 1997 rocked all of East Asia and challenged in profound ways the growing self-confidence of the region's leaders and peoples. It also challenged the debate about Asian values. Even today there is no unanimity among scholars about why such basically sound and basically well-run economies fell so drastically in value in 1997 and 1998. The preconditions, the imbalances, the structural problems are all easy enough to find, but they had been present while the region was enjoying decades of strong growth. In Thailand's case the essential structural misalignments had been publicly recognised for some time, although the Chavalit Government had repeatedly denied them.

Thailand, like numerous regional countries, had had its currency, the baht, effectively pegged to the American dollar. Unfortunately for Thailand, in 1994 the Chinese had substantially

devalued their currency and the Chinese were competitors with
the Thais in some exports. That this was so was an indictment
of Thai development policy. It represented a failure of Thailand
to put enough effort into post-primary school education and to
move Thailand's industrial production up the industrial food
chain to higher level exports with more value added in Thailand
itself.

At the same time the US dollar was steadily appreciating (and
the Japanese yen depreciating), so that the Thai currency itself
was therefore appreciating. This helped create a substantial trade
deficit for Thailand. Worse, however, was the effect of the
currency peg combined with pressures for financial deregulation
on Thai investment behaviour. American interest rates were
substantially below Thai interest rates. The longstanding currency
peg convinced lenders and borrowers alike that there was no
serious currency risk. Thus the temptation was irresistible for
people to borrow in dollars and lend in baht. As with any
booming market it did not take much brains to be able to make
speculative profits, at least on paper. The more you lent the more
you made. It also worked the other way. The more you borrowed
the more you made, through capital gains on your assets. Inevitably in such a situation much of the borrowing and investment
went into real estate speculation. A vast property bubble built
up. The quality of investment plans was not examined sufficiently
by banks. Property supply and construction activity far exceeded
demand.

The combination of a vast property bubble with a big trade
deficit pretty well inevitably led the speculators to home in on
the baht. The Chavalit Government handled the situation badly.
It denied there was a problem. It claimed it would never devalue
the currency. It wasted a vast portion of the country's foreign
reserves in a futile defence of the baht. And then, just after
denying yet again that it would devalue the baht, it did indeed
float its currency, leading to a massive devaluation. But by this
time the Chavalit Government was in chaos. There was no
effective strategy to accompany the devaluation and no effective
communication with the domestic or international markets, who
reacted very adversely. As soon as it became clear that the baht
was heading downwards Thais in their droves joined foreigners

in getting rid of their baht. Thai businesses, which had presumed there was no currency risk, had vast unhedged loans in US dollars. They immediately tried to convert their baht into dollars to protect their debt situation.

Thus a terrible deflationary spiral set in, a spiral which was to become all too familiar across the region in the ensuing months. As a result the baht lost more than half its value. So there was a full-blown currency crisis. Everyone knew that many Thai companies would have trouble servicing their loans and so Thais and foreigners started to sell their stocks. Thus phase two of the crisis was a stock market crisis. And with stocks and oversupplied property forming such a big part of the security backing for so many loans this quickly transformed itself into a full-blown banking crisis. The Chavalit Government was completely unable to cope and called in the IMF. However, the Chavalit Government had become almost paralysed by then and it was just a matter of time before it fell apart, to be replaced by a Democrat Party–dominated government led by Chuan Leekpai.

'Bahtulism', as it was quickly dubbed, spread rapidly throughout the region. Most South East Asian nations had developed their own property bubbles. The economies of Indonesia, Malaysia and the Philippines competed in manufactured exports so similar to Thailand's that a raft of regional devaluations became inevitable, as otherwise Thailand's devaluation would have given it a massive competitive edge over its South East Asian neighbours. The other nations also had their unhedged loan problems and thus followed similar patterns of economic crisis, though to widely varying degrees.

It was in the midst of this crisis that I went early in 1998 to see Prime Minister Chuan Leekpai. If there was ever an arrogant Thai it certainly wasn't Chuan. Small, dapper, bespectacled, infinitely polite, in command of reasonable English though preferring to do formal interviews in Thai through a translator, Chuan looked that day to have every ounce of responsibility for the fate of 70 million Thais resting on his narrow shoulders. He still looked young, almost unnaturally young, as he always does, but there was an unmistakable gravity in his face, and for the first half hour of our meeting he perched on the very edge of his sofa and endlessly folded and refolded his hands. He had every reason to look concerned. Many Thais had already lost their jobs and credible non-government organisations were estimating that unemployment would reach at least three million. And this in a country with no substantial government-provided social safety net.

As he sat and talked to me Chuan's mind must have returned to the threat all this posed to the existence of the modern Thailand we had come to know, the Thailand of rapid economic growth, flourishing democracy and endlessly expanding opportunity. In some ways Chuan was an unlikely figure to be cast as his country's leader in a moment of desperate crisis, an unlikely occupant of the cockpit of history. He had previously led a Thai government, from 1992 to 1995, a government which had been regarded as clean but ineffective. But in an environment in which restoring international investor confidence and ending crony capitalism and finance sector corruption were the overriding imperatives, Chuan's Mr Clean reputation probably made him the Thai leader with the best chance of success.

What was perhaps most notable in our discussion, especially in terms of Asian values, was the direct way Chuan spoke about his nation's shortcomings. He embodied the wholly democratic idea that in a crisis it's best to tell the people the truth, to force them to take responsibility collectively for their situation, not to seek external causes, scapegoats or excuses. Chuan's words to me could not have been clearer in this regard: 'Above all we Thais must bear in mind that this problem arises primarily out of our own doings and that primarily it has to be resolved by Thais ourselves. Its origins may have come from outside, in terms of attacks on the baht, but if we had been strong enough we could have resisted these attacks.'

Chuan was in the midst of administering an extremely tough IMF program, which involved not only the closure of almost all of the nation's finance companies and the merger or effective closure of numerous banks but also brutally high interest rates and a harsh Budgetary retrenchment. Again, about this package he was blunt: 'The program with the IMF was entered into voluntarily by Thailand. We therefore have an obligation to follow it as closely as possible.' Chuan renegotiated some aspects of the IMF program, especially its overly harsh Budgetary contraction, but there was no real doubt about the sincerity of his government in its determination actually to implement the IMF program.

Chuan did call attention to one aspect of what might be regarded as Asian values in asserting that Thai society would be better equipped than some others to cope with the inevitable social stress that would accompany economic recession. He told me: 'Thai society has some special characteristics which will help to cushion the severe impact of unemployment so that it will not have the dire consequences it has in some developed countries. The unemployed will have the option of going back to their extended family networks, to be back with their fathers, mothers and relatives. Perhaps we will not find the phenomenon we so readily observe in the US of the unemployed on the streets, homeless and destitute and looking for shelter. I believe there will certainly be social effects from our economic crisis, but these will be absorbed by the characteristics of Thai society. It will not be as severe as it could have been.'

This is perhaps the Asian values debate at its sharpest end. The countries of East Asia have avoided providing a welfare state not only because of its Budgetary implications but because they believe it undermines the strength of the family which is the strongest social glue there is. Virtually every East Asian state and its leaders take pride in the enduring importance of the family and in its strength as compared to the family in Western societies. By this they generally mean the extended family. The lack of a welfare state contributes to the high household savings rates, as saving for a rainy day is the nearest thing to unemployment benefits, health insurance and (often) an old age pension that there is. The lack of a government network of support centred on the individual reinforces the importance of the extended family as the essential safety net. Chuan's comments indicate that East Asian leaders regard this as an immediate, practical matter, not merely a pious social aspiration.

In Thailand the continuing existence of a big rural sector in the economy, and the physical presence of a geographically large rural hinterland, meant that the physical safety net of the extended family was in place in that, as Chuan indicated, it was assumed that many unemployed city workers could go back at least temporarily to live with relatives in rural areas. There might not be jobs, or at least not formal full-time jobs, in the rural economy but at least there would be a roof over their heads and enough food to eat.

But Chuan was also prepared to admit that distinctive Thai culture had its weaknesses as well as its strengths. If Thailand was to emerge successfully from the economic crisis, and if it was to implement fully an IMF-style liberal reform, especially of the financial sector, then there would need to be substantial cultural and political changes in Thailand.

The flipside of the extended family network is that such networks also operate automatically, almost unconsciously, in business and finance. When a man applies for a loan the first thing the proverbial Thai banker asks is: Do I know this person, is he from my part of the country, what connections do I have with him, what connections can I build with him? The first question is not: What is the creditworthiness of this loan application, does it satisfy objective rules and criteria, is the business plan convincing? Requiring Thais to fundamentally change this behaviour will require substantial change in Thai culture.

Here Chuan was more equivocal in our discussion: 'I don't believe it will lead to a wholesale change of Thai culture, but certainly there will be changes to the way we work within a system which will be more standardised internationally. Managers and directors in charge of the finance sector will have less leeway to bring in personal considerations in their decision making.'

Chuan was perhaps underestimating the degree of cultural change needed if Thailand were to fully embrace Western standards of accounting and business practices. In a sense, the question is how universal these standards are and how particularly Western they are; that is, whether their imposition constitutes a case of Western cultural imperialism. The reason for arguing against that proposition is that, while these standards in their modern embodiment may have originated in the West, they do involve universal values, such as straightforward, honest and fair dealing. More particularly, it is Thais themselves who have become sickened by their country's chronic corruption and who feel the burden of the injustices this corruption imposes on their society. While change at the top may be forced by the IMF, there is a vast groundswell of indigenous opinion in favour of the corruption-related elements of reform.

Nonetheless, there is a danger in Thailand's situation of a backlash against the international economy, against the forces of globalisation, and perhaps generally against the West and most particularly against the United States. Many Thais were bitterly disappointed that the US did not participate in the IMF bailout package for Thailand. Chuan acknowledged this sentiment in our conversation but did not quite formally endorse it himself. He said: 'There is that anti-American feeling among some groups of Thais, even among the mass media. These people feel that the US and Thailand have cooperated very closely in the past on many issues, even during the period of the Vietnam War. So people thought the US would be more speedy in their reaction when Thailand entered a crisis. But I don't think this is a matter of one side being at fault. Perhaps the US did not foresee that the crisis would spread as rapidly as it has.

'The US made an excuse which was not very helpful. They said they could not act when the crisis occurred in Thailand, because they were hamstrung by a congressional restriction.'

Chuan's comments are revealing. He would not himself be formally undiplomatic towards the Americans. That would have been both un-Thai and un-Chuan. But it is clear that many Thais who regarded themselves as pro-American were nonetheless bitterly disappointed at what they saw as American neglect and the relatively low value they believed Washington placed on America's friendship with Thailand. It is clear that the regional crisis massively increased America's power over the region, but at the same time it led to increased anti-American sentiment in the region.

Yet it is a sad and impotent anti-Americanism, and it is mixed with a deep recognition of America's awesome power. It reminds me of the anti-Yankee sentiment you could find in much of Latin America in the 1980s. Whenever that futile sentiment found expression in policy it led to poor results for the country concerned. Eventually the Latin Americans abandoned most of the anti-Yankee posturing and rhetoric, not because they were won over to admiration for the ideals and institutions of the

United States, but because they realised that basing policy on anti-Yankee posturing was profitless. However emotionally cathartic it may have been it led nowhere constructive, it achieved nothing useful. Eventually pragmatism took over and Latin America benefited from its liberalisation and increased cooperation with Washington. South East Asia in recent decades has had a record of very strong pragmatism in its leadership classes and they are unlikely to allow the undeniable anti-American sentiment in their societies to dominate policy. Nonetheless it bears watching.

Thoughtful Thais responded to the misfortunes of 1997 and 1998 by trying to use them as a catalyst to bring about constructive change in their society—to entrench a popular dynamic against corruption, to renovate their democratic institutions, to modernise the darker aspects of their financial practices and to effect broader cultural change to emphasise fairness and transparency as opposed to 'personalism'. In this they were trying to achieve particular cultural and political ends for their society, as well as making themselves more effective participants in the global economy.

Dr Suchit Bunbongkarn of the Faculty of Political Science at the University of Chulalongkorn is one of Thailand's most distinguished commentators and academics. He served on the commission to draft a new constitution for Thailand, a constitution designed above all else to reduce corruption and vote-buying. He is one of many Thais who, while not downplaying the human suffering that the economic crisis brought in its wake, also saw the opportunities it offered for reform and renewal.

We talked in an Italian restaurant secluded in a quiet Bangkok garden, only 50 yards from traffic and smog, but mentally, aesthetically, a universe away. 'We need both economic and political reform,' he told me. 'We also need reform of the bureaucracy. This is very difficult but the economic crisis gives us an opportunity. The bureaucracy is too large, inefficient and corrupt. Under the new electoral system we hope corruption will be less. For the first time we have an Election Commission, with real autonomy, independent and powerful.'

To listen to sophisticated Thais talk about corruption is a

bracing experience. They are honest and corrosive scathing about the practice of corruption in their society. Consider the following description of the phenomenon, printed in the *Nation* newspaper in 1996:

> The Budget is like a popsicle that's passed around. Everyone gets a lick at it when it comes their way, so that by the time the one at the end of the line gets it, there's little left . . . Most of the time corrupt politicians and officials escape punishment. In fact, most of them continue to prosper and command respect in society.

This devastatingly honest description of the previous method of Thai Budget making comes from Bonn-ua Prasertsuwan, the former Speaker of the Parliament and deputy leader of the Chart Thai Party. He estimated that something like 50 per cent of Budget project funds disappeared into corrupt purposes. Yet perhaps the most interesting aspect of corruption in Thailand is the way it has become a bigger and bigger issue in mainstream politics. And this process was certainly well under way before the economic crisis hit. In Pasuk Phongpaichit's very useful book, *Corruption and Democracy in Thailand*, she makes the point that corruption was perhaps the dominant political issue in the 1988–1991 period. The government of the day (led by Prime Minister Chatichai Choonhavan) faced numerous no-confidence motions in which the Opposition focused overwhelmingly on the alleged corruption of government members. Thus it is Thais themselves who are determined to get rid of corruption from their own society. This is a powerful rebuttal of those Western analysts who argue that corruption is inherent in Asian values and thus in Asian societies and their political systems. Indeed, the military even cited corruption as the primary reason for getting rid of this government in a coup in 1991.

Yet subsequent experience did not justify the military's action. Nor does the history of corruption under military rule in Thailand bear out the notion that suspending democracy and instituting military rule is an effective long-term way to avoid corruption. As Pasuk argues:

> The military has raised the corruption issue as an excuse for its attempts to retard democratic development while it searches

round for new strategies to conserve its political position in the long term. In the long run, however, the checks and balances of a full democratic system and the development of a civil society will prove a more effective means to control corruption than the intervention of a man on a white horse . . . it appears that the Thai electorate agrees with this conclusion.

Dr Suchit, like others, believes that, notwithstanding the dislocations brought on by the economic difficulties, Thailand has reached a stage of stability in which the necessary reforms can proceed without causing vast social upheaval: 'Social unrest here will be quite manageable. Protests will come, the crime rate will increase, but it will be manageable.' Like Chuan Leekpai, he sees Thailand's rural sector as essential to its social stability: 'A downturn affects the industrial sector most. The agricultural sector has been getting better and can absorb a lot of people. During the boom period they came to Bangkok and left parents at home. Thailand's safety net will be the rural sector.'

He saw a possible backlash against globalisation but did not think this would be the dominant theme in Thai life: 'Some people complain that liberalisation and globalisation give big benefits to rich Western countries which exploit our weakness, in our market and in our management, when we are not ready. But we cannot turn the country back from the liberalisation. We have to strengthen ourselves to deal with it. Everything started in the 1990s—free trade, the World Trade Organisation, the ASEAN Free Trade Area. But liberalisation doesn't mean everything is totally free. There is still a need for some regulation.

'Some sectors do feel that liberalisation is the cause of their problems but most blame our own mismanagement, among the leaders of the country. In the boom period there was tremendous self-confidence, if we compared ourselves with Latin America or Africa or even, in terms of growth rates, with Europe. But now for the long term I think we will be more realistic, more cautious about investment, less arrogant.'

Nonetheless, the economic pain that began in mid-1997 is in a sense a wholly new experience for Thailand. It is not that poverty is new. Thailand has experienced poverty before. But poverty after a prolonged period of prosperity and booming economic growth—that is new. For many of the unemployed, unemployment is a wholly new experience. They don't know how long it will last. Moreover, although the extended family is still there, the long boom has frayed or displaced some of the traditional psychological props that traditionally help people to endure poverty—especially the consolations of Buddhism, Thailand's dominant religion.

But the newness and the shock have also bred humility. For example, some analysts argue that the military is less tempted to a political response partly because they realise that the new global economy is so complicated that it is not amenable to simple solutions in which the primary question is merely a question of will.

Part of the problem for Thailand has been the cultural divide between the politics of rural areas and the politics of Bangkok. Bangkok is a big sophisticated city. It produces a political class much like the political classes of many other countries, some good parts, some not so good parts, but on the whole conversant with policy issues, somewhat internationalist in outlook, in touch with the modern economy. Thailand's vast rural hinterland, however, tends to be much more in the grip of regional parties wholly free of ideology or even elementary policy, which exist as traditional vote-buying machines which are the breeding grounds of corruption and which make the financial cost of winning a Thai election exorbitant. Thus an old saw has it that Thai governments are made in the countryside and unmade in the city. Traditionally, Thai political parties lacked any significant ideological or policy base and represented regional interests and personal fiefdoms. The reforms of the constitution in 1998 are meant to address and heal that divide in the political culture. But it is likely to be a long-term affair. Partly, again, this is a result of Thailand's failure to do enough about its education system beyond universal primary schooling. While rural Thais embody countless human virtues, lack of education makes it much harder for them to be sophisticated, responsible voters. In one sense this has meant in the past that roughly half of the Thai political class is not really fit to govern a modern trading economy heavily dependent on international capital flows. The encouraging thing is that many, many Thais recognise this.

As you might expect in a country subject to such vast Western influence, Dr Suchit, like many other commentators, does not believe that the conscious notion of Asian values has been very important in Thailand: 'Asian values as a concept was overplayed in Singapore and Malaysia, but not much in Thailand. You don't hear that it [the economic crisis] is a threat to Thai culture. Rather it will strengthen Thai culture. In the boom times we imported Western consumer culture and individualism. Now people think perhaps we forgot about aspects of our own culture. We need to work together to reinvigorate the idea of Thai indigenous culture. Of course, Thai culture is a mix. There is a traditional Thai culture which has existed for centuries. During the boom period the middle class tried to change the nation's culture into Western ways. But Thai culture still exists; for example, personal ties are most important. Everything has to go with personal ties, even in banking.

'Now, working together and tolerance will be more important. There might be more routine confrontation than there has been in the past. In the past Thais didn't confront one another. The economic downturn will probably cause more confrontation. In traditional culture you never said anything blunt to each other.

'It isn't easy for anyone to change the culture away from personal ties. Many middle-level bankers and so on study in the West and know everything in the textbook about managing by objectives etc. But they are still very Thai. They need the school and family networks. But Thais are very pragmatic.'

It would be too simplistic to say that personalism as such is a good or a bad thing in business, or in creating a less corrupt commercial and political culture. Thai personalism doesn't necessarily look all that different from 'customer-focused banking' which has recently become popular in the West. Rather it has been applied corruptly in Thailand's recent past. The challenge, as always, is to take an underlying cultural dynamic and mould it and apply it in a way which serves the whole society and which is consistent with a modern and honest economy.

An academic with a generally different view from Dr Suchit's is Dr Likhit Dhiravegin, who was a deputy minister in the last days of the Chavalit Government and who was politically aligned with the New Aspiration Party. He believes that the economic downturn was 'a very serious crisis' which threatened 'the morale, pride, sense of self-worth of everyone—poor and rich, academics, business people, peasants . . .'

'Immediately we have lost one thing—national pride. I came to dread the idea of going abroad. I was ashamed. Every two or three days I would find myself getting depressed. The coming in of the International Monetary Fund meant that we had lost fiscal sovereignty. Even regarding the change of government [from the Chavalit Government to Chuan Leekpai's Government] I believe the IMF played a role. When I saw a *farang* [a white person] come into Government House with a briefcase under his arm to tell the government what to do it made my heart ache. You can't help feeling, in the initial stages at least, that the Caucasians are taking over. People in general feel confused, lost, unsure of the outcome, and we've lost our confidence.'

Like most intelligent men caught in a situation of turmoil, Likhit was better at framing the questions than providing the answers. His speculations on the effect of economic downturn on Thai culture were perhaps pessimistic but they were not defeatist. 'People will hold fast to Thai culture. But talk of the Asian miracle, that's another thing. If the situation gets better quickly that might be OK, pride might be restored. If not, then confidence in the Asian way—personalism, patriarchy, feng-shui etc—will be discredited. Nothing succeeds like success, nothing fails like failure. Through the indoctrination of Hollywood movies, combined with this [economic downturn], Asians and Latin Americans may feel inferior deep down.

'A nationalistic reaction may really be a manifestation of an inferiority complex. National pride is often a self-defence mechanism but deep down you know your country is undeveloped. And those who studied in the West also feel superior. Their syntax and method of thinking is very Western. Globalisation is not really globalisation. There is always a centre of colonisation. Now it's the United States, Japan and Western Europe. Globalisation is Westernisation. The International Monetary Fund, the World Trade Organisation etc—all this originated in the West. It's all modelled and patterned after the US and Europe.

'Take a boy from Egypt, Guangzhou, Thailand, or London— give them the same education and each will produce an atomic bomb. Civilisation belongs to mankind . . . Monks and priests controlled everything in the West until the Renaissance. We have not really had the Renaissance in this part of the world. Think of the traditional Chinese gentleman with long fingernails who cannot touch material and therefore cannot make experiments. The Chinese used gunpowder for firecrackers, not for practical purposes. The Indians are mystics. The Chinese believe in Taoism—living with nature. The West believes in controlling nature. Even in medicine the Chinese were against surgery—don't cut the body.

'The Japanese try to combine Western and Asian influences. We try to combine these two as well. But for us there's a patron/client relationship as well as the need to embrace Western accounting methods. The thing we used to be proud of, combining Western and Asian—can we continue to do this in the same proportion as in the past?

'The four little dragons (Taiwan, Singapore, Hong Kong and South Korea) were either insular or peninsular, Sinic (except for Korea), Confucian and politically marginal. Is this a pattern or not? We just followed their lead.

'Technology is critical and this must come from basic science and from education—putting money into it. People must have scientific minds. Without science and technology, what do you have to sell? Does this region really have scientific minds? These are big questions and no one wants to ask them.'

Dr Likhit was in a gloomy mood when he made these remarks to me in early 1998, although he was certainly very good company in the nearly empty coffee shop of Bangkok's Plaza Hotel. His reflections were worth recording at some length because all kinds of Thais are reflecting on exactly these same questions, coming at them from different angles, reaching different conclusions; many people being sensibly tentative, like Dr Likhit, in coming too early to firm conclusions. But it all demonstrates what a convulsive event the economic downturn was. All the old assumptions were challenged. Yet the place of culture, of Asian values, was central to the reconsiderations.

One thing Thais seem agreed on is the continued relevance, place and utility of the monarchy in their Constitution and broader national life. The monarchy is a unifying and stabilising factor and one that has proved decisively beneficial in more than one crisis. Yet even here this tradition has fluctuated throughout Thai history and it may be the exemplary personality of King Bhumibol himself that has had much to do with the extremely high standing of the monarchy.

If the monarchy is a built-in stabiliser for Thailand there are a few built-in destabilisers. Even after the downturn Thailand remains far more prosperous and peaceful than most of its neighbours—Myanmar, Cambodia and Laos. (Only Malaysia to the south, among Thailand's contiguous neighbours, is at a similar or more advanced stage of development than Thailand itself.) Instability or hostility from Myanmar or Cambodia has traditionally been of great concern to Thailand. As the 1990s drew to a close Thailand faced innumerable challenges policing the Myanmar insurgencies on its borders, and the situation within Cambodia remained inherently unstable. A big issue for Thailand was illegal labour from Myanmar. The Thai authorities were keen to clamp down on this in order to free up jobs for their own citizens. But the border with Myanmar is long and porous and almost impossible to control. The Thai authorities could drop a group of illegal workers from Myanmar across the border and before the Thais had returned to base the illegal workers would have walked down the river and come back over the border again.

Thailand has a huge national interest in the prosperity and stability of its neighbours but its capacity to influence its neighbours in a positive fashion has been slight. There is a deep irony in all this. Thailand is often criticised, generally privately, by other South East Asians for effectively 'selling out' to Western consumerism. The critics are mostly thinking of the smog and pollution of Bangkok, the tackiness, brutal exploitation and ubiquity of its sex industry and the exaggerated materialism of the 'Buppies' in the 1980s and 1990s. There is even sometimes a feeling that Thailand's democracy is 'un-Asian', that it produces unseemly and raucous political discourse. Yet people from most of Thailand's neighbouring countries struggle to get *into* Thailand, not out of it. And even before the economic crisis, Bangkok had made serious efforts to clean up its act. It may just be that rapid development always looks a bit messy in any country much bigger than Singapore.

One of the most encouraging features of the economic downturn was the absence of any serious internal racial hostility. Sino-Thais are the most thoroughly integrated Chinese community in South East Asia. A few politicians made scattered comments about 'foreigners' within who had become rich while ordinary Thais remained poor. But such comments were ridiculed in mainstream Thai political debate. Thais themselves seem determined that race will not be a destructive issue among them and are much less hung up about racial purity than are many other nations, both within Asia and outside it.

The fact that the Thai style is not as declamatory and ideological as that of some of its neighbours does not mean that Thais don't care about ideological issues but simply that their approach is different, generally perhaps more calm and tolerant, as befits a Buddhist nation. Thailand has been a good participant in the region and has mostly provided a decent life for its citizens. Its pragmatism is a virtue, not a weakness. It does have profound issues of culture and of political and business practice to confront. That there is such a vibrant dialogue on these issues within Thailand itself is not the least of the reasons for optimism regarding its future.

10

JAPAN'S DILEMMA: A LUKEWARM YEN FOR URGENT CHANGE

SHINJUKU SUBWAY STATION IN the middle of Tokyo is one of the biggest railway stations in the world. It is a vast labyrinth of tunnels and exits and intersecting railway lines and platforms. Although it is conveniently signposted in English and Japanese, the sheer volume of people passing through Shinjuku at any time can be a little overwhelming to the foreign visitor.

It is a cold night in winter as I walk up the stairway to the east exit. Emerging from the stairs is a visual shock—more than that, a positive assault on all the senses. The first thing I see is a giant video screen, displaying some kind of high-energy narrative advertisement. Around that are countless other huge video commercials amidst a sea of neon. In the little forecourt at the top of the stairs, spruikers, touts and sales men and women of all types shout out their wares. There are girls in miniskirts, micro-minis, everywhere, even in winter.

The visual impression is stunning. People say that Shinjuku served as a visual model for Ridley Scott's *Blade Runner* movie and it certainly feels that way. Walking a block or two straight ahead from the subway I am in the middle of a seething red-light district—what used to be called 'Soapland' after the endless massage parlours.

'Hello!' shouts one huckster. 'All Western girl, topless bar, free whisky and breast-touching, five thousand yen.'

'Hello!' shouts another. 'Chinese girl OK, cheaper than Western, Japanese girl, only four thousand yen.'

Of course, such districts are pretty similar the world over. And

191

it would be wrong to characterise even the east side of Shinjuku purely by its red-light district. It also boasts some superb book-shops and the usual range of high-tech, high-glitz Tokyo shop-ping, as well as a grand old Shinto shrine and, beyond the gaudy district, an intricate latticework of tiny laneways filled with minuscule wooden bars suggestive of an older Tokyo.

But the biggest contrast is with the west side of Shinjuku. As you emerge from the stairs on the west side you enter a serene and dignified district of office buildings and orderly Japanese salarymen in blue and grey suits. A short walk away is the vast, monolithic Tokyo City Government building and behind that Shinjuku Central Park. The contrast between the two sides of Shinjuku has been much remarked but it offers a metaphor for the choice Japan faces at the close of the 20th century. It is a choice between the unregulated amorality and commercial vitality of the free market, on the east side of Shinjuku, and the dignified, solid, but rather drab power of the Japanese bureaucratic state, on Shinjuku's west side.

East and West, market and bureaucracy, reform and continuity, vitality and order, growth and stagnation—over many trips to Japan over many years I hear the debate on Japan's future framed in these dualities, these contradictions, these stark alternatives, right through Japanese society. For throughout the 1990s Japan has been facing sweeping social and economic change, attempts to manage that change and attempts to resist that change, which seem bound to transform forever the type of society Japan is.

Former Liberal Democratic Party powerbroker and sometime Opposition leader Ichiro Ozawa has argued in his book, *Blueprint for a New Japan*, that the challenge is for Japan to become a 'normal nation'. When he wrote that he had partly in mind shaking off the shackles of the pacifist Constitution that Japan adopted, under American tutelage, after World War II. This would be radical enough and Japan's slow moves to adopt a more assertive and 'normal' foreign and security posture have been one of the important developments of the 1990s.

But Ozawa also had in mind a comprehensive renovation, almost a revolution, in the way Japan orders its domestic society and civil life. He wrote of 'the huge gap between what appears to be our high income and what is in reality a poor standard of living . . . our inferior housing, impoverished social capital, high prices, long working hours, severe exam competition and many other things'. Ozawa's plaintive words reflect a widespread mood in Japan, that despite the nation's economic power it is somehow or other missing out on some essential, or at least highly desirable, aspect of the good life. They also reflect the change in the view of Japanese of themselves from the 1980s to the 1990s, a change which also reflects the view of the rest of the world of Japan. In the 1980s the view was widespread that Japan would emerge as number one, ahead even of the United States, in economic power at least and perhaps even in some other kinds of power. But then came the bursting of the Japanese bubble economy and the long stagnation in Japanese economic growth, exacerbated by the regional economic crisis that broke out in 1997. With that came an increasing questioning of the priorities of Japanese life, in particular the emphasis on production above all other virtues. Some of this was Westernisation, especially of Japanese youth, but much of it was just the seemingly inevitable consequence of affluence and alienation.

But how strong is the desire among Japanese for their country to become a 'normal' nation? For Japan to become what the West regards as 'normal' would require a revolution. First, it's worth pausing for a moment to consider just what an astonishing nation Japan is already. It is unique in a host of ways. For example, despite being in recession or near recession for most of the 1990s, its unemployment rate did not rise above about 3 per cent until 1998. It is perhaps the only fully developed economy to endure prolonged recession without high unemployment, although by the end of the decade its unemployment rate had increased substantially. Its per capita income of nearly US$40 000 is the highest of any big economy in the world and higher than that of the United States itself. Notwithstanding the stagnation in its economy it is the world's biggest aid donor. Crucially it still accounts for something like 30 per cent of the world's savings, a truly staggering figure which by itself confers enormous economic power, and it has consistently the largest trade surplus of any nation on Earth. These are familiar enough features of Japan but it is worth remembering that they are also signs of power, and features that many countries in the world would like to emulate.

In international analysis these days it is common to think of China as Asia's next superpower, the centre of Asia, the great metropolitan power of Asia, with the littoral and archipelagic states as the hinterland. There is a lot to be said for this view as a view of the future, or perhaps a political view. But in truth, in economic terms it makes more sense to think of Japan as the giant metropolitan power and the rest of Asia as *its* hinterland. After a decade of rapid economic growth in China, and longer in many of the regional tiger economies, Japan still accounts for 70 per cent of all of East Asia's production. As I say, the idea of Japan as an economic colossus is familiar but it is worth remembering just how big a colossus Japan is, and has remained, despite the poor growth figures of the 1990s.

But throughout that decade a determination seemed to grow in Japan, albeit excruciatingly slowly, that fundamental change was needed. Increasingly, the policies of all the country's major political parties converged on reform—deregulation and decentralisation of both the economy and the broader society. Of course, the impediments to reform were awesome, but the political convergence demonstrated that only reform had real legitimacy as a motivating idea in Japanese politics. That being the case, even while reform is agonisingly slow, it is likely to proceed eventually.

The 1990s were also a decade of devastating scandal and corruption in Japanese politics. But while such scandals are commonplace for Japanese politicians, the spread of the scandals to the bureaucracy, and the exposure of the corruption and incompetence of many parts of the bureaucracy, was a truly shocking development and one which did more to shake up the system than any of the revelations of scandal among the politicians themselves. Alienation became evident in voting patterns, especially in consistently declining voter turnouts. In the 1996 national elections voter turnout declined to barely 60 per cent of the eligible population. And some eccentric protest votes were lodged. At one election in the mid-1990s the good citizens of Osaka elected a professional comedian as their mayor.

But it was a sullen rather than hysterical alienation and if anything it was not a backlash against reform so much as an expression of impatience that reform was so slow and of scepticism that the existing crop of politicians could carry reform through. Moreover, Japan tried every alternative other than deregulation to break out of its economic stagnation. It spent the 1990s pumping huge amounts of money into the domestic economy to generate domestic demand, pushing government debt out to a preposterous and unsustainable level of more than 100 per cent of the gross national product. Ryutaro Hashimoto as prime minister came up with a big reform package involving administrative reform to restructure, downsize and curtail the power of the bureaucracy, and financial deregulation as the leading edge of a broader program to reduce the role of government in the lives of ordinary Japanese. Keizo Obuchi continued and accelerated the process. Of course, there were many reverses, reform was delayed, the bureaucrats kept much of their power, and after a thrashing for the LDP in an upper house election, Hashimoto resigned, but there was no doubting the direction of reform.

Again Ozawa is instructive, recalling his shock when he first went to the Grand Canyon in the United States and saw a 400 metre drop with no fences around it: 'In Japan there would be fences, no entry signs and park attendants who came running to warn people away.'

In truth, even with the reform program well under way, Japan remains one of the most highly regulated societies in the world. The weight of social expectation and conformity to national norms in people's lives is enormous, as it is in the economy. By the late 1990s one wisecrack doing the rounds of Tokyo had it that what China's casino economy needed was a good dose of socialism, whereas Japan's highly regulated economy needed an injection of capitalism.

Nonetheless, Japan is changing. The more it embraces deregulation and internationalisation the more uncontrollable, and profound, those changes will be. And the more fascinating. Because in some ways Japan represents the other great defining pole of human organisation besides the United States. It does this in a way that Arab or African or even Chinese societies do not because it is so obviously, in the broadest sense, a successful society. It is the one great successful alternative to the Western experiment. It is the one Asian country to modernise without, so far, westernising, although of course it has an intimate knowledge of Western

culture. It is remarkable that Japan has not held more interest for
the Left in the West and for nationalists in Asia, because,
notwithstanding its US-friendly rhetoric and pro-Western position
in the Cold War, Japan actually did what so many third world and
socialist leaders talk of but so few achieve: despite all its problems
it provided economic security for its people and achieved global
economic influence without embracing a version of the Western
lifestyle, without giving up its national identity.

But of course many Western liberals talk of communalism
without having any stomach for the authoritarianism that effective communalism requires. In classically liberal Western societies
like the US, the market, tempered by social disapproval and
voluntarism, is the key agent of social regulation. In socialist
societies it was the raw and brutal power of the state. In Japan
it is still overwhelmingly custom that is the social regulator. Japan,
uniquely, has achieved a modern economy with a feudal social
structure.

But many Japanese believe that this is now changing fundamentally. 'I feel great seachanges occurring in Japan,' Jun
Kurihara, the senior economist at the Fujitsu Research Institute,
tells me. Kurihara's personal experience illustrates his case. A
brilliant young economist with a moon-shaped face and roly-poly
body who bounces around his office with irrepressible energy, he
worked for the competition, the Mitsubishi Research Foundation,
for 10 years. Like many Japanese he had expected lifetime
employment at Mitsubishi, but he was headhunted by Fujitsu.
He was attracted by their generous financial terms and by the
opportunity to speak out more in his own name.

Sitting in a plush visitors' room overlooking the magnificent
Bay of Tokyo (Kurihara, like almost every other executive in
Japan, does his actual work at a desk in a vast room with his
colleagues) he says that 'deregulation' has become a cliché in
modern Japan. But he identifies three rapidly accelerating trends
that Japanese society will have to accommodate. The first is the
rapid ageing of the population, which will produce vast social
change and alter the way employment is organised, and which
perhaps more than any other single factor threatens the sus-
tainability of Japan's economic miracle. Second is the trend
towards globalisation, in which a rising Asia could threaten

Japanese manufacturing competitiveness, but which also offers economic opportunities to Japan. This trend of course was greatly interrupted by the regional economic crisis, although it should re-emerge as Asian economies recover. And third is the increasing importance of information technology. 'When it comes to manu-facturing, the old Japanese system works, but when it comes to knowledge workers, it doesn't work well,' Kurihara says.

Similarly, he says, 'the Japanese education system is good for shop workers but not for information workers. The government has been in a cul-de-sac. All these vast Keynesian stimulus packages have not produced a robust recovery. Japan is literally facing a crossroads. There are two options: to stick to traditional methods and remain closed; or, like it or not, to open the Japanese market and Japanese society.'

For most of the 1990s Japan's markets *were* opening (admit-tedly very slowly), even though it retained an enormous trade surplus. For much of the decade, before its currency devalued against the American dollar, Japanese imports were rising faster than exports and much faster than the economy overall. Even for much of the 1980s, when it was accused of being relentlessly hostile to imports, Japan imported, per capita, about the same value of goods as most West European nations. Given the chance, Japanese consumers do like to buy cheap foreign goods.

But although views similar to Kurihara's in some form or another are widespread in Japan, not everyone welcomes the accompanying social change that deregulation has wrought. Japan's postwar success was built on the overwhelming power of bureaucrats to guide and direct the economy, as well as the creation of company unions that were industrially tame in exchange for lifetime employment, thus forging a management–labour–bureaucracy alliance of vast productive power. The model eventually outlived much of its usefulness, partly because of the new mobility of global capital (not least Japanese capital itself) and the almost genetic inclination of money in a globalised environment to seek the best returns. The old Japanese freedom from seeking short-term profit in exchange for seeking long-term market share became a liability.

But the strengths of the Japanese model were still formidable. There was the high savings rate, which furnished plentiful and cheap investment capital. Before the stagnant 1990s this was mixed with the determination to measure corporate success by market share rather than short-term profit level. Thus managers were freed of labour pressures and profit pressures and could concentrate on building their businesses long-term. In addition, Japan was given access to the American market, it kept its own market at least partly protected and it was freed of the burden of having to pay for its own military security.

Despite the enduring strengths of the Japanese model, it was plainly fraying badly by the 1990s. Perhaps the worst feature of Japan's economic management was not purely economic, but political. The Japanese political system just could not make tough decisions in a timely fashion. With the bureaucracy discredited, the politicians were unable to take up the slack. No one could inflict the necessary economic pain on any powerful sector of the economy in order to produce reform. The failure of the Japanese authorities to clean up the bad debts that bedevilled the banking system was the key failure in global economic management throughout the 1990s. Similarly, most of the huge stimulus packages were wasted on unproductive infrastructure projects which were both a payoff and a disguised subsidy to the politically powerful construction sector. Indeed, many of the infrastructure projects in the stimulus packages were disguised income transfers from the city to the countryside, the LDP's stronghold.

Nonetheless, real change is coming to Japan. Many of the pillars of the old order are beginning to crumble. Japan is having to adapt. The symbol of the change came in 1990 with the stock market crash that burst the so-called 'bubble economy'. It resulted in a vast and prolonged deflation, which shattered what had been previously the three great certainties of Japanese economic life—that real estate prices always rise, that stock prices never fall in the long term and that the Japanese economy always grows. Ever since, Japan has been working out how to cope with the burst bubble, the bad loans and the strong yen. The foreign pressure, or *gaiatsu*, has all been in one direction—Japan must deregulate, open up its economy, let market forces reign. And, like Kurihara, many, perhaps most, Japanese basically agree with some version of this advice.

But the inability to take rapid action led to a serious loss of

Japanese prestige and credibility throughout the rest of East Asia, especially in South East Asia. In particular, what really upset the rest of the region was Japan's feeble response to the economic crisis. It generously donated more than $40 billion in aid and currency support. But that was not what the region was looking for from Japan. Rather it wanted Tokyo to re-energise the Japanese economy, to become a locomotive for regional recovery and to soak up a large quantity of regional exports. Thus while no one really suggested that Japan directly caused the regional crisis although the devaluation of the yen certainly contributed, there was a very strong sentiment that Japan's feebleness exacerbated it. Worse, the chief intellectual force articulating a strong program of reform for Japan was the US Treasury—much more so than most Japanese politicians. There was a great deal of humiliation in all this.

Shinji Sato, who was the minister for international trade and industry for a time in the 1990s, told me before the onset of the regional crisis that he thought that contemporary reform was driven much more by the Japanese for their own reasons than as a response to external pressure, and that this fundamentally distinguished the contemporary push from previous efforts. He told me: 'We had been pursuing deregulation before . . . But that was different. That was under international pressure. This reform is being undertaken with a sense of crisis; without this reform, undertaken under our own hands, Japan might sink into oblivion in the 21st century.

'Two particular factors have urged us to pursue deregulation and economic restructuring. One is the loss of vitality in our economy due to the ageing of our population. The other is the hollowing out of Japanese industry with heavy investment made by Japanese firms outside Japan.'

In fact, Sato was far too sanguine. In the months after our interview, reform continued to stall and the role of the United States in the Japanese reform debate grew.

Interviewing Sato was instructive in other ways. He was a senior Japanese politician and a competent man. Yet when I interviewed him he virtually recited key sentences out of the speeches he was scheduled to be making at that period. There was almost no cut-and-thrust of conversation, no real intellectual engagement in the interview. This is a sign of a serious deficiency in the Japanese governing class. Japan desperately needs a cadre of leaders who can speak English and engage in the great, international, CNN-mediated policy debate. No doubt it is unjust that more Westerners do not speak Japanese. No doubt it is unjust that English remains the predominant language of international policy debate, especially, perhaps, in Asia. But these are the facts. For a country of Japan's enormous power it is grotesque that it lacks a leadership capable of putting Japan's case in the great international public relations competition of a globalised economy. Inscrutableness and relentless policy consistency were useful assets in much of the Cold War period, and perhaps Japanese politicians positively benefited from the insularity that surrounds them and the difficulty the international media has in exposing them to really detailed scrutiny. But the modern economy has changed. The information technology revolution has transformed not only international politics but also international investment flows and even strategic decisions. The Japanese need to be much more proactive—beyond their famously expensive lobbying firms in Washington—in actually selling their message.

The process of economic change in Japan is not without serious social pain. If Japan does deregulate and open its markets its companies will have to become far more flexible, far more able to expand and contract rapidly. Many more will have to restructure, vacating areas where foreign producers are much cheaper and building on new industries. But this would undermine the traditional lifetime employment system in medium and big companies, which is at the heart of the Japanese social contract. This could have serious political consequences because, as a result of its experiences in the 1930s, Japan is still rather phobic about unemployment.

I decided to explore the way these issues affect the lives of a few individual Japanese.

Mrs Masue Y, 50, describes herself as a housewife, though she works part-time every day for an international marketing firm. We meet in a tiny Japanese restaurant high in an office building in Otemachi in central Tokyo, and share a meal of steaming *tepanyaki* as she tells me her story. In her own estimation, she and her family have recently emerged from a grave crisis. Masue's husband, now in his mid-50s, works for a very big Japanese company. He works in computer software and has been with the company since he was a young man.

She recounts her family's crisis: 'My husband was 53. A lot of major companies had to face restructuring and senior staff like my husband were targeted. The alternatives he was offered were to leave voluntarily with a redundancy payment and some help to find another job or to stay on at a massively reduced salary. They advised him to leave and he nearly took their advice. I insisted that my husband stay on despite the massive pay cut. Otherwise, I knew, he couldn't find a job well paid enough to run the house. Also, I know my husband. I knew he couldn't easily cope with a new work environment. Every day I asked, I begged him to stay on. Eventually he agreed. His company was fairly hard on him for a while because he had stayed on against their advice. During that time he had health problems and his mother complained to me that it would have been better for him to leave and cope with a new work environment.'

Getting a hard time from the company is fairly common when the company wants the worker to leave but can't bring itself actually to sack someone. It is called bullying and can take several forms. Workers can be given desks facing windows with absolutely nothing to do but stare out the window all day. Or they can lose their desks altogether, or long-time white collar middle managers can be sent to do manual work. The company does not sack the unwanted worker, but in a society in which men generally derive their sense of worth from their work, such treatment can be devastating.

As well, many Japanese receive as much as 30 per cent of their annual salary in two bi-annual bonuses. These can be cut or eliminated without the company having technically cut the worker's pay.

In the case of Masue's husband the story had a happy, and entirely Japanese, ending, indeed an ending which is virtually inconceivable in a Western society. After a relatively short period of bullying, the company sent letters to the wives of workers who had been asked to leave, asking for ideas on what they should do next. Masue wrote back saying that she didn't mind her husband's reduced salary but would they please stop harassing him.

And that is exactly what they did. The company president wrote to Masue apologising for the company's behaviour and her husband was restored to a place of honour in the firm, although still at a reduced salary.

The story is deeply instructive from several points of view. It illustrates the absolute centrality of the husband and his welfare in the Japanese home. But it also illustrates much about Japanese corporate culture. Eventually the company did reduce its wages bill by the required amount, but no one was sacked. Anyone, such as Masue's husband, who really needed the security of their long-term employer was allowed to stay. Perhaps most telling of all, no Western company could possibly act with that degree of consideration towards its long-term employees. Not only would it be impossible to reduce their wages, but sending out letters of apology would open up a company to all kinds of litigation. In Japan there are very few lawyers and the codes are mostly unwritten, but they are binding nonetheless.

Despite all these anti-competitive, sentimental and inefficient practices, Japan keeps much of its economy efficient by the most telling, basic, practical and drastic measure of all, it orients it overwhelmingly towards exports. I travelled on the gleaming Shinkansen bullet train to Nagoya to visit Toyota City and the fabulous Toyota car plant. There I saw the most advanced robotics and perfectly refined and synchronised production of automobiles—although it was interesting that, at the time I visited, human beings were actually making a modest comeback on the assembly line because they were more flexible than robots for some tasks and not much more expensive.

All the same, Japan has deliberately organised a good deal of its domestic economy *inefficiently*, with the conscious aim of providing employment. (This, incidentally, means that if Japan ever does get round to serious reform there's lots of growth and new efficiency still to be had in the economy. The fact that a system is inefficient means that there is a big return on improving its efficiency.) This cross-subsidisation of society, the deliberate use of surplus wealth in efficient sectors to provide social stability through de facto job creation schemes, should, as I say, have made Japan of far more interest to the Left in Western societies over the last four decades. But then the Left, intellectually if not politically, was asleep for much of that time, especially as concerns economics.

I have seen over the years countless examples of Japanese job creation. A typical case was of a small bridge being constructed over a canal in Tokyo. The bridge was to be barely ten metres in length. Last time I saw it, work had been under way for 18 months and was scheduled to go on for another 18 months. By no stretch of the imagination could this be called efficient, but without such practices the men involved might not have work. Part of the genius of Japan has been in making such make-work schemes seem meaningful, requiring their participants to work very hard, shrouding them with the mystique of national practice and the cultural value of Japaneseness. In most societies overt make-work schemes are demoralising and even demeaning to their participants. While Japan's schemes are inefficient and in many ways hinder the reform of the economy, they do have justifications beyond providing income to their participants. Japan may well need to change all this, but there is no point in denying that it has had its positive side.

To get a better idea of day-to-day life in a Japanese company I visited the Tokyo head office of a plumbing and household goods wholesale firm, Hashimoto Enterprises. The firm was founded in 1890 by the great-grandfather of the man who was its president when I visited, Masaaki Hashimoto. At the time of my going there it employed 530 people in 16 branches around Japan.

A most charming and hospitable businessman, Hashimoto tells me he supports the deregulation process as necessary for Japan, although his company will be affected by deregulation and foreign competition and has already experienced price wars and the flatness of the Japanese housing market, which accounts for 70 per cent of his sales.

Just visiting his company is an education in the culture of Japanese company life and management style. The Tokyo office occupies seven floors of a smallish building. The top floor is devoted to a staff canteen, which has the look and feel of a rather attractive middle-range restaurant. Everyone lunches there every day for about 400 yen (a few dollars).

At first glance, Hashimoto's own office looks imposing, with a bust of the founder, leather sofas and similar such accoutrements of corporate success and status. But that is only where he receives visitors. He later shows me the desk where he actually does his work. It is at the edge of a large working room he shares with dozens of colleagues. Most of the desks have computer terminals. Hashimoto's desk is efficiently crammed with paper and barely bigger than anyone else's. He takes me on a tour of the building and every floor is the same. Computers are in use everywhere, there are no partitions and no visible signs of rank. There is no trade union.

I ask him how he feels about the quality of life in Japan. 'I believe Japanese people enjoy being middle class and middle-class consciousness is held by most people,' he replies. 'If you look at clothing, eating and housing we have achieved high quality in clothing and eating. Increasing the quality of housing is the next challenge and a must if we are to cope with ageing society and to conserve energy.'

I also ask him whether, with all the change around him in corporate Japan, he would ever sack workers. Again his reply is instructive: 'I have no idea to sack employees, no matter what happens. I wouldn't sack a worker under any circumstances, unless there was criminal activity involved. Our policy is not to sack people. This policy applies to almost all Japanese companies. If profits decline we would unilaterally cut all workers' wages rather than sack them.'

He accepts, too, that the role of women in the workforce is changing, although generally women have been the first to suffer in the recession—the first to be let go and the last to be hired. The disparity between women's earnings and men's is large in Japan. Hashimoto says that his company is increasing the range of opportunities available to women, but explains the problems as he sees them—at the same time revealing the extremely conservative cast of the Japanese corporate mind on gender issues. 'The difference in wages is not between men and women as such but comes from the different jobs they do. A university graduate in this company must be ready to work overtime or be transferred to different cities. We have a group doing sales, then another group doing clerical work. So of course females are assigned to the clerical section. It is from that that the difference in salary comes.'

It is easy to get lost in the infinite paradox of social change in Japan. Michiko S is a lecturer in international relations at Dokkyo University, outside Tokyo. In her late 20s, she is an example of the trend for women to marry later. She is an internationalist by training and inclination, having spent two periods of study in the United States, which she loved for its openness and relaxation, the sense of life being so much less intense than in Japan. Like others of her age she expresses great cynicism about Japanese politics and politicians. Yet, despite her sophistication and success, she lives at home with her parents and considers that when she marries she will work only part-time. That is what Japanese men expect, that is what Japanese society expects. She accepts without apparent protest that this is the way Japan is.

What emerges from the comments of Michiko S and Hashimoto, and the story of Masue Y and her husband, is just how much continuity the Japanese expect in their society, how conservative they are at all levels. Deregulation, internationalisation and opening markets will change Japan profoundly and probably permanently, but at the end of the day it will still be Japan. It is very unlikely ever to resemble Los Angeles.

One of the most forthright and powerful defenders of the idea of Japaneseness—of Japan as a distinctive and successfully different capitalist society that should not sacrifice that distinctiveness—is Dr Eisuke Sakakibara, the famous 'Mr Yen'. I went to interview him when he was vice-minister of the Ministry of Finance, the most powerful arm of the bureaucracy in Japan.

To meet a series of Japan's top bureaucrats—directors-general, deputy ministers and vice-ministers—as I have done on numerous visits to Japan, is really to meet a series of modern princes: extraordinarily powerful men, the elite of the elite and, in their intellectual ability to range across policy areas and their general air of self-confidence about policy, a striking contrast to most of their ministers. In Japan the bureaucracy traditionally attracts the best talent in the nation, although that may be changing. Most of them come from the law faculty of Tokyo University, or Waseda

University, or one or two other elite institutions. They have been the most brilliant students at school, then the best performers at the best universities. They devote their prodigious working lives to the science of governing Japan and then, at age 55, in a process known as 'ascending to heaven' or *amakaduri*, retire to the most senior corporate advisory and executive roles, recycling their vast accumulated expertise in Japan's interests. They are extremely formidable. In recent years, especially after revelations of corruption scandals involving senior bureaucrats, Japan has had an extensive debate about whether these men are too conservative, too inbred and narrow a group to wield such vast influence. Yet, taking the long view, they have as a leadership class shown the ability to manage Japan. Only in the 1990s has the stagnant Japanese economy called their collective wisdom into question. But as a class they will be difficult to dislodge from the commanding heights of their society.

At our meeting Sakakibara fully supported his government's deregulation package and was eloquent in his defence of financial deregulation in particular. But he stressed the limits of the kind of reform that Americans especially always press on Japan. 'I'm not a laissez-faire economist,' he said. 'I don't necessarily support the philosophy of Reagan or Thatcher. No country has completely followed laissez-faire.

'For example, we should always secure employment. Not laying people off is part of the social contract in Japan. I would not like to see Japan become a country where we had only convenience stores and supermarkets. We need small shops and restaurants. I would rather live in a country like France with many small restaurants than a country where fast food dominates. It's a question of culture. If you really know the market you would never place 100 per cent confidence in it. The market always overshoots. We should adopt some Anglo-Saxon features but not all of them. Since the Meiji Restoration [the period in the 19th century when Japan opened up to the outside world and modernised itself] we have adopted some Western measures in modernisation but retained the key elements of Japanese culture which make Japan unique.

'Stability of employment is a key to Japanese stability. By securing employment you can raise morale, productivity and competitiveness. France has remained France. Germany has remained Germany. I did a comparative study of the big five economies. Japanese corporate governance is quite like Germany, or even France. The United States and the United Kingdom are the other extreme. You could classify Western economies into two types. I would not say Japan is the outrider. The US is the outrider, although a successful outrider.'

I found slightly different emphases among the different princes of the bureaucracy. Hisashi Hosokowa, vice-minister of the Ministry of International Trade and Industry when I met him, seemed to be more enthusiastic about the need for root-and-branch reform, perhaps reflecting the internationalist influences in MITI's outlook compared with the focus of the Finance Ministry on regulation and control. Hosokowa (no relation to the former prime minister referred to below) put it bluntly: 'Japan is undergoing tremendous change right now. Japan is playing a survival game for its own sake, but it will help other nations as well.'

Morihiro Hosokowa, who between July 1993 and April 1994 led the first non–Liberal Democratic government in nearly four decades in Japan, is evangelical about the need for root-and-branch reform. When I interviewed him last, in 1997, he was a senior figure in the Opposition. It has been fashionable in much Western commentary to write Morihiro Hosokowa off as a dithering lightweight who achieved nothing and was brought down by an all too familiar corruption scandal. I think that assessment is fundamentally wrong. Although it is true that Hosokowa did not fulfil the promise of his government, his achievements were substantial. Above all he allowed Japanese voters to contemplate a non-LDP government, even to elect such a beast, without the sky falling in. He also began the liberalisation of the rice market, which had proved too hard for all his predecessors. He carried the process of apologising for and coming to grips with Japan's history in World War II further than any of his predecessors and he oversaw political reform which, by dispensing with multi-member electorates, should in time help to remould Japanese politics into a more conventional policy choice between large political parties.

Good-looking, athletic, the soul of courtesy and solicitousness, he is the most charming Japanese politician I have met, and he retains immense residual popularity. The interpreter for our meeting had been begged by her children to get his autograph. Moreover, while interpreters are routinely nervous when involved in interviews with big shots in Japan, Hosokowa's image is so benevolent that this is not at all the case with him. Hosokowa is sceptical of the quality of reform his successors have been able to provide but steadfast in his espousal of the necessity for reform. He told me: 'There is a general desire for change among the Japanese people but it is not receiving full expression. People are not happy with the current situation but this does not lead to immediate reform. People are angry but they are quietly angry. There are many problems—the quality of housing, the long working hours, the difference in living costs from other countries. People should be more angry.'

Although there is good reason to be optimistic over the very long term about the process of reform in Japan, Hosokowa is right to be impatient and angry at how long it all takes. Japan's failure through the 1990s to force its banks to pay the adjustment costs for the bubble economy of the 1980s prolonged the period of adjustment and deepened the pain its economy was forced to endure.

One of the most contentious areas of debate in the creation of a 'normal' society in Japan is foreign and security policy. Here in a way the expected roles in Japanese politics are reversed. The right-wingers, who are often resistant to reform on domestic and economic issues, are in favour of Japan breaking free from its pacifist World War II constitution and asserting greater regional leadership and taking on a greater security role. The domestic liberals, on the other hand, are deeply suspicious of anything that smacks of Japan's militarist past.

The government of Ryutaro Hashimoto was by Japanese standards quite adventurous in foreign policy and pushed Japan down the 'normal nation' road much further than it had gone before. Hashimoto's foreign policy activism was seen in his desire for summits. He proposed a regular annual summit between Japan and China, between Japan and the Association of South East Asian Nations and between Japan and Australia. It was a sign of his desire that Japan provide more leadership in regional and even global affairs; also evidenced in his continuing if fruitless efforts to get Japan a permanent seat on the United Nations Security Council.

There is an odd contrapuntality between Japan and China in this broad foreign policy process. Japan has become a great, global economic superpower, more or less by accident, and China is well on its way to becoming such a power, but entirely intentionally. The partial parallel is that both are having to learn painful lessons about how to deal with the consequences of their own power. Japan is somewhat further into the process.

It used to be fashionable in the West to assert that Japan's failure to come to grips with its past, specifically its crimes in World War II, had crippled its foreign policy and prevented it from exercising international leadership. That assessment was at least partly wrong.

Japan's foreign policy over the last 40 years, up until, say, the mid-1990s, has been extremely effective in securing its national objectives. The misassessment by foreigners came from not understanding what those national objectives were. The objectives were admittedly narrow and did not include global leadership. Rather they included gaining full acceptance as a legitimate member of the international community, the creation of a benign security environment, which was provided for by the Americans, and promoting an international order that allowed Japan's trade and investment to flourish.

Far from being crippled and ineffective, measured against its own national objectives Japan's foreign policy was spectacularly successful. Moreover, Western assessments of leadership in Japan were fundamentally misconceived. Japan did not produce a John F. Kennedy, or even a Lee Kuan Yew, but Japanese society was not without leadership. While its leadership was not individualistic or charismatic, it was institutional. The Japanese *bureaucracy* provided the leadership, including that in foreign policy.

Institutional leadership has some advantages, and some disadvantages, compared with individual leadership. The Japanese bureaucracy, for example, has a vast institutional memory which it can apply in its own interests. Japanese trade negotiators, for instance, even at very senior levels, work in the trade bureaucracy for decades, whereas their American counterparts are lucky to last even the four years of a presidential administration.

But that is the old model. Now Japan is confronting new realities. It still regards the American alliance as fundamental to its own security. As Hashimoto declared: 'The most important factor for peace and stability in the Asia-Pacific is, I firmly believe, the presence of the United States in Asia.' Towards the end of the 1980s the Japanese were hoping to elevate their relationship with the United States to that of a 'global partnership'. But after the rancorous trade disputes of the first few years of the Clinton administration that idea was quietly dropped.

Nonetheless, Japan still has to manage its enormous influence. Despite the slowdown of the 1990s Japan remains the world's largest aid donor and largest investor. Given the level of its savings it is likely to remain the world's largest investor, and given that foreign aid is unpopular in the United States it is likely to remain the world's biggest aid donor. These are two immensely powerful international levers.

Translating even such strong levers as these into more direct foreign policy influence will require a new style, and a new approach, from Tokyo. But Japan faces some constraints on its actions, some of which served it well in the old dispensation but should now be got rid of. One is its pacifist constitution, which it is slowly reinterpreting out of existence. The generic difficulty, however, is finding a new framework for increased foreign policy activism.

Part of the solution may be the United Nations. After Japan was admitted to the UN in 1956 it adopted a heavily UN-centric rhetoric. This acted essentially as a rhetorical cover for a wholly pro-American foreign policy. But the UN and its works retain significant legitimacy within Japan, evidence of an element of Japan's national identity which is internationalist and outward-looking. Tying some of the new foreign policy activism to the UN, therefore, can be a useful way of moving Japanese politics along to accommodate a more activist foreign policy.

The UN, though, is ultimately too diffuse for Japan's regional economic and security priorities. Developing new economic struc-tures for the region is helpful from Japan's point of view. Its natural economic bulk allows it to play a big role in such bodies. That is why Japan has been so keen on the Asia-Pacific Economic Cooperation forum and the Asia-Europe summit process. APEC of course has the extra benefit for Japan of helping to tie the United States into constructive involvement in East Asia.

The US relationship still remains the key element of Japan's view of itself in the world, certainly of its security outlook. Hashimoto had an immensely successful summit meeting with President Clinton in 1996. It followed the tragic incident of the rape of an Okinawa schoolgirl by two American servicemen. The Clinton administration was shocked by the anti-American reaction within Japan to that incident. Similarly the Japanese, at the official level, had their minds focused anew on the importance of the US alliance by China's belligerent actions in the Taiwan Strait during the Taiwanese elections. Both leaders therefore refocused on the security dimension of their relationship. This process resulted eventually in revised guidelines for the security treaty.

The process, formally called the revision of the US–Japan defence guidelines, is one of the most important security developments in Asia since the end of the Cold War. It allows the Japanese to provide logistical support, evacuate refugees and engage in mine-sweeping tasks, intelligence operations and virtually everything else, short of actual combat, in support of US military operations in Japan and 'surrounding areas'. This is basically designed to allow the Japanese to offer full non-combat support to the Americans in the event of fighting on the Korean peninsula. However, a great debate broke out within Japan, and between Japan and China, over whether these guidelines could apply to American action in Taiwan or the Taiwan Strait. Some Japanese spokesmen said they would, some said they wouldn't. Ultimately, the official Japanese line was to say that Japan supported the 'one-China' policy but expected the Taiwan issue to be settled peacefully. This is exactly the formulation the Americans use.

The Chinese objected strongly to the renegotiation of the US–Japan defence guidelines because they recognised that this process involved a fundamental transformation of the US–Japan alliance. It was no longer simply an American security guarantee for Japan but a bilateral alliance for the whole region, although still one that stopped short of committing Japan to combat participation in support of the alliance. But the revision did take a giant step towards creating reciprocity and partnership in the alliance, a giant step towards moving Japan to becoming a more 'normal' nation, with the normal security prerogatives and responsibilities of a normal nation.

This process has many obstacles, not the least being the Japanese system's extreme slowness when confronted with a difficult decision. Another is lingering regional sensitivities.

In the long run, such concern is less likely to be a serious problem in South East Asia than in North East Asia. It is difficult to judge how sincere are the continued laments about Japan's failure to apologise sufficiently for World War II in the rest of Asia. My impression is that South East Asians use it, though more rarely these days, to gain some kind of leverage in their dealings with Japan. Professor Seizaburo Sato of the Institute for International Studies in Tokyo told me he thought that anti-Japanese sentiment in Korea had become a 'ritualised' part of Korean politics and was based on 'old emotions' and the emotional style of Korean politics. But China's anti-Japanese sentiment he found 'more Machiavellian', designed to gain some advantage over Japan.

There must surely come a time when Japan's neighbours can no longer credibly use events of more than 50 years ago to win tawdry economic and diplomatic points today. Japan is the most stable democracy in Asia and its record of five decades of impeccable international behaviour must ultimately start to influence its neighbours' perceptions of it.

Moreover, the region needs Japanese leadership. It may well ultimately need Japan to perform security tasks on its behalf. For all that, Japan's sense of itself as a normal nation is an essential prerequisite. However, probably the single most serious and negative diplomatic and international political consequence of the economic crisis has been Japan's loss of regional prestige and leadership. Tokyo ought to work consciously and forthrightly to recover its position in this.

But the rest of the world, too, must come to view Japan as a normal nation. Attempting to interpret Japan has been a profound challenge for Western economic, political and social analysts. Japan in this sense, as in many others, is unique. It is the only open, accessible society about which Western scholars cannot agree even as to the fundamentals of how it works. There is a vigorous Western debate on the intentions of the Chinese leadership and the future of the Chinese economy, but serious Sinologists are in broad agreement about how the place functions. The same is true of India or Russia or most other places. But Japan has so comprehensively baffled the Western mind that there is a serious scholarly debate over how Japan actually works.

There are two main schools of Western economic analysis of Japan. The orthodox economists believe that Japan is a modern economy like any other though with certain very unusual features. Most of these features, they believe, are market-distorting mechanisms which retard Japan's economic performance. The revisionists, on the other hand, believe that Japan is a thoroughly mercantilist state, utterly unlike Western economies and designed to enable the use of state power to direct the economy and to maximise exports and minimise imports.

In fact, both schools have some insights to offer. The orthodox economists can point to the poor performance of the 1990s to demonstrate that even Japan cannot escape the laws and consequences of economics and that the old Japanese paradigm clearly has its limitations. The revisionists, for their part, do well to remind us of the vast underlying strength of the Japanese economy and the great elements of control and continuity still present in the Japanese approach.

But overall the nation's experience figures too little in mainstream Western discussion. And it is in any event dominated too much by economists. Japan is important to us all. More than that it has elements of beauty and grace to contribute to the human condition. In the great discourse about human values there is a distinctive Japanese contribution. It is unwilling to put itself at the head of some new economically achieved Greater East Asian Co-Prosperity Sphere. It is unwilling to lead a campaign for specifically Asian values if that means the rejection of Western values. Rather it is an amalgam of Asian and Western experience. It is a nation which refuses to make the choice between Sumo wrestling and baseball, its two most popular sports. Instead it says, perfectly sensibly, that it can have both. Culturally it owes a profound historical debt to the Confucianism it inherited from China. Yet it adapted and transformed that Confucianism. More recently, like much of East Asia, it has been deeply influenced at every level by its exposure to the United States. It once adopted the slogan, 'Out of Asia and into the West'. It would not adopt such a slogan today. But in insisting on its Japaneseness, and giving that Japaneseness a contemporary and humane definition, it is pioneering a new relationship both with the rest of Asia and with the West.

In the entirely subjective view of the author, Japan's greatest weakness is not economic rigidity or social feudalism but rather its conception of citizenship as being intimately linked with ethnicity, as evidenced in its unwillingness to accord full citizenship rights even to its Korean minority—in the case of some families, even after generations of residency. With Japan's birth rate way below replacement level, and a demographic crisis looming in which an ever smaller proportion of workers will have to support an ever larger proportion of retirees, Japan should look again at the issue of immigration and the contribution that immigration could make to its own development and to the countries that might send migrants to it.

There is something of a paradox in Japan's attitude to citizenship. The nation has made a considerable effort to internationalise itself, by making English compulsory at school, by importing increasing numbers of native English speakers to assist in teaching English at school, and by sending more and more of its own students overseas for periods of study. The idea that citizenship should rest solely on blood is counterproductive. It is not only offensive to the humanitarian and universal values that the new Japanese society is striving to achieve; it also means that Japan risks losing its dynamism as a society. This is a radical idea but Japan's leaders, and its friends, need to think unconventionally. In short, Japan needs a vigorous immigration program.

Japan offers the world more than karaoke and sushi, although certainly its popular culture has made remarkable inroads internationally, particularly but not exclusively in Asia. Indeed as a child two of my favourite television shows were Japanese—the cartoon, *Astro Boy*, and the adventure series, *The Samurai*. These two shows formed my first view of Japan, that it was technologically advanced and possessed of a culture of considerable antiquity, heroism and grace (though I may not have expressed it that way as an eight-year-old).

Sumo and baseball, kimonos and miniskirts, the mystique of the economic colossus and the seeming timidity of the foreign policy tyro—Japan's multitudinous, enthralling and contradictory Asian and Western values are a work in progress, a dialectic which has not yet reached synthesis, a harmony of many voices. It is utterly unique. But then, so are many countries. Is Japan in some fundamental way different at its heart? Is it uniquely unique?

It's a question we have always asked about Japan. And it's a tribute to Japan's complexity and mystique that we ask it still.

11

KOREAN CONFUCIANISM: THE HARD VARIETY

KOREA, SO THE OLD saw has it, is the one society in the world in which Chinese go broke and Japanese look lazy. It is also destined, after the inevitable unification of North Korea and South Korea, to be one of the first division players in Asian security, a big nation with a long land border with China, almost certainly with a nuclear weapons capacity inherited from the otherwise derelict North Korean state, and with a burning nationalistic ambition. It will take some years to recover from the Asian economic crisis, but of all the crisis-hit countries Korea resumed economic growth most quickly. After all, prior to 1997 it produced four decades of probably the fastest economic growth in recorded history. By the beginning of that year it was the 11th largest economy in the world.

South Korea is often regarded as the most thoroughly Confucian of any of the East Asian societies, even more so than Japan or Taiwan. It is instructive that Korean cities, such as Seoul or Pusan, are virtually the only sizeable Asian cities without Chinatown districts, though this wasn't always the case. It is partly that Chinese traders have found the competition too intense and have moved on, but there is also an element of Korean insularity at work, a lack of welcome for non-Koreans who wish to make Korea their home. This doesn't contradict the fact that in some ways Koreans are among the friendliest and most helpful of people for the temporary visitor.

The wariness about foreigners living in their midst—certainly about Chinese and Japanese—is not too difficult to explain.

216

Korea's history is one of repeated turmoil and invasion, a perpetual battle to stave off its two giant neighbours, as is often said, like a porpoise caught between two whales. But in the last 40 years Korea has changed as rapidly as any society on Earth. Its per capita income in that time, at least before the economic crisis began, leapt from US$80 to more than US$10 000. This is one of the most rapid exits from poverty of all time.

People in the West should know much more about Korea than they learn from the television series *MASH* or from vague memories of the Korean War or from the knowledge that South Korea makes a lot of cars and North Korea is a loony dictatorship. They need to know more about Korea not only because of its economic potential (notwithstanding the recent crisis) and its strategic centrality, but also because of its intricate and august culture, which is bound in time to play a more prominent role in the great human discourse.

The rapid economic change produced rapid social change in Korea, even before the economic crisis, and resultant stresses and challenges for that ancient Confucian culture, which are as fascinating as those occurring anywhere. The evidence of social and cultural change is everywhere in Korea, but because it was for so long accompanied by rising wealth levels it did not produce great social dislocation, beyond the ritual demonstrations and political confrontations on the streets, which by regional standards were not extreme, certainly in the 1990s. But there was always plenty of muted grumbling to be heard by a patient enquirer.

I travelled out to the solidly middle class Sangye district, about 45 minutes drive north of the centre of Seoul, to meet a Mrs Park Kyung-ja, a 55-year-old who proudly told me she had been a full-time housewife for 37 years. She originally came from Pusan, on Korea's southern tip. Her husband came from North Korea; he fled south at the time of the Korean War. Her eldest son lives in the United States. In her life she has seen Korea in war and in peace, in desperate poverty and unimagined riches and in newfound economic distress. She told me that in all that time I was the first foreigner ever to enter her home.

Not that she has ever had anything against foreigners. But Korea was for so long isolated, and is still so homogeneous, that the average Korean can live a full life without ever encountering one. Mrs Park's home is a three-bedroom apartment on the sixth floor of a big apartment building. In the US or Britain or Australia, or most Western societies, the building would be considered monolithic and bleak, characterless, and probably just waiting to be vandalised or to have its lower portions daubed with graffiti. In Seoul, though, it is neat and prosperous, children play unsupervised and unmolested in the playground and graffiti is nowhere to be seen.

Inside, Mrs Park's apartment is spotless, pleasantly if not lavishly furnished, with only one thing setting it apart from the average Western apartment—its striking religious iconography. Like millions of other Koreans, perhaps 30 per cent of South Korea's population, Mrs Park is a Christian. But she is still a very traditional Korean woman, not least in terms of hospitality. A succession of traditional drinks precedes a feast of Korean dishes as our visit (I am accompanied by an interpreter) is considered an obligation, and an opportunity, to dispense hospitality.

Conservative and traditional as she is, there has been more than a touch of rebellion in Mrs Park's life. Her husband is a retired school principal. Having fled the north, he was without money or family, two normal prerequisites, when they decided to get married. There was much opposition from her family and only after a long time was the husband accepted.

'There is an old Korean saying that a son-in-law is like a 100-year-old guest, you must treat him nicely,' she says. 'Eventually they accepted him.'

Mrs Park appreciates her personal affluence and the democracy her society enjoys but is querulous about some of the cultural influences in the new Korea: 'There are a lot of Western influences in Korean culture now. For example, home is a place where you should rest. When a husband goes to work he gets stress. Home should be a place for him to rest. But modern couples get husbands to do chores around the house. It's too much stress for them. I've seen couples that I know from church getting divorced over such trivial things. It's very bad.

'I see a lot of Western shows on TV now. These and Western movies are a bad influence. I see on cable TV a lot of kissing and touching of skin. I've even seen with my own eyes young people in the street kissing and touching and everyone stares but it doesn't make any difference to their behaviour. In my opinion the Western way of kissing and touching is not so good. The Korean way is to look and see the eyes to tell feelings. The Western way is to touch and tell the other person you love them so much. But if the Western way is so good then why are there so many divorces in the West?'

These sentiments may sound to Western ears positively ante-diluvian, although they are probably more common in the West among a similar age cohort to Mrs Park's than the Western media normally allow. But in Korea they are very widespread attitudes. The question is, if the Korean economic progress resumes soon and is sustained for decades, will Korea lose this conservatism? Will it lose the very things that make it Korean? The Korean Government in the 1990s regarded its policy of *segyehwa*, or internationalisation of society, as a high priority, but many Koreans feared their society could lose, in their embrace of the West, something of what makes them special. Of course, there are some traditional traits of Koreanness which it would be no bad thing to lose. Although Koreans are generally friendly and helpful to foreigners, their nationalism is intense and can quickly turn defensive and ugly. Sometimes it is irrational. In 1996 an American soldier was attacked in the subway because he was touching (not in any particularly lascivious manner) a Korean woman. The woman turned out to be his wife.

Despite Mrs Park's conservatism and her belief in the impor-tance, the centrality, of Korean etiquette and culture, there is one thing which for her easily wins in any contest of importance with the concept of nation. That is the concept of family. If her son decides to stay permanently in America she would be quite happy to go there and live with him and her grandchildren, sacrificing all the familiarity of the national home, to re-establish the familiarity of home as the extended family.

But while Mrs Park's views are widespread, especially for those in her age group, younger Koreans often have a different take on the social and political change around them. Cho Hee-ock was a reporter with the Yonhap News Agency when I met her. In her early 30s, she was married with one daughter and was eight months pregnant. We met at the Seoul Press Club.

When she married, in 1986, South Korea was still substantially authoritarian. Ordinary folks were not permitted to travel abroad so she and her husband had their honeymoon in Korea. Now, like many two-income Korean couples, they love to travel, though this of course was tempered when the economic crisis came along. Every year before the crisis, however, they went overseas for a short holiday, generally a week or ten days: Paris, London, Rome, Geneva, New York, Washington, Singapore—the cities she has visited trip off the tongue. Liberalisation, both political and economic liberalisation, made this possible. To that extent, all young middle-class professionals tend to be social liberals, up to a point.

Cho would like to go abroad for longer periods but a week or ten days is generally as much as she can take off work each year. Theoretically she gets longer holidays than that but, as she says: 'Most people don't take their full holiday entitlement. If you do, you find it counts against you when promotions come round.'

The Korean work ethic is indeed ferocious, at least as strong as Japan's, which until the end of the 1980s was Korea's model for economic development. Of course, there are plenty of stories of wasted time and declining productivity as the work hours drag on and on. But there is no doubt that the average Korean works hard, and the ambitious Korean furiously hard, and long.

Parents, whether conservative or liberal by Korean standards, instil this work ethic in their children early. Cho sends her daughter to *hakwon*, or cram school. At nine years of age, the daughter goes three times a week for tuition in English, once a week for special classes in computers and twice a week for piano lessons.

'English language will be good for her work, for school, for university entrance,' says Cho. 'There will be many areas in which Koreans will need English.' Indeed, just in case the little girl gets dozey with all her free time, Cho is looking for a private tutor for further English lessons, to make sure her daughter is fluent. Mrs Park, a generation earlier, gave her son similar motivation. Every night, she says, she went to church and prayed that he would get an American university education. With the weight of parental expectation and devotion like that, what son would fail to do his best?—although the downside of such motivation is that the psychological penalty of failure is severe.

The automatic identification of what is best with what is American was characteristic of Mrs Park's generation, even if they resented or distrusted American social values. They had seen what US technology and knowhow could do during the Korean War. They also knew who won the Korean War. Cho's generation has a different view, although they still recognise the commercial importance of the US. Nonetheless, Cho's hesitation about the embrace of things Western takes a different tack, is concerned with different issues, from those which vex Mrs Park. She is more concerned with quality-of-life issues than with the loss of traditional values.

'I do not see economic growth as totally a good thing,' Cho tells me. 'In order to achieve economic growth you have to sacrifice the environment, plus our mental outlook and quality of life. I would like more leisure time and time with my child. I travel an hour each way from my apartment each day. My daughter would like to live in a house but I am afraid of burglars.'

Skip another generation down from Cho and you find less concern with Western dilution of the Korean mind or character and considerable cynicism about Korean politics and national life. Chang Hyun-soo was a fourth year student at Korea National University when I met her, studying Korean language and literature and intending to become a school teacher.

Like Generation X students everywhere, she acknowledges that there are fewer student demonstrations than there used to be, but then, as she rightly points out, there is very much less to demonstrate about. And, she says proudly, she and her fellow students still demonstrate sometimes. In fact, the tradition of student demonstrations, which were important in the long struggle for democracy in South Korea, if anything were overdone in the 1990s. Occasionally students preposterously demonstrated in sympathy with the Stalinist North Korea and its dictator, Kim Jong-Il. They were sometimes prepared, too, to resort to violence—the occupation of buildings and violence against riot police being a speciality—over trivial grievances. There were an emotionalism and a willingness to pursue confrontation that were disproportionate. But these were not particularly frequent occurrences. Importantly, the economic crisis did not produce a dramatic surge in student militancy.

Chang comes across as a levelheaded young woman and reflects a growing sobriety among students: 'Like Western students, a lot of Korean students are worried about their future. A lot of graduates have difficulty finding work connected with the courses they took. I do not think being influenced by Western culture is a bad thing. It means we are getting nearer to other people and other countries.'

She is moderately cynical about Korean politics, and unimpressed with the 'three Kims'. These are Kim Young-sam, the veteran democracy campaigner who joined the ruling party in order to secure its endorsement for his 1992 presidential bid, and who was president, with his former prestige in rapid and terminal decline, when I interviewed Chang; Kim Dae Jung, the grand old man of Korean democracy; and Kim Jong-Pil, another party leader and former prime minister with an intelligence background, who became prime minister once again after Kim Dae Jung became president. But the cynicism about the 'three Kims' seems to indicate a wider cynicism about the structures and personalities of Korean politics.

'The three Kims are too old,' Chang says. 'They should all move on. Some of my friends admire Kim Dae Jung but I would prefer younger people.'

Very much unlike her elders, Chang does not exhibit much overt nationalism and is highly critical of what is almost the state religion in Korea—dislike of the Japanese. 'Not only older but younger Koreans have bad feelings about the Japanese. This is a bad complex by Koreans. We should get rid of these feelings.'

Not the least of the reasons I have found Korea enthralling in the 1990s is the combination of extreme, high velocity change with stubborn, sinewy cultural continuity. The power of culture is almost overwhelming in Korea and yet Kim Young-sam named his party the New Korea Party and promised a new Korea. But the constant rhetorical emphasis on a new Korea belies the pervasiveness and strength of the old Korea. Mrs Park's younger son is a successful professional man in his 30s. Yet because he is not married he automatically lives at home with his parents. In how many other societies as affluent as Korea is the strength of family so pronounced?

These days South Korea has every right to be called a democracy, with a free press, free political parties and a wide range of autonomous civic organisations. As you travel its wide but clogged roads, its gleaming office towers, its state of the art factories (albeit burdened with vast over-capacity), its vast industrial conglomerates, its ancient temples and magnificent gardens, you meet a wide range of opinion on many issues. You also meet consistent courtesy and consideration for the welfare and comfort of a visitor. Yet the strength of majority opinion on some issues is somehow overwhelming, stifling, especially in relation to certain prejudices, in particular anti-Japanese sentiment.

One night I went out to dinner at a traditional Korean restaurant with a senior government official. We bonded after the Korean fashion over a few drinks and the talk became confiding. We talked of the vexed issue of race. As an educated man, the official told me, he himself was not at all racist, but he was of course scared of black people, especially in the dark. This had nothing to do with racism, he said—it was just natural that people would feel that way.

When you hear preposterous remarks such as this, from the most senior Koreans, you begin to understand what Korean intellectuals mean when they talk about *segyehwa*, or becoming a developed society generally, as requiring almost a revolution in the Korean psyche. And indeed attitudes to race, the notion of citizenship based on blood, and the underlying fear and intolerance of outsiders, are together the greatest single weakness in Korean culture.

Nonetheless, Korea is a much more attractive society than it is generally given credit for. You feel somehow that its people never quite get the press they deserve. After all, it is one of the safest societies in the world and its achievements clearly dwarf its failings. It's a bit like the historical claim you often hear that ethnic Korean guards were among the most brutal in Japanese war camps. Whether this was so or not, Korea was not an aggressor nation and it seems somehow a double injustice that they suffered both the terrible reality of Japanese colonisation and the reputation for brutality in Japan's service. These people are not getting a fair shake.

On a clear, beautiful spring day I journeyed out of Seoul to meet one of the country's leading novelists, Yi Munyol, a professor of literature whose deeply serious, allusive novels have sold millions of copies. Yi is not exactly a social novelist, certainly not a social realist; his novels are allegorical, dense and poetic. He is nonetheless an acute social observer. Consider this account of the pace of change in Korea: 'The changes of the last 20 or 30 years should really have taken place over two or three centuries, they're so big and so rapid. The generation gap used to occur over 20 or 30 years. Now it's people just a few years apart who feel the generation gap. Both the older generation and Generation X might have difficulty with some of the changes. The older generation is not familiar with the psychology of modern people and are still tied to tradition. Generation X have their lives dominated by television and computers. It's hard for them to understand older people in their own society.'

Yi himself embodies the countless contradictions of Korean life. His father defected from the south to the communist north when he was three years old, which gave him a difficult childhood. As a novelist he has never regarded nationalism as a driving force in his work, yet he is conscious of an increasing trend for writers to look to Korean tradition for literary inspiration. Yi himself has publicly warned of the dangers of abandoning tradition too quickly.

The first of his books to appear in English was called *Our Twisted Hero*. It is an allegory about Korean politics of the 1980s, set in a school classroom. In many ways it resembles George Orwell's *Animal Farm*. The class students, it seemed to me, represent the South Korean people and their teacher the Americans. The class is dominated by a ruthless bully who is eventually exposed under pressure from the new teacher. It is a beautiful little tale, with no overt political references, and with the life of the school and all the daily terrors of which a classroom is capable, superbly rendered. Just as in *Animal Farm* it is the authenticity of the farm setting that anchors the political message and gives it such power, so in *Our Twisted Hero* it is the convincing psychological and social atmosphere of the school that makes the allegorical political content so telling.

Writing this book in the 1980s was a mildly adventurous thing to do. Now of course everything is much more liberal politically, yet there are still some areas of backwardness if not feudalism in South Korean society which are quite shocking. I spent several days talking with some Korean feminists, who painted a bleak picture of the status and opportunities afforded to women. And this was borne out by the fact that there were hardly any women in parliament or in top corporate positions. Korean women famously were long required to submit to the 'three obediences'—obedience to parents in childhood, to husband in marriage and to eldest son in old age. The relations between the sexes are of course changing but not necessarily all that rapidly. In the savage economic recession of 1998 and beyond, women were let go from companies first, and of the women the young women were let go earlier than the older women. It was not just assumed that the young women would have parents and probably an extended family to look after them, or that most families were ultimately dependent on a primary male breadwinner; there was really also an underlying assumption that men had a greater right to work than women had.

Many problems persist for women. The young women around the central areas of Seoul look impossibly glamorous, and are often heavily made-up and fashionably dressed. Several young Korean women tell me that this is because of the overwhelming social pressure on single women to fit a stereotype of glamour and beauty if they are to attract a husband. Korean girls at an all-girls high school look perfectly normal and come in the usual variety of shapes and sizes. But once they get to a co-ed university the pressure to be slim, if not abnormally skinny, intensifies and eating disorders abound.

Many forms of institutional discrimination, long outlawed in virtually every Western society, are only now being addressed in Korea. According to Mih Ye-roh of the Women's Development Institute, the abuse of spouses, almost entirely the abuse of wives by their husbands, is a huge problem, very widespread and wildly underreported. In traditional Confucian terms it is regarded as a private matter, a matter to be dealt with within the family, rather than a social issue. It is proving hard work to change this particular attitude.

Laws have only recently been changed to give Korean women roughly equal rights with Korean men. And customs, the way people really live, typically take time to catch up with new laws. Women are now permitted by law to take out bank loans, a great advance, but because so few women own property, which is almost always held in the husband's name, very few women do take out loans. To take another example, a far more disturbing one, the bias in favour of sons is so great that many women have female foetuses aborted. Korea has possibly the highest male–female ratio in the world. This is particularly striking in the case of the birth of a third child in a family. Parents often don't mind having one boy and one girl as their first two children, but feel that if they are going to go to the trouble of having a third child it had better be a son. This feeling is so widespread that, for the third child in a family, two boys are born for every one girl.

'There are many good parts of our traditional culture that we would like to keep,' says Mih Ye-roh. 'But there are some bad elements that we want to change, such as the tradition of women being confined to the home.'

Yet for all that Korea still gives you the impression of being one of the more civilised societies on Earth. With considerable psychic pain it is making an effort to face up to the ugly sides of its inheritance, while desperately trying to hang on to the things it believes are good. Despite the economic problems of the late 1990s it has made an impressive transition to being a modern economy. It is hard to believe that as recently as the mid-1980s it was authoritarian and undemocratic. It is hard to believe, too, that all this progress, all this genuinely magnificent achievement, lives still under the awful threat of nuclear conflagration.

Whereas for much of the rest of the world the end of the Cold War has meant liberation from nuclear terror, for Koreans it is a daily part of their lives—although it is something they don't seem to allow to interfere too much with the business of living. The world is paying more attention to East Asia and that is good. But most of the attention has focused on the two giants, China and Japan. Perhaps Asia's next giant is even now stirring. At the time of reunification the world will suddenly discover Korea. Yet it is a society that merits being discovered earlier than that, and in its own right as one of the interesting fusions of Asian values and Western dreams, not just for its security dimensions.

One reason why Korea doesn't get the press it deserves is that it has had the greatest difficulty in cleaning out its political system of corruption and nepotism, especially the corrupt collusion of business and government, a kind of Korean version of Chinese *guanxi*—connections. This results partly from the lack of a democratic tradition and partly from what was effectively continuous rule by one party, albeit under different names, from the end of the Korean War onwards until 1998. The presidency of the veteran democracy campaigner, Kim Young-sam, had promised to change this. At the start of the decade Kim had thrown in his lot with the ruling party—despite its tainted reputation— and with its support he ran for and won the presidency in a fair election in 1992, becoming the first civilian president in decades.

I met Kim Young-sam several times during his presidency. When I first interviewed him in 1994 his hair was jet black; when I met him again in late 1997 his hair had gone grey. Of course, this had more to do with hair dye than with stress, but there would have been every reason for his hair to turn stark white over that period. Rarely can any democratic leader have experienced so many setbacks in so short a time. Once the hero of Korean democracy, Kim Young-sam ended his term in office with his reputation significantly diminished, his administration sunk in corruption, his son and two immediate presidential predecessors in jail, and the split in the ruling party so great that Kim Young-sam left his own party rather than campaign for its endorsed candidate. And to top it all off his country's economy was suffering a severe debt, liquidity and competitiveness crisis. Then his detested rival and opponent in 1992, Kim Dae Jung, won a smashing victory in the presidential poll. For Kim Young-sam there was an element of terrible tragedy in all this, for few can doubt Kim Young-sam's basic decency and political goodwill.

But there is a deeper tragedy for the nation in Kim Young-sam's fall. Korea, as has been mentioned, is often regarded as perhaps the most thoroughly Confucian society in Asia. Yet one of the central tenets of Confucianism is that the leader, the ruler, should embody the moral virtues, embody those virtues the nation holds dear. This places an enormous emphasis on the personality of the leader himself. In the American or British or Australian systems we like our leaders to be good men and women but we rather suspect that sometimes they're not, and when they are occasionally exposed as having feet of clay we take consolation in the system as a whole—even see their exposure as evidence of the system working. That is not to say it is unimportant in the West to have leaders of moral substance; but there is a compensating faith in institutions, a feeling even that a good system compensates for mediocre or even bad individuals.

But in a deeply Confucian society such as Korea the leader's personality is all important. Indeed, while he is president the leader is treated like a king. Yet eventually the presidents always come to grief. Every president of the Republic of Korea, before Kim Young-sam, faced disgrace in retirement. They either went into exile, were assassinated or went to jail. This syndrome has contributed powerfully to the failure of the Korean political system to mature into one of which the people can be proud.

The presidents occupy a building known as the Blue House. It is constructed to observe Confucian injunctions regarding design and harmony, and stands in a tranquil and even majestic complex of parks and buildings. If your physical environment influences your thinking, Korea should be a well-governed society. The Blue House itself enjoys a most favourable disposition by Confucian standards. It is at the foot of a mountain and overlooks a river, the Han, and the city of Seoul. The buildings have high, Korean-pagoda-style roofs; there are several gardens, green and soothing to the eye without being overdesigned, and there is a 300 metre jogging track. Close by is a beautiful 'evergreen' house along traditional Korean lines, which is always cool and with its high ceilings gives the effect of spaciousness. Yet the jostling Western and Asian influences are present even here. In one corner sits a giant television set, the biggest I've ever seen, and from the ceiling hang huge chandeliers. It is in this small wooden building that the Korean president often entertains foreign heads of state. Near to the 'evergreen' house is a pretty carp pool, where you can feed the fish if you have a mind to, and an exotic aviary.

But the Confucian forms cannot conceal what have often been

corrupt and irregular practices, to which the nation is fundamentally unreconciled—otherwise there would not have been such regular post-presidential retribution. Kim Young-sam had seemed to offer a clean break from all of that, but in the last two years of his presidency it all fell apart. In 1992 Kim enjoyed an approval rating greater than 80 per cent; by the end of his term it was less than 15 per cent.

How did it all go so wrong? Kim Young-sam's story tells us much about modern Korea and the immense challenges remaining (despite its impressive achievements) if it is to fully modernise its highly conservative society.

For most of his life, Kim Young-sam was a professional politician. As a schoolboy he wrote out signs proclaiming himself a future president. He first achieved election to the National Assembly at the tender age of 26. Right through the 1970s and 1980s Kim was an authentic hero of democracy. He was frequently in and out of jail on political grounds, a committed parliamentarian, one of the most flamboyant and effective opponents of the harsh military dictatorship that ruled South Korea. In 1983 he nearly died after 23 days on a hunger strike to protest against an unlawful transfer of power. He was a formidable politician and, partly as a result of pressure exerted by him, the military decided to hold a free presidential election in 1987.

But hubris intervened. Kim Young-sam and Kim Dae Jung, both great democracy activists, sometimes collaborators, more often rivals, destined it seemed to dance an endless minuet with each other, ran for president. Neither would defer to the other. They got 55 per cent of the vote between them (gaining very nearly identical shares of the vote), but this allowed the military's candidate, Roh Tae-Woo, to win the election with just 36 per cent.

Kim Young-sam then took one of the many radical gambles of his career. He merged his party with the ruling party, giving it a majority in the parliament and securing its endorsement for his presidential bid in 1992. Again his main opponent was Kim Dae Jung, but this time, as we've noted, Kim Young-sam was the decisive victor. He promised a 'new Korea' and an end to the 'Korean disease'—the pervasive corruption, the lawlessness at the top of the system and the absence of complete legitimacy in the whole government framework.

He started his presidency magnificently. He was a breath of fresh air. He publicly declared his personal assets and later made this compulsory for senior officials. He said he would not accept donations or play golf while he was president, as golf was so often the backdrop of corporate cronyism and corruption. He introduced substantial laws to back up his anti-corruption crusade, in particular the 'real name' banking law that made it compulsory for Koreans to use their real names in banking transactions. This was seen at the time as a significant blow against corruption and the black economy. He began the process of liberalising Korea's agricultural markets and helped complete, ratify and implement the Uruguay Round of trade liberalisation. He lowered the nation's tariffs. Korea joined the Organisation for Economic Cooperation and Development, the symbol of developed nation status.

Kim Young-sam became an enthusiastic player in the Asia-Pacific Economic Cooperation forum. After the intense and, for Kim, wholly novel personal diplomacy involved in the 1994 Bogor APEC leaders' meeting and the leaders' commitment to implementing free trade, Kim and his aides devised, on the post-APEC flight to Sydney, a whole policy of globalisation for Korea. Called *segyehwa*, it became a touchstone of his presidency. He continued Korea's democratic revolution, reinstating local elections, taming and reorganising the military so that it was no longer a decisive political force. He tried hard, though without much success, to pursue greater dialogue with North Korea. And he committed himself to economic liberalisation.

But underneath, mostly unseen by the public, there was a cancer eating away at his administration. While there was no suggestion that Kim Young-sam took money for his personal profit, his administration was riddled with corruption. It began with the jailing of the two former presidents. The courts discovered that Roh Tae-Woo had accumulated a slush fund of hundreds of millions of dollars. Kim's reputation suffered because, in the period after he amalgamated his political forces with the ruling party, he had for a time been a close political ally of Roh's, though there were always tensions between them.

One of Kim's most senior aides was charged with corruption. The leaders of Korea's biggest chaebols, or conglomerates, were convicted of massive bribe-giving. Each new revelation seemed to set off an entirely unprecedented set of detonations. Eventually the scandal spread to Kim's family, and his son, Kim Hyun-chul, was jailed for allegedly arranging bribes.

Meanwhile the economy, for so long among the fastest growing in the world, hit a trouble spot by 1996, with growth slowing markedly. Kim's economic reforms had run into stiff resistance and been only halfheartedly implemented. The enormous chaebols had been built up initially to give Korean firms the size and clout to compete on the global market. But while they had succeeded in doing that, they had also acquired disproportionate economic and political power within Korea, such that it was impossible effectively to reform economic policy without affecting their interests—and they were extremely averse to change. Moreover, their growth strategy—securing market share at all costs and diversifying widely—had been effective in the era of supercharged growth but inappropriate in a more highly competitive environment in which each dollar of capital needed to be used efficiently. They had also contributed to over-investment and over-capacity in the economy, particularly in the automobile manufacturing sector.

There were other problems too, some structural, some cyclical. The labour movement, which had grown truculent and radical in the years of decaying military rule, was achieving unsustainable wage increases. The national debt had ballooned out to several times its foreign reserves. Billions of dollars were owed to Korean banks by failing chaebols, some of which were technically insolvent. Then came the stupendous Asian crash of late 1997 and early 1998. Not altogether justly, Kim Young-sam was widely blamed for this by his countrymen.

Kim Dae Jung, Kim Young-sam's long-time rival, made a bitter end of term assessment of his opponent's presidency. At his Il-San home Kim Dae Jung told me: 'People believe Kim Young-sam didn't practise democratic leadership, but rather a one person dictator style. He also corrupted the merit hiring system of government. But after the general frustration with his government, the Korean people are really frustrated by his economic policies. The economic failure is the most crucial point for the Korean people.'

In an earlier conversation in 1996 Kim Dae Jung had gone so far as to call into question South Korea's basic democratic credentials. 'I don't believe Korea is a democracy,' he said at that time. 'President Kim Young-sam has failed to implement democracy. During the election in 1995 the ruling party committed every type of election fraud, spending money everywhere and exploiting the activities of North Korea in the Demilitarised Zone. Television is totally under the control of the state.'

When I spoke to him last, in late 1997, Kim Young-sam was still able to talk confidently of the 21st century as 'the Asia-Pacific century' and to express confidence in the Asian economy. But there was no ringing declaration on Korean politics and his administration's achievements, such as there had been when I interviewed him in 1996. Then he had said: 'The severance of the collusive link between politics and business by the civilian government's reform program is creating a business climate which guarantees transparent, healthy and fair competition. This is the most important factor in building a strong economy.'

For much of his presidency it seemed that Kim Young-sam was able to make such pronouncements with some credibility, at least as policy aspirations. By the end of his term such statements would have sounded like a sick joke. And it is in that reality that the tragedy, not just for himself but for his nation, of Kim Young-sam's presidency lies. A decisive opportunity to change the dysfunctional Korean political culture was lost.

The man who replaced Kim Young-sam as president, Kim Dae Jung, must be regarded as also facing an uphill task in attempting to reform the political culture. And most of the good things that could be said about Kim Dae Jung could have been said about Kim Young-sam at the start of *his* presidency.

One morning, very early, I drove out to Kim Dae Jung's home in the new development area of Il-San, about 15 kilometres north of Seoul, towards the nearby North Korean border. It was a comfortable enough two-storey bungalow, not particularly big or lavish, solidly middle class rather than flashy. I was invited there for breakfast. With a Korean friend who arranged the interview, I arrived about 6.30 am.

In accordance with Korean custom we discard our shoes at

the front door and enter a little sitting room, where a couple of Kim's aides are watching American baseball on TV (truly Americans have conquered the world, or at least Asia, with their baseball and basketball broadcasts). After a minute or two we are shown into the dining room and Kim and a couple of aides welcome us to breakfast. The meal is a cultural fusion. There are, roughly in this order, boiled potato, corn on the cob, Korean porridge, cornflakes, sausages, ham and eggs. Mrs Kim comes in to meet us, but breakfast is an all-male affair.

Kim looks well for his age, though he walks with a small but noticeable limp. He is ready for the day's work, attired already in a flawless blue suit; he looks imposing with his suspiciously jet-black hair and naturally grave face. This is a lived-in face. It was George Orwell who said that every man has the face he deserves after the age of 50. Kim's face mirrors a life of struggle.

Kim Dae Jung stoutly rejects the idea that democracy is a Western concept foisted on a culturally unsuitable region in Asia. 'Democracy is very possible in this Asian region,' he says. 'For a start we have philosophies and traditions which can be linked to democracy.' In a famous article in the journal *Foreign Affairs*, Kim explored Confucian and Buddhist ideas that he thought were sympathetic to democracy, such as the Confucian notion that the ruler should govern in the interests of the people, and the Buddhist stress on the worth of every human being.

'Secondly, Asian societies are now becoming information industry societies. Alvin Toffler once said that Korea should implement genuine democracy if it really wants to develop an information industry because the information industry can survive and develop only where there is democracy. Authoritarian rule would cut the flow of information. Economic development these days requires democracy.

'And thirdly, Asian peoples themselves have been eager to realise democracy. The majority of countries in Asia are now democracies or becoming democracies—India, Japan, Korea, Thailand, Bangladesh, Sri Lanka, Pakistan, Nepal, the Philippines.'

It is easy to dismiss Kim as a Pollyanna on the matter of Asian democracy, especially on the alleged link between Confucianism and democratic practice, yet it is true that in the last 15 years democracy has replaced military or martial law regimes

in South Korea itself, Taiwan, Thailand, the Philippines and
Indonesia. And there has been no lack of Asian democratic
heroes, men and women like Kim himself, or his one-time
colleague at Harvard, Benigno Aquino, or Aquino's widow, Cory,
or Myanmar's Aung San Suu Kyi.

Like most of Asia's democrats, Kim is a strong supporter of
the American military presence in the region. This relationship
is easily and inaccurately caricatured as neo-colonialism and many
authoritarians and would-be authoritarians play the anti-
American, nationalistic card as hard as they can. Yet it is natural
that Asian democrats would have a proclivity to favour alliances
with the world's most powerful democracy in order to maintain
Asian security and stability. Kim Dae Jung is forthright on these
issues: 'Strong military ties with the US are essential to prevent
North Korean aggression. Even if both Koreas are united, the
presence of 100 000 American troops in Japan and Korea is
essential to maintain peace in North East Asia. If American troops
were to withdraw, there could easily be a strategic contest between
China and Japan and this would be the greatest threat to peace
and security in the region.'

The effects on South Korea of 40 years of nuclear neurosis
are hard to unravel. According to many commentators it has
made South Korea politically a much more conservative society
than would otherwise have been the case. On the other hand,
like most frequent visitors to South Korea, I am always struck
by the normality of the place, by how little day-to-day attention
people pay to North Korea and its unfathomable, opaque policies,
its dark, muttered threats and its occasional obscene gestures,
like those of a demented ape in the gorilla enclosure at the zoo.

I am drawn, whenever I visit Korea, to the truce village of
Panmunjom, the only official contact point between the two
Koreas, in the Demilitarised Zone. I have visited the place again
and again but find its pull irresistible. And something in the
atmosphere of the place always gives you a clue to how things
are going between the two halves of Korea.

Standing on the little knoll at Checkpoint Three at Panmunjom,
late in 1997, listening to North Korean propaganda blare out from
a huge loudspeaker system, I could see the stark silhouettes of the
North's 'propaganda village', so called because it has no inhabi-

tants, only buildings designed to show the South Koreans how paradisiacal life is in the North. There is also a huge flagpole with a 30 metre flag, designed to be bigger than any flag in the South. The only problem is that it has a 600 pound dry weight and it takes a gale to move it, so it almost never flies. Another triumph of socialist engineering.

From insanity in small things to insanity in big things—the North has it all. On this day there is unusually heavy security. Our tour of the border is delayed and shortened and the little group of Asian journalists of which I am a member is accompanied not only by a US military guide, which is customary, but by an armoured transport vehicle with more American soldiers inside. Similarly, our visit to the Armistice Commission Hut, where officials from North and South meet to discuss routine border matters, is not only shortened but has what appears to be an entire platoon of American soldiers, in the company of a senior officer, standing by. Only later do I learn the real reason for this extra security.

That morning a North Korean soldier had been shot dead in the Demilitarised Zone. He had advanced towards the southern end of the DMZ and been told to stop, but instead had raised his rifle as if to fire. At that point South Korean soldiers had opened fire and killed him. I spent the next week or so in South Korea talking to officials from the foreign minister down, and tried to find out what the North Korean soldier could possibly have been up to. No one had any conceivable explanation for his behaviour.

Some time before that I had interviewed Choi Joowhal, a defector from the North, to find out a little more of life in the last Stalinist redoubt. Choi had been a senior official in the North Korean Government, allowed to travel to China and Russia on trade missions. In China he had, through mere accident, become acquainted with a South Korean businessman who had taken him out for a couple of meals and a few drinks. In the intricate and obsessive system of everybody spying on everybody else, this had been reported back to Pyongyang and Choi had received a summons to return. He knew this meant that he would be in real trouble on his return so he defected instead.

When I met him he was a sombre, even sad, figure. He was

one of an increasing number of senior officials defecting from the North, indicating that the lunatic kingdom of the Dear Leader and the Great Leader is in perhaps terminal decline. Choi's air of melancholy was not too difficult to explain. He had a well-grounded fear for the safety of his family. And although he didn't mention it there must also have been a certain amount of fear for his own fate.

There were other elements in Choi's predicament as well. One was that he had no friends or relatives in South Korea. So at the time of maximum psychological stress in his life he was completely alone. Meeting Choi brought home to me the appalling human cost of the division of Korea, with ten million families divided between North and South. An official from the National Unification Ministry told me that no people have ever been as determined as Koreans to achieve unification: 'The Korean people want it [but] not because of the security threat posed by the North. This has little or nothing to do with it. Rather it's because the Korean people have lived as one nation for the last 1300 years—as one people, with one language and one culture. It's a desire to reunite the national family.'

Most South Koreans, and certainly most Americans, Chinese and Japanese, would like to avoid a precipitate collapse of North Korea. The danger of some military miscalculation in such a scenario is high. And the short-term financial costs to South Korea would be staggering, running into hundreds of billions of dollars. There would be acutely difficult questions, such as how to deal with potential floods of internal refugees, whether to maintain an internal border between North and South, how to revive industry and how to organise meaningful elections in the North. The preferred strategic option is for the North to engage in a prolonged period of economic reform along the lines of China. This would give the North a prolonged period of rapid economic growth and thus hopefully diminish the staggering difference in economic level, and perhaps more importantly the psychological outlook, between North and South. But as its economy sinks ever deeper into crisis, the problem is that the North seems wholly incapable of embarking on such reforms, even if it were so inclined. The failure of its proposed special economic development zone near the Tumen River is testimony to this.

Professor Jung Kuhyun, of the East-West Institute at Yonsei University, takes a radically different view, arguing that the collapse of the North is both likely and desirable. 'I am a believer in the earlier collapse scenario—the earlier the better,' he says. 'The earlier it happens the lower the cost will be. I don't think any happy scenario is possible. North Korea is already a bankrupt country. Without a massive resources infusion from outside it will collapse. This infusion of resources is not possible while it remains North Korea.'

Professor Jung's view is distinctive because of its emphasis on the costs of continued division, whereas the discussion normally concentrates on the potential costs of reunification. Chief among the costs of continued division is the diversion of resources to the militaries of both sides. In a best-case scenario the addition of North Korea would provide vast new areas of land, mineral resources and a huge and cheap new labour pool to boost the Korean economy.

But the gap between the two societies could hardly be greater. Choi, the defector, tells me that in North Korea the population is told that people in South Korea are so poor they are starving, that millions cannot afford even to send their children to school but must send them to work instead. Anyone who has travelled knows the regime is lying to them, he says. But most North Koreans have not travelled.

Although Choi was in no sense an intimate of dictator Kim Jong-Il he knew enough to know that Kim Jong-Il was competent and in charge. This emerged clearly from defector testimony over the years, whereas earlier there was a strong suspicion that Kim Jong-Il may have been mentally or physically incompetent, so reclusive was he.

When Choi defected he thought reunification was not too far away. He thought that either there would be a short war in which North Korea would be crushed or there would be economic collapse. 'Government officials, soldiers and police don't experience food shortages,' he says. 'But you cannot imagine the hardships of people in the villages, even villages on the outskirts of Pyongyang itself.'

North Korea's aim in ten years of fitful diplomatic effort has been to create a split between the United States and South Korea.

Joe Nye, the former US assistant secretary of defence and the author of the Pentagon's East Asian military strategy, told me at a conference in Seoul that he believes two elements are essential in effective American policy on the Korean peninsula. The first is to make sure that Pyongyang believes that launching an attack on South Korea would result in the absolute destruction of its regime. The second is to ensure that, while both the US and South Korea retain tactical flexibility, there is no prospect of North Korea's significantly dividing them.

In contrast to the North's sporadic and ineffective Machiavellianism in foreign policy, South Korea over the last decade has pursued extremely effective foreign policy. The centrepiece of this was normalising relations with China, which formed the basis for the huge trade between South Korea and China. South Korea is respected in the United Nations and involved in every diplomatic game of consequence in East Asia. It has totally outflanked North Korea on that score, while Pyongyang has made no gains of any consequence among Seoul's traditional friends.

There is one area, though, in which Seoul's diplomacy has been distinctly lacking, and that is Japan. Koreans are paranoid and obsessive about Japan. No one should underestimate the suffering that Koreans went through at the hands of the Japanese, but you'd think that 50 years of impeccable international behaviour by the Japanese would have started to register with the Koreans. Instead, you will almost find them blaming the Japanese for the weather. I remember one senior official in Seoul telling me in the mid-90s that South Korea and Japan had made vast strides in international cooperation but that nevertheless it was appropriate that pop songs and other elements of Japanese culture be banned from Korea. This was because Japanese culture was inherently dirty and would pollute the society if allowed in. Similarly, you do not find many Japanese cars on the roads. The Koreans have made a positive art form of slowly going through the remaining Japanese buildings in Seoul and ceremonially blowing them up, one by one, always with a baleful Japanese ambassador in attendance.

Yet all this emotional anti-Japaneseness is not only immature and unproductive in itself; it blinds Koreans to the profound strategic interests they share with Japan, and indeed the profound values the two societies have in common. Both countries are democracies, perhaps the two best established democracies in East Asia. Also, culturally both countries are profoundly similar, though both get upset if you say this. Both are allies of the United States and dependent on the US for their security. In effect they are part of a de facto multilateral alliance with each other, centred on America.

In both societies there is an irresponsible tendency to leave the creation of a regional order to the Americans, even though both claim they want a greater role in shared decision-making. If the Americans ever do leave Asia, Japan and Korea would have no one to turn to but each other, especially as a moderating balance to China. Korea after reunification would have a long land border with China and might find it a more complex neighbour to manage than it imagines. Both Korea and Japan have huge economic stakes in China, but instead of each trying to play China off against the other they should be seeking to develop the most solid and intimate association with each other right now.

To do this would require two things. It would certainly require a more forthright strategic dialogue between Korea's leaders and its people. But it would also require political leadership from Japan. Japan makes the development of this relationship more difficult by its continued niggardly treatment of its Korean minority and by the tendency of its politicians from time to time to say preposterous and offensive things, such as that Korea benefited from Japanese colonisation—statements which are always withdrawn and apologised for but which leave lingering bitterness among Koreans.

But Korea's outlook towards Japan is changing, just as the nation itself is changing, forced into change not least by the economic crisis of the late 1990s. The other force for change in contemporary Korea is its president, Kim Dae Jung. One of the most important things about Kim Dae Jung is that he told his people the truth about the causes of their economic malaise. In late 1998 I went once more to talk to Kim, who has been generous in giving me his time over the years. This was our first meeting since he had been elected president.

In the sitting room in which he receives guests in the presidential Blue House, Kim has two huge photographs. One is of his addressing a joint sitting of the two Houses of the American Congress. Another is of his, also in the US, greeting Se Ri Pak, South Korea's champion woman golfer who became the most popular woman, probably the most popular person, in all Korea.

The photos tell you a lot about Kim—the citadel of democracy, the populist touch, the pervasive American motif. Kim, aged 74 when I meet him that time, still limps from a long ago assassination attempt by South Korean Intelligence. He is in many respects the most radical leader South Korea has ever had. A lifelong democracy campaigner and dissident, a veteran of six years in prison and eight under house arrest, the survivor of at least two assassination attempts and a kidnapping, Kim is the man whom history has chosen to lead his country through its most severe economic crisis in nearly 50 years.

When I meet him the statistics are glum—the economy shrinking by 8 per cent in a year, unemployment officially at 1.7 million but probably nearer 3 million—yet Kim himself remains a bundle of energy and optimism. But by late 1998 the signs of social distress are easy to find in Korea. Opposite my five star hotel is a public park—each bench is occupied by people sleeping rough. The hills around Seoul are also unusually busy. Men who cannot bear the shame of unemployment dress for work each morning, but spend their days wandering the hillsides.

South Korea was profoundly shocked by one case that received heavy media coverage. An unemployed, divorced man chopped off the little finger of his ten-year-old son. He pretended it had been done by a burglar, and his son supported his story. His objective was insurance money. Anyone would be shocked by this, but for this deeply traditional, family-oriented society, the experience was lacerating.

A lot of Koreans resent the severity of the International Monetary Fund's original reform program for South Korea. Kim tells me he supports the IMF in principle and that without its intervention many of the necessary structural changes in the economy, which cut across politics and vested corporate interests, would have been much harder to make. And the money the IMF provided was essential. 'The IMF has given us great help,' he says.

But he enters a qualification: 'Some IMF policies were inadequate. Especially they wanted too much austerity and too high interest rates.' This is a universal complaint about all the original IMF programs. The IMF later accepted the need for Budget deficits and expansionary policies, but the Kim Government simply did not have the money for the giant tasks it needed to undertake: refinancing the dysfunctional banks, creating a social safety net and stimulating the real economy.

In the first half of 1998 total demand for goods and services declined a staggering 28 per cent. A trade deficit was turned into a trade surplus only because the collapse of imports was greater than the collapse of exports.

In the face of all this, Kim at least had the guts to lay it on the line to his countrymen. He tells me: 'The cause of the crisis is that we did not practise democracy and free markets hand in hand. When you don't practise free markets you lose competitiveness. Our domestic crisis was due to bad loans. Banks were giving loans to questionable characters and many of these became bad loans. Businesses did not have self-control but tried to make their profits by linking themselves to power. We had a tremendous trade deficit, which brought [the need for] external loans and [meant] a loss of competitiveness. We came very close to a debt moratorium situation. Because of our lack of democracy, financial institutions came under the control of government.'

Kim's rhetoric is attractive and he gives the impression of being utterly determined to make the changes he talks about, but the power of the chaebols is awesome and their resistance to reform emerged as a key theme of his presidency. And in 1999 the economy did start to recover.

When Kim gets up to leave, his shuffling gait reminds me how old he is. His courage, though, is undeniable. His life, like that of his nation, has been one long series of impossibilities.

Notwithstanding the challenges of North Korea, of China, of Japan, of its own headlong rush into modernisation, I depart feeling broadly optimistic about Korea. People who work so hard, with so much basic goodwill and such a strategic positioning, are much more likely than not to succeed. As I've argued in this chapter, at the time of reunification the whole world will focus intensely on Korea. But in its fusion of Asian values and Western dreams, in its earnest discourse on human values and cultural inheritance, in its economic and social achievements and the fascinating mixture of Confucianism and Western influence it embodies, Korea deserves a much higher profile.

Come and taste the *kimchi*—the garlic and chilli are strong, but you'll get to like it.

12

INDIAN SUMMER?

VIBHU IS A FAST-TALKING, fast-smoking London advertising executive with a rich East End accent and an endless line in professional patter. But he's now living in India. He sits with his roly-poly body perched on the edge of a small swivel chair in the unbelievably chaotic and crowded offices of a big multinational, on the fifth floor of a tall office block in New Delhi.

'I can't think of a better word than "exciting" to describe this place,' he tells me, speaking in rapid-fire bursts. 'I love this place. It's a fact of life that this is a booming economy. I'm on the phone to the boys back home [London], you know, friends of mine who are surveyors, accountants, saying to them, come on, find an opportunity in Asia, come to India.'

Vib, as his friends call him, is a representative of what is almost a new, Brahminical caste in India, the returning NRIs (non-resident Indians) who come back to run the Indian operations of multinational companies and in the process become the shock troops of a revolution that is sweeping across Indian society, promising to transform one of the oldest and most culturally distinctive societies on Earth.

India's economic reform program, which began in 1991, is, despite all its setbacks and partial reversals in the late 1990s, shaking up Indian society in a way that nothing has done in modern Indian history since the gaining of independence in 1947. Inaugurated by former Congress Party prime minister P. V. Narasimha Rao and his finance minister Manmohan Singh, it has virtually abolished India's arcane licensing system, opened up its economy to foreign investment and trade, and cut and simplified taxes. In the late 1990s the reform process slowed down and it is an open question as to how committed and energetic future Indian governments will be in furthering the reform process, but no one is seriously talking of going back. The reforms that have been made are permanent.

Moreover, the direction of change seems established and future governments may accelerate or decelerate but they will keep moving in the same direction. Thus it is an ongoing revolution, born of a foreign currency crisis which at one point saw India with only two weeks' worth of foreign exchange reserves in the bank. The revolution is profound for it involves totally reorienting Indian economic thinking and behaviour, turning it away from 40 years of bureaucratic socialism and towards the free market.

'It is the best chance we have ever given ourselves, but also probably our last chance,' says Sunil Adam, the foreign editor of *Pioneer*, an innovative New Delhi newspaper. Adam's is a view widespread among Indian intellectuals and to be heard at any dinner party in Mumbai (formerly Bombay), New Delhi or Chennai (formerly Madras). The 1990s represent perhaps a critical decade in Indian history and many Indians are deeply aware of the significance of the issues on the table at the turn of the century. The economic reforms offer the chance to lift hundreds of millions of people out of squalor and poverty. They also offer India the chance to resume its rightful place as one of the big players on the world stage. But they could cause severe local dislocations too, as economic reform programs frequently have elsewhere. They could widen the already huge gap between rich and poor. But if they fail . . .

The economic reforms are transforming Indian life and society. For decades, indeed for centuries, poor but industrious Indians have been going overseas to work and to live, and generally to succeed—so much so that the Indian diaspora abroad numbers about 16 million. Now, in unprecedented numbers and with unprecedented influence, they are coming home, drawn by the chance offered by India's promising economic development.

Vibhu is a case in point. He left India with his parents at the age of four. His father, a doctor, practised medicine in England. Vibhu grew up an Englishman. Then, in his mid-30s, he came back to India at about the age at which his father left.

'In a sense home is England and in a sense I've come home to India,' he says, the Cockney cadences falling somewhat incongruously from what appears to be a wholly Indian physiognomy. 'I'm in a very fortunate position to be able to use what I've learned in my 30 years away. I was a bit worried at first that people would say: "Who is this guy and what does he think 'e's doin' tellin' us what to do?" But there's been none of that. Everyone is falling over themselves to learn, to know what's going on overseas. I don't make any apology for my return to India. I'm setting benchmarks in salary levels, job conditions, career opportunities.

'This was a tailormade opportunity for me. I was a low-risk investment for my employer. Being of Indian origin, experienced in the United Kingdom market, single, and with family here, I was less likely to say after two months that I wanted to go home. As for the quality of life in India, where else would I have servants? I have a chauffeur to drive me around. I'm on an invite list, ambassadors and all the rest, that I'd never be on in London.'

The NRIs are a significant economic force in India, both as managers and investors. By the mid-1990s, if the NRIs had been considered as a single foreign-national unit, they would have formed the largest foreign investor in India, ahead of the United States and Japan. To some extent they are replicating the role of the overseas Chinese in China's rapid economic development. They are also the perfect managers for multinational companies seeking to do business in India. In joint ventures in China there are frequently two managers, a representative of the Western firm and a local Chinese. In India the post is often unified in one NRI.

The NRIs know India. Vibhu can understand, though only haltingly speak, Hindi because that's what his parents spoke to each other at home in London. That degree of cultural knowledge can be invaluable. At the same time the NRIs typically know the Western market and operating style as well.

But even more surprising in its way is the role the NRIs have played as investors. Many economists thought the NRIs would be negligible investors. Unlike the overseas Chinese, who were concentrated in territories near to mainland China—in Hong Kong, Taiwan and South East Asia—most NRIs live far away, in the US, Canada, Europe and Australia. And the Indian diaspora, though containing many traders, did not contain many industrialists. But the Indian economy's historic opening has proven too attractive for the NRIs to ignore. And for some at least, an element of benign nationalism, a desire to participate in the transformation of Indian society, is part of their motivation.

That sense of nationalism increasingly pervades many areas of national life, even advertising: 'Everyone knows that Indian women are the most beautiful in the world,' declared a television advertisement that screened frequently in 1995, 'so come spend a night with the most beautiful women in the universe as we televise the Miss Femina India beauty contest.' Two Indian women in the mid-90s won the Miss World and Miss Universe contests respectively and became super-celebrities within India as a result. They also challenged, even if in a fashion of which orthodox feminists might disapprove heartily, the traditional subservient, non-assertive role of Indian women.

But paradoxically—and again it is a development that traditional left-wing feminists may be ambivalent about—one of the biggest factors in changing, indeed liberating, the lives of many Indian women is the globalisation of the Indian economy and the entry of multinational companies into India.

Parvati is representative of the new Indian woman. She is 26 years old when I meet her and a graduate of Delhi University. She was educated before that at a convent school, not because she is a Catholic but because convent schools provide the best education. Unlike any of her female forebears she lives alone and independent, in a rented two-room apartment. She can afford this because she works for a multinational and earns a salary of about US$10 000, a prodigious sum by most Indian standards. Much to the distress of her parents she had a long relationship with an older Western man. She is determined that when she marries it will be for love, rather than as part of an arranged marriage, which is still the norm for millions of Indians. Her standard of living is quite decent by any international standard, although the Indian currency is so weak that she finds travel abroad extremely expensive unless she can stay with friends or relatives. In her apartment she has a water cooler and a fan but cannot yet afford airconditioning.

'You really need airconditioning in Delhi's summer,' she says. 'The temperature regularly goes up to 45 degrees Celsius. But anyway there are always power cuts during the day and often during the night as well.'

She bought one of India's national cars, a second-hand Maruti, for about $5000. 'But I'm going to get rid of it and buy a new one. It gives me more trouble than all the men in my life put together.' There is an eight month waiting list for a standard new Maruti, so Parvati will buy a more expensive version, which will cost her about $9000, for which there is no waiting list. Without working for a multinational she could never afford either an independent apartment or a car. Many Indians do not approve of women like Parvati. She approached an Indian bank to get a loan for her car. Unused to such requests, and a little shocked by her impertinence and presumption, they turned her down, despite her solid job and good income. She went to a foreign bank instead which looked not at her gender but at her work record and prospects and her income, and approved the loan.

Parvati's independence helps other women, not only by providing a role model for friends and relatives but by providing an alternative female source of minor wealth, patronage and support. Parvati has a female relative who is regularly beaten by her husband, a practice which is appallingly common in India and about which Indian authorities are extremely slothful and negligent. When the beatings get too bad Parvati's relative comes and stays in her apartment for a few days. This is hardly an ideal solution to domestic violence but it is at least a small extension of freedom and independence both for Parvati and her female relative. In time, if India's economic growth continues, this kind of social change will become much more widespread.

All this independence would be impossible without the multinationals. For a time Parvati worked for a European embassy. She describes the European diplomats as 'a bunch of wankers' and says they erected invisible but inpenetrable barriers between themselves and their Indian colleagues. She finds the commercial sector much more racially relaxed, with far fewer barriers between Indians and foreigners. Parvati has discovered what millions have discovered throughout history—though money can be cruel, there is a kind of democracy about it. Its aristocracy and class gradations operate along only one axis, the making and possession of money. It is substantially colour blind, gender blind, class and caste blind. That is not to say that the pursuit of money should become the highest personal or social goal, but rapid economic growth does have a strong track record in breaking down all kinds of barriers.

Parvati is understandably positive about India's economic reform program: 'I can do things now I never could have done five years ago,' she says. But her conversation is laced with extreme cynicism about Indian politics, which she regards as corrupt and incompetent in equal measure. Her hope is just that the politicians don't mess things up. Like so many Indians of her generation, she yearns for yet more change.

The creation of a new India will nonetheless be a slow process. Wherever you go, the old India is still around. It sought me out one day in the most unlikely setting, Connaught Place, the most upmarket shopping area in New Delhi. Connaught Place is a huge circular park ringed by a series of radial roads lined with old, seemingly identical, colonnaded buildings. I am there in search of a decent bookshop. The area is crowded and boisterous with a vast array of goods on sale. After a few minutes wandering around I find myself accompanied by a strikingly beautiful child, a little girl aged I guess about four or five. She is wearing a grubby but still quite beautiful child's version of the traditional Indian sari. She doesn't say anything, doesn't even put her hand out, but she stays close to me, and her huge, dark almond eyes stay fixed on mine.

I walk away briskly, thinking that no good can come of a Western man having unsupervised contact with an Indian child, full of the traveller's paranoia and embarrassment in such a situation. Still without saying anything, or making any gestures, she follows. Eventually I give her a pitiful 10-rupee note (which is worth somewhat less than 50 cents). Immediately her eyes are off me and she scampers away, to give her small takings to an older woman, presumably her mother, sitting passively in the middle of the sidewalk at the next corner.

For women and children such as these the economic reforms probably haven't changed things much, beyond bringing a few more affluent foreigners their way. Will the economic reforms ever bring much benefit to people such as my small companion from Connaught Place? Eventually, argue Indian Government officials, increased employment opportunities will flow through. The raw figures for economic growth after the reform program had taken hold were impressive. In the late 1990s India's economy managed a consistent annual growth rate of 6 per cent. Given India's performance in the past, this was a fantastic achievement. But the stalling of reform meant that the growth rate never lifted off to a true 'tiger' rate of 8 per cent or more—a rate that would rapidly create a huge, politically powerful middle class which would have sufficient clout to see that the reforms were followed through. India kept getting to the brink of economic liftoff only to stall, with good growth but not anything like its true potential.

Nonetheless, the global economy was by the late 1990s starting to take real notice of India. The country's exports grew in some years of the decade by 20 per cent. Certain industries, such as capital goods, grew by 20 per cent a year. Inward foreign investment was measured in billions of dollars instead of hundreds of millions. Corporate profits grew rapidly. Huge infrastructure projects, despite the fact that they always involved countless problems and controversies, drew in foreign participation. These were big developments and big numbers and, if they continue, they will make India an economy that no one can afford to ignore. And the evidence was that the international community was starting to wake up to India's potential, notwithstanding the outrage at India's conducting a series of nuclear weapons tests in early 1998. Foreign government and business and investment delegations made hundreds of pilgrimages to India in the 1990s.

The experience with satellite and cable TV is instructive. Although the Indian Government later imposed a series of irksome restrictions, it did not overturn the basic policy of openness which led, incredibly, to India's becoming one of the most enthusiastically wired societies heading into the information revolution of the 1990s. In 1991 some 330 000 Indian homes received satellite or cable television. By 1995 more than

12 million homes did. Given India's average household size of 5.2, at least 60 million Indians were regularly watching satellite or cable television. Even this is probably a gross underestimate because so much piracy and illegal cable reception go on and because many villages have only one TV, which virtually everyone watches.

All of this aroused some nationalistic resentment and backlash in India. There was talk of a cultural 'invasion from the skies'. But as usual India's ancient capacity to adapt and absorb came quickly into play. The pay TV operators found that while there was a certain audience for standard international product, especially sports but also some soap opera and the like, there was a huge demand for Indian product too. Official Indian television had been a dreary state monopoly. The pay providers began producing Indian soap opera. The international phenomenon of MTV was too raunchy for mainstream Indian tastes. An Indian version was produced with an Indian host, some cuts to the raunchier video segments and increased Indian content. Nonetheless, the whole satellite and cable television phenomenon is a powerful force for social change in India.

Certainly, if you can gauge the likely success of a reform program by the enthusiasm with which a national elite embraces and espouses it, India's economic reform program looks to have a substantial future. India's elite recognises it as a very big opportunity. T. N. Ninan, editor of the *Business Standard*, described the economic reforms to me as 'epochal, pivotal'.

'Over time it will affect the whole of Indian culture,' he says. 'It has the greatest chance of anything in recent Indian history to make the difference in the lives of ordinary people.' He cites powerful consumer figures, such as sales each year of six million TV sets. In 1980 about 150 000 motorised two-wheel vehicles were sold. By the late 1990s more than 1.5 million a year were. Automobile sales have risen tenfold since the 1970s.

The interests and ambitions of Indians are changing because of the different patterns of work and the different levels of spending power brought about by the effects of the economic reforms. 'All the expansion in Indian journalism is now in business journalism,' Ninan says.

The reforms won in-principle support across the political

spectrum, although, as you would expect in Indian and most other democratic politics, every form of rent-seeking distortion and pork-barrel special pleading is undertaken by politicians seeking special privileges for constituents and other powerful figures. I spent an absorbing afternoon with Atal Bihari Vajpayee, who was then leader of the semi-fundamentalist, right-wing Hindu Bharatiya Janata Party (BJP), before he became prime minister. BJP activists were responsible for burning down the historic mosque at Ayodyah and setting off Hindu–Moslem riots, in an appalling act of sectarianism.

Yet Vajpayee, who went on to become prime minister on two separate occasions, is a moderate, reasonable and deeply cultured man. He is known to represent the moderate wing of the BJP. A large man with a leonine and regal look, dressed as he is in traditional rural Indian garb, he comes across as both warm and wise. These were my impressions when I met him and I don't retract them at all because of the nuclear tests. His office then, in New Delhi's extraordinarily grand Parliament House building, was modest. He speaks in an earthy yet fatherly manner about India's multitudinous problems. On the economic reform program, he is absolutely clear: 'We are in favour of economic reform,' he says. 'In fact we would accelerate the program and do it more vigorously. At the state level things are moving too slowly. We are also in favour of privatisation. The state should concentrate on education, health and nutrition. These areas are neglected in India. We have so many universities, but after 50 years of independence we cannot even make primary education compulsory. No party now can stop this process of privatisation and liberalisation.'

Vajpayee is probably right in this last assessment. The communist State government in West Bengal in the early 1990s saw a flight of capital out of Calcutta and into Mumbai in the State of Maharashtra. So the West Bengal Government got with the program, disciplining its unions, wooing foreign investment and supporting economic reform. Mugged by reality.

Vajpayee is also certainly the reassuring and moderate face of alleged Hindu fundamentalism. He is clearly a moderate and therefore not wholly representative of the more militant elements of the BJP. The Hindu–Muslim split is still one of the deepest fractures within India. The rise of the BJP to become a truly national party seemed to threaten to exacerbate this divide, and to further undermine India's cherished and admirable secularism, so long promoted by the Congress Party. Religion mixed with ethnicity is a potent brew, and religious conflict, between Muslim and Hindu, between Sikh and Hindu, and latterly between Christian and Hindu, is a perennial threat in India. There are real worries that the emergence of the BJP could change the symbolic nature of India, the signals the political system sends about the sort of nation it aspires to be.

On the other hand, the BJP's Hindu militancy should not be overstated. It does not favour a theocratic state. It favours cultural nationalism. Of course, in a country with a predominant religion cultural nationalism can often be a disguised form of religious preference. And yet when the BJP went into coalition government with the far more radically Hindu fundamentalist party Shiv Sena, in the State of Maharashtra, the administration was surprisingly pragmatic.

Over a long discussion Vajpayee argues that Hindu fundamentalism is virtually a contradiction in terms, Hinduism itself being so diffuse and syncretic. Yet, as the terrible Ayodyah mosque violence indicates, the arousal of passions of religious hostility among Hindus is certainly a possibility. Again it would seem that solid economic growth is likely to be one of the best ways to subsume religious tensions in a broader national increase in prosperity. But the Indian voices, from all religious persuasions, that argue against religious bigotry and explicitly see India's multireligious reality as a central part of the overall Indian identity, have also been important in keeping religious hostilities in check.

I travelled down to Bangalore to interview an ostensibly left-wing leader, H. D. Deve Gowda, who was when I met him the leader of the Janata Dal Party in his State and chief minister of the Karnataka State Government. He later became prime minister. Deve Gowda led the traditionally left-wing Janata Dal Party to a crushing victory over the Congress party in 50-million-strong Karnataka.

Meeting him is quite an experience. Over a period of a couple of days our interview is on again and off again several times; it is rescheduled and rescheduled. But finally I am taken to his residence, a spacious two-storey bungalow in the heart of Bangalore. There I am shown into a large sitting room around all four walls of which sit a motley variety of petitioners and constituents, party workers, government employees, small businessmen, ordinary citizens with some grievance or problem they want the chief minister to address. It is a scene repeated in chief ministers' residences all over India. The chief minister might not see all of them, but will certainly see some of them. Most hope that just a minute of the chief minister's time will solve their problem.

After a relatively short wait I am ushered upstairs and amid some pomp and ceremony taken in to meet Deve Gowda. He is a great, bald-headed bear of a man, friendly and physical and informal. We are served hot tea and sweets in the Indian style and a substantial coterie of party workers, aides and hangers-on of various types stay to witness our encounter. Deve Gowda looks physically weary in the way political leaders often do but is hospitable.

In following Vajpayee into the office of prime minister, he anomalously held that office without being able to speak Hindi. He stayed prime minister for somewhat longer than Vajpayee in Vajpayee's first term but was always leading an unstable coalition. He is a horse-trader of a politician but there is no shame in that. Indians are good at politics and a lot of them have something of the style of a Lyndon Johnson. Deve Gowda agrees to see a foreign journalist on the day that I meet him because he has one overwhelming message that he wants to convey to the outside world.

'I want to be very clear as far as private capital is concerned. I'm going to support economic liberalisation,' he says. 'I will actively seek foreign investment. It will help us use our government resources in priority areas like education and health. If they want to come and start an industry, construct a highway, collect a toll, let them do it.'

His left-wing credentials notwithstanding, he even offers the relative passivity of his State's unions as an attraction to foreign investors. In taking basically the same line on such matters, Vajpayee and Deve Gowda are not selling out their respective ideologies. Instead they are demonstrating an intelligent pragmatism, a pragmatism of necessity, a desire to take advantage of the realities of the globalising economy, rather than the ideological and theoretical and bureaucratic nostrums that have too often informed Indian policy-making. There is a democratic deficit in a globalising economy, in that national and provincial governments are forced into a relatively narrow range of policy options, and must deal with the consequences of forces over which they have very little influence. But it is of no use to bemoan this democratic deficit if such bemoaning gets in the way of making the best arrangements for the people a politician represents. Democratic politicians do not deserve criticism for this pragmatism but rather praise, for the alternative of trying to hold out against the global economy produces merely poverty, backwardness and isolation.

Bangalore itself is a marvellously globalised city. Although it suffers from the serious problems of overly rapid growth, it encompasses much of the vision splendid for India's future. A rapidly growing metropolis of more than five million, it is the most colourful city in India by night, with a positively East Asian profusion of bright lights. It was for a while in the 1990s the fastest growing metropolis in Asia. It is the centre of India's huge computer software industry. India has (after the United States) the second biggest computer software industry in the world. Computer software design and adaptation fit perfectly with the strengths of Indian culture, the creativity of the Indian mind, the proverbial verbal fluency, the ease of manipulation of symbols. Bangalore also houses high-tech elements of India's defence industry, which, with ballistic missiles, nuclear weapons and regional servicing of Russian defence equipment, are substantial.

Bangalore is a city bursting with technocrats and yuppies, with huge art deco apartment complexes sprouting up in the centre of the city. While the pace of growth has put its services under severe pressure, Bangalore remains a city of great beauty and charm. It has expansive city parks and has retained, like many Indian cities, magnificent colonial and pre-colonial architecture. The sense of so many different ages of man brought together in the one time and place, the extraordinary psychological and technological distance that it is possible to travel in one day, is a big part of Bangladore's, and India's, perennial appeal to all foreigners who visit.

Winston Churchill, for one, spent some of his happiest days in Bangalore. He found its climate, at 900 metres above sea level, mild and attractive by Indian standards. In his autobiography he wrote:

> Although the sun strikes with torrid power, the nights, except in the hottest months, are cool and fresh. The roses of Europe in innumerable large pots attain the highest perfection of fragrance and colour. Flowers, flowering shrubs and creepers blossom in glorious profusion. Snipe (and snakes) abound in the marshes; brilliant butterflies dance in the sunshine, and nautchgirls by the light of the moon.

If you add to Churchill's description a vast high-tech industrial park, a bit of urban squalor and a lot of frenetic construction activity, you pretty much get the idea of modern Bangalore.

Of course, the rush from neighbouring States of Indians seeking to share its wealth is changing Bangalore rapidly. As India develops it will face ghastly problems of too much traffic and too much pollution but, bad as these problems can be, they are infinitely preferable to too much starvation or too much desperate poverty.

As the 1990s drew to a close the great muddle of Indian politics was seriously slowing down the reform program. Chronic rigidities, such as the labour market, appeared to be beyond anyone's power to reform. It is still all but impossible for big companies to sack people. Grotesque restrictions apply to land use. These restrictions may have once been motivated by considerations of fairness or redistribution of wealth but they have become dreadful supply side constraints on the creation of wealth. They impede and damage the Indian economy. They are exploited by rent-seekers and they make everyone poorer. They are also an irresistible breeding ground for corruption.

One of the worst rigidities imposed on the economy is the system of caste reservations, whereby a certain number of civil service jobs, and in some States university places, are reserved for members of the lower castes. While this policy obviously had good intentions in its origins, it has led to a poisonous intensification of the politics of caste identity, the very opposite of what India needs. Moreover, higher caste people feel that they are being discriminated against and demand the reservation of jobs or places for their caste as well. The whole system is corrupt and evil. It cuts directly across the idea of advancement by merit and it reinforces the centrality of the caste dynamic in Indian life, whereas enlightened Indian leaders from Mahatma Gandhi onwards have been trying to ease and diminish the impact of caste.

Pranab Mukherjee, a former commerce minister and a heavy hitter in the Congress Party, tells me that he believes much more active and effective public selling of the reform program is needed: 'Economic reform means higher growth, more jobs and more development,' he says. 'We have to do more to get that message out.' He also nominates as an urgent task the need to change the mindset of India's army of bureaucrats, many of whom have grown up in an atmosphere of control and regulation.

Some have broken free. After coming up through the Indian Administrative Service, Mr Bhargava became the managing director of the giant, state-owned Maruti automobile company. From his panelled skyscraper office in downtown New Delhi, where I met him, he now urges the government to privatise altogether. He is almost an absolutist on these matters, an evangelical, and he has the passion of the convert: 'The public sector won't survive in India. Its culture is too inefficient.'

Yet the mentality is changing in the bureaucracy, and at the lower levels as well. I have had occasion to deal, as a foreign journalist, with several arms of the Indian civil service and generally find them helpful, certainly compared with many other Asian bureaucracies. I put this once to an acquaintance in the government service, saying that I could not quite believe the tales of gross inefficiency and epic obstruction that I had frequently heard. 'Ah, my friend,' he replied, 'before I joined the Indian Administrative Service I had some very bitter experiences myself. I determined that no one would ever have cause to think that of me.'

Within the Indian political and intellectual tradition there are of course powerful and sincere voices that question, if not downright oppose, the program of economic reform. Anees Jung, a member of the international board of UNESCO, is one such woman. Born into an aristocratic Muslim family in Hyderabad, brought up in strict purdah, she went on to become one of India's most renowned feminists and author of the bestselling *Unveiling India*.

I meet her in her small but elegant apartment. By no means rich, she is nonetheless attended by servants and lives in a gated and guarded compound, a not at all untypical arrangement for middle-class Indians. 'I'm very optimistic about India,' she says. 'I see such strength in the people. To keep a country rolling along with our traditions, and yet be modern—it's not easy. We are changing, but we are changing within the parameters of our tradition.

'I'm a bit worried about the economic reform program. The strength of India lies in the countryside and I wish our economic policies would concentrate on the country. When you're really worried about whether your field will have enough rain to feed you, when you walk all day with poverty, when you walk all day with agony, your perspective on economic reform is different. Education and health are the two greatest factors for India. When women are more educated they don't want more than two children.'

Health is certainly a critical and immediate challenge for India. Apart from a few complete basket cases in Africa, no country has a smaller proportion of its population (about 15 per cent) with access to clean sanitation. And India remains a remarkably filthy country. In the plushest suburb of New Delhi, in Janpath Street right outside Sonia Gandhi's palatial compound, I see a man unselfconsciously urinating on the sidewalk. In Delhi's crowded streets the cars share the road with 17 000 head of untended cattle—seen anywhere, lazily mooching around looking for food, unimpeded but unassisted—and with elephants and a variety of horse-drawn and camel-drawn vehicles.

India is indeed a nation of bewildering contrasts—of an exponentially growing middle class, of space programs and ballistic missiles, of Silicon Valleys and magnificent architecture, but also of shocking squalor, filth, poverty and cruelty. It is perplexing for the visitor. The men tend to speak like a cross between Winston

Churchill and P. G. Wodehouse, a graceful, fluent, inventive and completely distinctive idiom of English. India's is a verbally gifted culture. The women, the overwhelming majority dressed in exquisitely coloured traditional saris or Punjabi suits (harem trousers covered by a flowing, calf-length blouse) are models of grace and visual eloquence.

These superficial observations are merely the most obvious manifestation of a profound truth about India—that it remains one of the great cultural treasure-houses for the entire human race. Apart from Australia, my home, the two countries that I have actually lived in for substantial periods of time are the United States and China. The US, China and India strike me as peculiarly and powerfully similar countries, despite all their obvious differences. In a way, the feature they share puts them in a league entirely by themselves among all the nations of the world and they ought to be able to find a way to build on this unique similarity. The feature of which I speak is the sense that each gives you of being a complete universe unto itself, a whole, functioning cultural, political and (to some extent) economic system, fantastically rich and diverse internally but coherent, which tends automatically to regard itself as the appropriate universal standard, the prism through which all of human experience ought to be viewed and evaluated. If you live in Calcutta, in Shanghai, in Chicago, you can invite your soul to contemplate the vastness and complexity of humanity and never leave home.

China, America and India—you could spend a thousand productive lifetimes in each and come nowhere near exhausting their cultural possibilities. It is not just size I am speaking of here but a continuous cultural richness, as well as a sense of achieved national unity within a context of startling diversity.

India's modern achievement in this particular regard ought to be more widely recognised. The great failure of Indian governments since 1947 has been the failure to ignite economic growth and development. It is a tragedy for India that it became independent just at a moment when bureaucratic socialism was the preferred economic strategy among Western intellectuals— and its initial governing class were intellectuals heavily influenced by the West. Partly as a result of this it simply pursued the wrong growth model for several decades, with appalling consequences for the Indian people.

But the half-compensating achievements of that generation and their followers ought not to be denied or downplayed either. India contains within itself at least as much cultural diversity as the whole of Europe. It has 20 000 caste groups and 600 languages. It has an astonishing panoply of religions and religious influences, with Hinduism arguably the world's oldest continuous religion. It also contains the second or third largest population of Muslims in the world. Its ethnic diversity is at least as great as anything found in Europe. A Tamil, a Bengali, a Punjabi—these are radically different people. Yet it has achieved a broad political unity, which is genuine and borne deeply in the hearts of the people. Moreover it has done all this as a functioning democracy. Other Asians often comment privately that India would have done better as some kind of authoritarian regime. Yet that was not really an option in India. Indians love their democracy, imperfect and frequently corrupt as it is. Indians are determinedly political. They hold political opinions. They express political opinions.

And an Indian election is a wonder to behold. The national elections in 1996 involved 600 million voters and 14 000 candidates. Despite everything that can be said against Indian administration since 1947, probably only a democratic and federal system could have produced any effective administration in India at all. And the attachment of Indian culture to democracy and freedom of expression is one of its enduring features, and enduring strengths. It is a wholly admirable trait.

The Indian verbal gift is partly responsible for a stunning recent comeback by India into international consciousness. In particular this is happening through the international triumph of Indian literature. I developed a taste for Indian literature in the 1990s when it made a fantastic impression on the global consciousness. Sadly, I was limited to Indian literature published in English, but the Indian gift of English is so great that this is itself a huge representative body of work telling us much about India. As for many people, with me it began with Vikram Seth's incomparable *A Suitable Boy*. I thought it the best English language novel published in 1993, even if the haughty literateurs who judge the Booker Prize didn't understand its merits.

What is perhaps most captivating to Western readers of
A Suitable Boy is its mixture of rather disturbing familiarity and
mystifying exoticism. It is set in post-independence India
and revolves around the lives of four Indian families—the
Mehras, the Kapoors, the Khans and the Chatterjis. This novel,
in a great tradition, is about everything—politics, religion, race,
culture, love, marriage. It bears all the comparisons made for
it—Tolstoy, Jane Austen, George Eliot—except of course that it
is infinitely more fun to read than those are.

India's increasingly popular literature is part of the road back
from the partial cultural isolation that the country endured for
so long. The length of Seth's book—1349 pages in one edition—is
no disincentive once the story is begun. As I came to its close I
felt, as I hadn't felt since childhood, that deep sadness at the
ending of a book.

Seth's viewpoint is so interesting from so many angles. Here
are all the psychic dilemmas of post-colonialism. Seth's affectionate but critical dissection of India's upper class lays this issue
bare. One character, Arun Mehra, can tell you three good children's toy stores in London and is up with every word of English
literary life. Yet he is mortified when it comes out at a dinner
party that he has never been to London. Seth has captured
perfectly the psychological condition of post-colonialism, whatever the formal constitutional status of independence.

Then there is *A Suitable Boy*'s heroine, Lata Mehra, around whose
romantic dilemmas the whole novel swirls. Lata is completely
Indian, reveres even as she questions tradition, rejects at great pain
modernist notions such as mixed marriages, accepts parental discipline well into adulthood—the very picture of the traditional
Indian girl. Yet she is also fabulously familiar to the Western reader.
She is a curious, intellectually well-endowed university student. To
cheer herself up she reads the novels of P. G. Wodehouse. Her
brother-in-law, Pran Kapoor, a thoughtful, serious, ethical academic,
is obsessed, as are most of the male characters in *A Suitable Boy*,
with India's performance on the cricket field.

But the novel also contains scenes of melodramatic Hindu
religiosity. Characters can effortlessly move between the mental
worlds of Wodehouse and Krishna, not remarking at all in their
own lives that this is, at the very least, a distinctive mobility.

Increasingly, in the 1990s, the world became familiar with this unique mental universe. Indian writers in English, whether at home or abroad, have that intriguing insider/outsider quality. As writers in a post-colonial society many of their terms of reference, much of their mental furniture, is inevitably foreign.

This is perhaps even more true of writers of the Indian diaspora, which is an increasingly powerful cultural force in its own right. I have particularly enjoyed Rohinton Mistry's stories, which range from the purely Indian experiences of a group of predominantly Parsi tenants in an apartment block in old Bombay to the perplexing challenges facing the Indian migrant in a Western society. Sunetra Gupta, in a novel of aching melancholy and pure pain, *Memories of Rain*, rends our hearts with the cross-cultural issues involved in infidelity in a racially mixed marriage, between an Indian woman and a Western man. And late in the 1990s Arundhati Roy's *The God of Small Things* achieved a worldwide success and won the Booker Prize in 1997.

This global literary resurgence of India is a great gift which India has given the world. It is born at least partly, nonetheless, of the ambivalence in India's identity, its working out still of the issues of post-colonialism. This has been, until recently, something of a hindrance in India's integration into Asia, beyond the South Asian region which India utterly dominates.

India's national and historic circumstances today are being transformed by two great dynamics of immense historic consequence. These are the end of the Cold War, and the economic reform program that India itself embarked on in 1991. The nation is also being drawn out by a third historic dynamic which has only been tangential to its story so far but will become much more central if India is to succeed, and that is its determination to become reconnected to East Asia.

When India became independent it was expected to become a leading Asian nation. Its traditions of learning and political rhetoric, the erudition of its leaders, its familiarity with English (then as now the international language), its sheer size, the antiquity of its civilisation, its commitment to democracy, the ethical inspiration of Mahatma Gandhi, its intimate knowledge of and connections with the West—all these should have conspired to make India the natural leader of Asia. Instead of which, India tragically withdrew from and became irrelevant to the greatest stories in Asia—the rise of Japan, of Korea, of Taiwan and Hong Kong and Singapore, later of China and South East Asia. India adopted a development model which with its licence-raj and countless obstacles to international trade was the opposite of the East Asian export-led, globalising development model. It is only relatively recently that a wholesome sense of embarrass-ment, indeed shame, at India's poor development record com-pared with that of East Asia has come to inform its political leaders. Since the onset of the economic crisis in East Asia, which has not greatly affected India, this has been replaced by some pride at India's continued solid economic performance. Provided this is used to continue to impel sensible economic policy, that need be no bad thing.

Historically, what was much worse was India's self-destructive behaviour in the Cold War. Although India was never exactly a client of the Soviet Union, and always prized and maintained its independence, a curious anti-Americanism infested its foreign policy and, broadly, it chose to support the Soviet side in the Cold War. The US was not blameless in this either. However, for India, its choice was simply one of the great historic mistakes that any democratic leadership has ever made. Although it greatly pains the nostalgic anti-Americanists of Asia and the West to hear it said, those Asian nations that had the closest connections to America did the best in terms of development and economic growth. The stand-out examples are Japan, South Korea and Taiwan, all of them intimately, profoundly and for a long period under the influence of the US, all of them accorded access to the American market, all of them recording some of the fastest economic growth in the history of the human race.

India and America, the world's biggest and second biggest democracies, should have been natural friends. The Indians saw the US favouring Pakistan but did nothing effective to further their own cause in Washington. They took almost a perverse pride in constantly poking the US in the eye. But whatever satisfaction this may have given to Indian politicians and the very Eurocentric Indian foreign service, it did absolutely no good for the Indian nation. Washington was almost equally to blame for failing to give due weight to India's democratic achievement, and more fundamentally failing to make the leap of imagination required to see India as a potential great power, to try to draw it out into the world, to find a dignified place for India in the international system commensurate with its size and importance.

India also retreated from its involvement with East Asia. It became absorbed in its multitudinous disputes in South Asia, preoccupied with its creepy relationship with the Soviet Union and greatly taken up with worthless posturing about Non-Alignment and in the United Nations, but it missed the transforming emergence of East Asia.

Some in East Asia believe that India never recovered psychologically from its British colonisation, that it adopted British prejudices, and looked up to the Europeans and down on South East Asians in particular; that even its anti-Americanism involved a good deal of apeing of British attitudes of superiority. Certainly, there was about Indian intellectual and political life a self-consciously bookish air which seemed to disdain the practicalities of economics and commerce.

In any event, it was not until the Cold War was over, and its own economic reform program well under way, that India turned its attention towards East Asia. It had some commercial and diplomatic success, attracting some significant investment and becoming a formal dialogue partner of the Association of South East Asian Nations. But its diplomatic failures were more notable; for example, the consistent failure, after years of effort, to be allowed to join the Asia-Pacific Economic Cooperation forum, even after Russia, which is by no means an Asian nation, was allowed to join. Similarly, it was not invited to join the Asia-Europe summit process, a truly remarkable exclusion for the nation of Nehru.

Partly this has to do with the Indian diplomatic style. It is so verbally fluent that it has become inherently disputatious, inherently prone not only to seeing fine distinctions but to endlessly arguing them; and it is regarded as being, in itself, an impediment to coming up with workable agreements and speedy action.

But at a deeper level it is a sign of India's failure to connect with East Asia. India of course has vast human, intellectual and cultural resources to contribute to the great international discourse on values, on how we all live, separately and together. But its failure to take positive account of the Asian values of its neighbours to the east, its failure to become an integral part of the Asian economic miracle, is both emblematic of and a key to a broader failure of the nation since independence.

In some respects, India in 1998 took the most radical action since independence to achieve international relevance again, and that was conducting a series of nuclear tests which made it clear to the world that India was a nuclear weapons power. The cause of nuclear non-proliferation is so overwhelmingly important that India's action must be regarded as extremely irresponsible. And yet New Delhi had a case.

It had watched with horror the growing size and sophistication of China's nuclear arsenal. It had likewise watched with horror the help China gave to Pakistan in that country's efforts to become a nuclear weapons state. With both of these difficult neighbours India had fought wars. Moreover, the United States had let Russia into APEC in order to placate it over NATO's expansion. Yet the US had kept India, a democracy in good standing, out. And no one was willing to let India, a nation of nearly a billion people and the source of so much of the world's culture, join the United Nations Security Council, the Group of Eight Industrialised Nations (which anomalously includes Russia) or any other of the world's major councils. We are constantly told that the world must engage China, but the leading powers, especially the US, have done too little of consequence to engage India. Yet possession of a nuclear weapon seemed to give any and every other international regime leverage.

The reason why this line of argument is unsatisfactory is that every nation that feels slighted or neglected could equally deploy it to justify the acquisition of nuclear weapons. But the fact that New Delhi chose to go down that path is a failure not only of Indian leadership but of American diplomacy—and of European and Asian diplomacy too, for that matter.

India is too big and far too important to ignore. The world needs India's civilised and civilising traditions. It needs to offer India a rightful place at the big tables of decision-making.

Krishna is stirring. We'd better pay attention.

13

THE ASIAN SUPERPOWER:
AMERICA AND THE
FORMATION OF
ASIAN VALUES

A Chinaman is unprogressive. He remains a Chinaman as long as
he lives and wherever he lives. He retains his Chinese dress, his
habits, his methods, his religion, his hopes, aspirations and
desires. He looks upon foreign methods, appliances and
civilisation with scorn as inferior to his own.

Hawaiian Board of Immigration, mid-19th century

HAWAII . . . MY JOURNEY STARTS there, as every journey from
Asia to America should. The Chinese were there before me.
They have been in Hawaii more than 200 years, longer than they
have been in Singapore in any significant numbers, as long as
Europeans have been in Australia. They once made up a quarter
of Hawaii's population. Now they are one of its numerous
substantial minorities.

In this way Hawaii is more quintessentially American than
any other State in the Union. For in Hawaii everyone is a
minority. There is no majority racial group, and that is America's
future; perhaps it is the future of most countries. It is also
America's genius, its dream and its promise—its special contribution to mankind. For nothing is so idealistic as the American
commitment to the idea that nation has nothing to do with
ethnicity, that every race and no race, every ethnic background
and every mixture of ethnic backgrounds, can partake fully of
the American dream. It is the single value that sets America most
apart from Asia, and yet it is also the single value that makes
America most attractive to Asians.

265

Hawaii is of course special for many other reasons. It is truly the most dazzling location on Earth, a munificence of beauty which can almost be said to be overdone. For all of us, brought up on American popular culture, there are particular resonances in Hawaii. Driving into Waikiki for the start of a nationwide speaking tour of American campuses (in connection with a book called *Tigers* which I'd written on Asian leaders) I could not get out of my head the theme music from *Hawaiian Eye*, a fabled cop show of my childhood, or the ridiculous catch-line of the equally fabled *Hawaii Five-O*: 'Book 'im, Danno!'

Hawaii's ethnic mix—Chinese, Japanese, Filipino, Hawaiian, Caucasian, black—makes it one of the most cosmopolitan places on Earth, and in some ways the most Asian State in America. Its economy is tied to the Asian economy so much that when the great Asian downturn began in 1997, Hawaii too experienced recession.

But its connection with Asia is inescapable and has generally been to the benefit of both Hawaii and Asia. I went to Honolulu's Chinatown to meet one of the leaders of the Hawaiian Chinese business community, Warren Luke, the proprietor and chief executive of a family bank and a diversified family business heavily involved in real estate. His great-grandparents came from Guangdong in the 1850s, when many Chinese were brought to Hawaii to work on sugar plantations. Hawaiian Chinese, Luke says, try even more consciously than mainland Chinese-Americans to observe their Chinese traditions. This leads to some paradoxical results. Luke himself does not speak Chinese because just after World War II, when Luke was born, the Chinese community was fully concentrated on integration and proving themselves to be good Americans. But the next generation have found that their Chinese ethnic connections and cultural knowledge have an intrinsic value worth preserving. They have also found that these connections have real economic value in the international business environment. 'Everything now is networks,' says Luke. Therefore his sons have acquired some Chinese language in the course of an elite and international education.

While being proudly and uncompromisingly American, Luke is attached to his Chinese heritage: 'We follow all the Chinese traditions. Even if you don't believe, you go to temple when they say because it can't do any harm and you need every bit of luck you can get.'

Moreover, even for Luke's generation, the reputation of the ethnic Chinese for frugality was a positive benefit. When he worked in New York, he recalls, banks would tend to advance loans to customers with 'Oriental' names because they wouldn't default, and if these customers did get into trouble their families would help them.

The standard interpretation of the overseas Chinese, as the Chinese diaspora is called, is that it is predominantly a merchant class which retains a deep feeling for China, and Chinese culture, despite its extreme pragmatism and the various civic loyalties it has taken up in its nations of residence.

Luke himself, progressive, enlightened, five generations from China and hugely successful in America, would prefer his children to marry Chinese Americans: 'In most families there is a preference for the children to marry someone of their own race. If you come from similar backgrounds, eat similar foods, do similar things, it's easier in a marriage. But you learn to accept your children's choices.'

A Japanese-American friend of Luke's who is sitting with us, a man in his early 40s who drives a flash sports car, volunteers the fact that when he was in his 20s his family hoped he would marry another Japanese-American, when he was in his 30s they hoped his partner would at least be an Asian-American, now they would be happy if he married a female of any race at all. Luke and I chuckle at the humour, but the message is there: the society is not exactly colour blind, but it is reasonably relaxed.

When asked to nominate what Asian values mean to him, Luke gives the answer that many others also give: 'If you look at most Asian families, education is most important. It's the way you pull yourself up. Then there is respect, respect in the family, respect for elders. It's not only Chinese—you see it in the Korean and other Asian communities. And mainstream Americans are trying to get back to family values as well.'

It is fatuous for those who believe 'Asian values' is a meaningless term to argue that an emphasis on education and family values is also found in the Western tradition. If Asians believe that stress on education and fidelity to family are distinctive elements of their culture, then those Asian values, just by that fact alone, are a significant, animating force in the way they live their lives and make their contribution.

For another version of mainstream America's connection with Asia I journey over to a different part of Hawaii, to the headquarters of the Commander-in-Chief of US Forces in the Pacific. CINCPAC is the forward beacon of the American military commitment to Asia, a vast, sprawling establishment which commands the biggest theatre of operations in the world.

In the glory days of the Cold War, CINCPAC sat like a giant imperial overlord in Hawaii, almost as suspicious of Washington as of anyone in Asia. As the former Australian prime minister, Paul Keating, has commented, for much of the Cold War period American policy in Asia was really the policy of the US Navy. The Pacific was said to be an American lake and the awesome firepower of the US Navy dwarfed any possible challenger. The US now is susceptible to 'asymmetrical' challenges to its power, in which much weaker opponents use well-targeted weapons of great destructive force to potentially inflict unacceptable damage on US forces, or even US civilians. But in any kind of direct military conflict no one is likely to challenge American naval dominance in the Pacific for 50 or even 100 years to come.

CINCPAC still has the air of an imperial headquarters, not through any pomp or trappings of circumstance, but simply by its sheer size and the professionalism and attention to detail attendant upon its every operation. I am scheduled to see the admiral then at the centre of it all, Joseph Prueheur. In preparation, I am offered various opportunities to visit American warships and given a complete command briefing in advance—a professional presentation by a senior officer using extensive audio-visual props. Several intelligence experts, public information analysts and strategic players are also present, to answer any questions I have, evaluate each other's performances and, presumably, to impress me with just how seriously they are taking my interview with their boss. The strategy works. I am impressed.

In person, Prueheur is relaxed but focused on his message and, needless to say, completely on top of his brief. At that level, the American military is almost always impressive. He complains of being a little tired, having been up at odd hours consulting Indonesia's Armed Forces commander, General Wiranto, the night before. This is just a couple of weeks before the fall of Suharto and I am profoundly relieved that Prueheur is engaging in this kind of consultation. Much of official America doesn't realise how much it has at stake in Indonesia—how much the world has at stake—and sustained attention from Americans at Prueheur's level is unequivocally a good thing.

Prueheur acknowledges that part of his job is keeping the American political and bureaucratic East Coast establishment focused on Asia: 'We [have to] do a lot of marketing in Washington, given our Eurocentric heritage as a nation. At very high levels of our government, people have said that we did not have our eye fully on the ball regarding the baht crisis [the currency crisis that began in Thailand in mid-1997]. Compared to, say, NATO's expansion it was not a front-burner issue in Washington.'

Like soldiers everywhere, he likes to lay out his mission in logical steps: 'The economic system [of the Asia-Pacific region] rests on a political order which in turn rests on a security order. Security, stability, prosperity. So preventative defence is the first part. Then crisis response. Then being able to fight and win a major conflict.'

He then lists his five operational priorities: maintaining the defence relationship with Japan; building a better security relationship with China; helping to create conditions for a non-cataclysmic resolution to tensions on the Korean peninsula; trying to develop a military-to-military relationship with India (this was before India's nuclear tests); and responding to the security implications, for nations in the region, of the economic crisis.

Two things in particular strike me from what Prueheur is saying. One is the importance of not sending mixed signals to countries in Asia. This is especially difficult for a system as vast as that of the United States. Trying to coordinate the economic, diplomatic and military signals that the hugely complex, multi-agency American system generates is difficult.

The other is the great and growing need for what one might term military diplomacy. Prueheur was struck, and somewhat alarmed, that during the Taiwan Straits missile crisis in 1996 he didn't know personally his counterparts in Beijing. There was no one he could readily ring on the phone to overcome any misunderstandings or slips in communication further down the chain of command. He worked hard to remedy that situation.

In this age of the dominance of economics, it is much too easily forgotten just how much of America's position in Asia rests on its forward military deployment and its vast military capability more generally. America spends more on defence than the next five or six nations combined. Its military budget in the late 1990s was bigger than the entire economies of South East Asia put together. The most sophisticated militaries, after the US, are in Europe. No one in Asia comes anywhere remotely near the US in terms of military power. The Taiwan Straits missile crisis demonstrated this.

America's power in Asia has four interdependent elements: military preponderance, economic dominance, hegemony of popular culture, and historical association. Each reinforces the other and each looks likely to continue for a long time, despite, in recent years, the frequent mismanagement by Washington of its Asia policy. All four elements come together in California.

No place represents the American dream to Asians more than California does. From the yuppie uppercrust whites-only lifestyle of worldwide TV hits like *Beverly Hills* 90210 or *Melrose Place* to the staggering Asian success in West Coast universities, California dreaming is where many Asians would like to be. It's not that Asians necessarily approve of the lifestyle liberalism of California, but they certainly approve of its prosperity, and as residents California offers them the freedom to live a conservative lifestyle as well as a liberal one if they wish.

The Los Angeles riots following the 'not guilty' court verdict on the white policemen who appeared to beat the black motorist, Rodney King, in 1992 were the recent low point of LA's reputation in Asia. Across Asia at that time there was a certain smugness about America's inner-city problems, as evidenced by the comments of Lee Kuan Yew quoted in Chapter 4 on Singapore. Occasionally a Japanese politician in his cups would talk about America's problems with non-white minorities. In Malaysia defenders of the policy of offering preferences for *bumiputeras,* or ethnic Malays, would point out that there were no race riots in

Kuala Lumpur—with the unstated but heavily implied place of comparison being LA.

The problems of America's inner cities, combined with a 'declinist' school of thought based on the idea that America was suffering either from imperial overreach (as argued by Paul Kennedy) or from a lack of strategic industry policy along the lines of Japan (as argued by Chalmers Johnson and many others), led to a brief currency for the hugely mistaken idea of American decline.

But the sustained economic expansion in the US in the mid to late 1990s, with the surge of information technology throughout the economy, and the improvement in the unemployment rate especially, revolutionised all that. And the election of a brilliant raft of non-ideological mayors in America's major cities, who were racially inclusive but did not make racial job-sharing the basis of their approach to their cities' problems, added to the turn-around. The declinist school, it seemed, had rested on poor analysis.

For their part, Asians had always understood the extreme strength of American power, but the clear revival of America's cities drove the point home in popular Asian imagination.

Naturally, Los Angeles was my first stop after Hawaii in my journey across the US.

'Excuse me, have you been robbed lately?' The question, somewhat disconcerting, came from a young black man who had pulled up in a car beside me at a set of traffic lights in south central Los Angeles, the overwhelmingly black area that had been the epicentre of the race riots in the wake of the Rodney King verdict.

What struck me, as a first-time visitor to the area, apart from its being overwhelmingly black, was the high quality of the housing. If you didn't see the ubiquitous signs of the crime problem, among them bars on all the shop windows, you would take it for a very affluent neighbourhood. But the crime was pretty obvious. Along the main shopping streets, clusters of two or three people were fairly openly selling drugs. An Armenian companion (LA has lots of Armenians, mostly living in north Hollywood) told me that experienced Angelinos can tell the dealers by the way they move, the way they hold their bodies—ready for action. During my short drive through the district a police helicopter swooped overhead and police vehicles and personnel converged on the area. There'd been some disturbance; it turned out to be not very serious and the police dispersed.

But for most residents of Los Angeles, this is not the way they live. I don't think the enquiry at the traffic lights about whether I had been robbed lately was in any way hostile. Rather it was a friendly warning, a gesture of civic concern and fellowship, a good-natured way of telling me that I was being foolish in touring south central LA. I took the hint and went across to east LA where I found mainly Hispanic neighbourhoods. In some of these areas you could just as easily be in Mexico. Everyone in the street is Mexican, the signs and billboards are mostly in Spanish.

Determining where the real border lies between the US and Mexico is increasingly difficult. The economies continue to integrate under the North American Free Trade Agreement, while the physical border is extremely porous. People flow back and forth almost uncontrollably. Quite soon Hispanics will outnumber blacks and become the US's biggest minority.

Washington in fact is committed in principle to a free trade deal with the whole of Latin America. California, with its multicultural population increasingly drawn from both Latin America and Asia, is an area of particular interest.

Indeed, elites all over Asia should pay more policy attention to California. That at least is the thesis of Abe Lowenthal, the founder of the heavyweight Pacific Council on International Policy, based in Los Angeles. Lowenthal explained his thoughts to me over lunch in the boardroom of an LA bank, high up in a skyscraper in the small downtown area of the city. Despite the end of the Cold War being a decade past, America as a nation still has not worked out intellectually and politically what role it is going to play in the world. The last time it faced such a conundrum, after World War II, it solved it by convening small groups of wise men—in Washington, in New York and in a few Ivy League East Coast universities. That kind of elitist approach is impossible today and the new debate on America's global role is going to be much more open, democratic and messy. California, though, is far more conscious of Asia—through immigration, through the Asian involvement of West Coast businesses and through simple geography, than are the East Coast power centres.

Equally importantly, California has the biggest State economy in the US, it sends the biggest delegation to Congress, it dominates popular culture through Hollywood and leading edge technologies through Silicon Valley. Therefore if you are an internationalist in the Asia-Pacific, and you want to influence the US, you should put a substantial part of your effort into California. Furthermore, Lowenthal told me, California lacks the influential public policy institutions, especially those with an international focus, that the East Coast has in abundance. This comment is the Californian version of the old Asian lament, that America's interests are in the Pacific but its institutions are in the Atlantic.

The Asia-Pacific Economic Cooperation forum, founded by Australia in 1989, is one Asian effort at addressing this American institutional deficiency. But although America insisted on belonging to APEC from the very first day, its attention to APEC has been sporadic at best. Half the time the president can't be bothered attending the APEC summits and there is no sign that Washington gives APEC any significant priority. This is a pity because APEC is a beautiful structure for the US—it lays out the whole of the Asia-Pacific region for Washington and is premised on the idea that keeping the US intimately and constructively engaged in East Asia is in everyone's interests. But of course, while it pays lip service to multilateral institutions, the US, like most big powers throughout history, has been much happier dealing bilaterally; that is, dealing one-on-one with other nations. In a one-on-one dealing the disparity in size and power between the US and whoever it is dealing with is at its most significant, and this gives the US greater leverage. Despite the tradition of genuine idealism in American foreign policy, this preference for dealing from a position of absolute or maximum power has been strong among American policy makers and, sadly, has weakened Washington's commitment to APEC.

American idealism was on display for me at another venue in Los Angeles, the University of California. Speaking to an undergraduate class of about 200 at UCLA was a real pleasure because they were so receptive, so eager for new experiences. UCLA is a beautiful campus and its student body is very bright. It had had something like 33 000 applications for a first year intake of about

3000, the year I visited. A series of speakers that week, to whom the students all had access, included Kofi Annan from the United Nations, the former US National Security Adviser Tony Lake and the author Clyde Prestowitz.

What a dazzling array of experience and opportunity is offered to these students! By the time these kids graduate they will be well equipped for the global economy. Just the fact that they are enrolled at UCLA means that life has smiled kindly on them. And opportunity awaits.

But, bright as they are, their education when they first arrive at university has plenty of gaps. For they are, also, victims of Californian high schools. They are extremely good at manipulating symbols and working on computers, they are verbally fluent and especially good at asking questions, but they don't really know anything in depth and they haven't really read anything. The high school curriculum is so chopped up into tiny bits and pieces that the great integrating power of a liberal education is somewhat lost. I once heard Henry Kissinger remark that the present generation has the power to tap into astonishing amounts of information on any subject but no ability to integrate it into a knowledge of the past and no ability therefore to project it meaningfully into the future.

Of course, the kids at UCLA are the lucky ones. They will have these problems substantially remedied by the sheer quality of the education they receive there. The scale of resources available at an institution like UCLA is awesome, impressive by any standards.

Strolling around UCLA for a couple of days, two things are notable—the absence of blacks and the large numbers of Asians. The faculty members I talk to are in agonies over the decline in black enrolments, arising from legal decisions outlawing affirmative action in university enrolment policy. The staff are all committed to academic rigour and free, meritocratic advancement. But the ones I speak to are also deeply unhappy, truly distressed, about the lack of representation of African-Americans at UCLA. It's not good for UCLA and it's not good for the society as a whole, and it's certainly not good for the African-American community.

In conversations with many of the Asian kids they strike me

as pure gold-plated Americans, in accent, civic loyalty and in many ways in culture as well. But there's still an attachment of some kind to the Asian nations from which they, or their forebears, originally sprang. LA, they make me realise, is certainly one version of the future—cosmopolitan, vast, strikingly diverse. It's truly a global city and a powerful icon of the American dream.

But the American dream comes in many different varieties. After Los Angeles I travel to Penn State University in Pennsylvania. Pennsylvania, so the old saw has it, has two great liberal cities—Philadelphia and Pittsburgh—one at either end. And in the middle are Alabama and Mississippi.

This is no doubt unfair because in the middle, also, is Penn State. Again there seem to be few African-Americans in this heartland campus, one of the 'Big 10' in the Mid-West, the cradle of so much that is distinctively American in American civilisation. The Mid-West gets an unfair press internationally. It is often depicted as a rather hokey, narrowminded region. In fact its verdant plains are studded with dazzling metropolises—Chicago, St Louis—great cities and great centres of culture, learning and refinement.

Penn State, while apparently less diverse than UCLA or the American nation more generally, is nonetheless hardly homogeneous. I hear Spanish spoken in its corridors. I spend the night, through some oddity of local organisation, in a student hall and the rich noises of the campus provide a variegated accompaniment to repose, or attempted repose. First there is a sound of distant shouting, a dull roar almost like a football match or a crowd scene in an old-fashioned Hollywood blockbuster. Gradually the volume rises until I realise it is a march of women and some men chanting in that peculiar rally-rhythm of the demonstrating classes: 'No more date rape, reclaim the night! No more date rape, reclaim the night!'

Then there are various students running through corridors in the normal way. I turn the television on to observe an astounding program concerning women who have got pregnant by one of their brothers, and then ditched that brother to fall in love with another brother, taking incest beyond any reasonable bounds of abnormality. This must be a very small subset of sociopathology and I thrill with admiration for the energy and ingenuity of the program's producers in finding enough specimens to fill the half-hour. This is one of the talk shows for the exhibitionistically dysfunctional, a species of program in which America excels. This particular program involves what I later learn is a regular thing—an aborted fist fight between various of its participants.

But the most entertaining part of the evening comes when I turn in for the night. The walls are thin and next door, all through the night, a co-ed and her boyfriend discuss, in a kind of infinite, almost gruesome psychiatric detail, the various contours of their relationship and whether they truly need each other or not. In the US, the educated do not lead unexamined lives.

Penn State's students are less forthcoming, less obviously bright, than those at UCLA. But still they are a gifted and conscientious lot. Life is giving them inestimable benefits, in their being born in the richest country in the world, and in the vast resources being expended on their health and education.

Nothing could be a greater contrast with Penn State than New York. The first time I went to the Big Apple was way back in 1984. I remember rather timidly asking a cab driver whether my hotel would be a convenient place for him to take me. 'Aw get in the f. . . . this cab, man' came the response. But truly, on this later visit New York was transformed. I stayed in a modest hotel in the centre of Manhattan, near St Patrick's Cathedral. The first free hours I had spent just wandering around Manhattan. The sense of threat and menace from the 1980s had certainly disappeared under Mayor Giuliani's zero-tolerance crime policies and other city reforms. Without really being aware of where I was walking, I came across an area that looked vaguely familiar. Then I realised: it was Times Square. But where were the hookers, the drug dealers, the sex shops, the muggers? The place was so clean it looked as if you could eat your dinner off the sidewalk. 'Good grief, Giuliani,' I thought, 'this is New York, for God's sake!'

Later in the same day, walking in another part of Manhattan, I saw what I thought was a more traditional New York scene. Two black kids, teenagers, were chasing a white kid. Oh no, I thought, there's going to be a mugging here, maybe a homicide. What should I do? What *could* I do? But the two black kids caught up with the white kid and after a moment of good-natured horseplay all three collapsed in laughter. They were all friends. The pursuit had been innocent, a cheerful effusion of adolescent energy and camaraderie. This is the age of miracles in America.

That day I attended the late afternoon page-one conference of the *New York Times*, a venerable New York institution. Two of the stories vying for page-one treatment caught my attention. One was about local strip clubs complaining that they had been overly harassed by city anti-sleaze ordinances. They had to be at least 500 feet from a residence, school, hospital or the like. 'Can we describe these as mom-and-pop businesses?', one of the *Times* editors wisecracked.

The other story was that anti-Suharto student demonstrations in Indonesia were moving off the campuses and into the streets. Was this worthy of page one? My modest contribution to the history of the *New York Times* was to suggest very strongly that, yes, this certainly was worthy of page one.

One of the lead stories in the *Times* of that day showed just how cynical politics had become under the Clinton presidency. Clinton had decided not to fight Congress to get funding for needle exchange programs because the Republicans would demonise such programs. Yet the evidence strongly suggested that needle exchange programs reduced the number of infections, especially in the context of HIV-AIDS. As the *Times* journalist asked in the story: if the president, deep into his second term and already effectively a lame duck, not facing re-election, and enjoying a 60 per cent approval rating—if such a president will not fight for a life-saving health measure during an epidemic killing large numbers of Americans at home, just what *does* he stand for?

I pondered this as I left for the end-point and true destination of my journey across America—Washington DC.

Washington is a grand and imperial city. It is, paradoxically and perplexingly, the most important centre of the exercise of power in Asia, more important to Asia than Beijing or Tokyo or Jakarta or any other city actually located in Asia. The US Treasury was probably the single most important agency in the world concerning the Asian economic crisis. The International Monetary Fund, effectively an agent of American policy, is in Washington, as is the World Bank. The Pentagon, still at the centre of American policy, still one of the biggest single organisations of any kind in the world, radiates its power out of Virginia. The hardworking, but these days much less important, diplomats and analysts of the State Department toil in Foggy Bottom to process the vast interagency negotiations that constitute American policy. There is the Senate, the most powerful legislative body in the world, whose committee chairmen operate like quasi-independent princes in the vast Washington court. The National Security Council, the men and women at the president's elbow, providing the vital last brief to the chief executive before action. And the White House itself, the unique repository of history, hope, power and American resolve. And a thousand other agencies, countless lobbyists, dozens of thinktanks, a vast press corps, domestic and international, the most important diplomatic corps in the world.

If there is such a thing as a global capital today it is not New York, despite Manhattan's buzz and the presence of the United Nations, it is not Los Angeles, despite Hollywood and Silicon Valley, and it is certainly not any fading imperial centre like London or Paris. It is Washington, the city on the Potomac, the edifice to government in a nation congenitally suspicious and distrustful of government.

I lived and worked in Washington as a correspondent in the mid-1980s. To misuse a Maoist metaphor, the newspaper correspondent in Washington is a fish swimming in a sea of information. The selection every day is an embarrassment of riches—Jack Kemp speaking at a lunch at the Heritage Foundation, the president of India performing for the Press Club, Warren Christopher appearing at Brookings.

Asia suffers from Washington's Atlanticist bias and outlook. But be that as it may, Asians need to make a major effort in Washington. On this trip I go to see Stanley Roth, the Assistant Secretary of State for East Asia and the Pacific. On the floor of his office sit two posters, waiting to be hung on the wall. One is an election poster for Ferdinand Marcos, the other a newspaper front page from the day Marcos fled the Philippines in 1986. Roth, who was working closely in Congress at the time with the then congressional guru on Asia, Stephen Solarz, was up to his eyeballs in US efforts to assist Cory Aquino and hasten Marcos's departure.

But these days the State Department is not the key American

agency for Asia, trailing a long way behind both the Treasury and the Defence Department. Roth, like Madeleine Albright, the Secretary of State, seems a figure from the wrong era; the formulations about democracy and human rights seem too simplistic for the complexity of contemporary Asia. Roth is generous with his time and we discuss the issues of the day at length. Obviously he is a smart fellow, but he seems a little less self-assured, certainly more prickly, than his immediate predecessor, Win Lord. And, despite his position, he does not really impress as a first-division player in Washington.

Across town at the newly opened Nixon Centre I meet a man who was always a first-division player, Henry Kissinger. He is speaking at a seminar to commemorate the 25th anniversary of the fall of Saigon, that icon of American involvement in Asia. In a sense Kissinger has always been competent at dealing with Asia because he has always viewed it through one single but universal prism, the prism of power.

Kissinger's book, *Diplomacy*, is the best book I've ever read that deals with American foreign policy, although it deals with much else besides. *Diplomacy* is a scintillating mixture of systematic analysis, cultural intuition and telling personal anecdote. Kissinger takes almost a physicist's approach to international relations, in that he sees the task of diplomacy as an endless attempt to create stability, or equilibrium, in the international system. This is best achieved through promoting a stable balance of power so that the dominant nation of the day is constrained by an alliance of lesser nations.

The great exception to this systems analysis is the United States. Balance-of-power thinking is almost second nature to Europeans, but deeply foreign to Americans. Kissinger sets up the two poles of American foreign policy in the 20th century as Theodore Roosevelt and Woodrow Wilson. Roosevelt represents the classic realist or balance-of-power approach to foreign policy, superior to any other president of the 20th century, superior in this respect even to Nixon. Wilson, on the other hand, represents the approach of foreign policy idealism.

Kissinger is correct to recognise Teddy Roosevelt as the first American president psychologically and politically equipped to make America a great, global power, which is exactly what he did. Much of the discussion of America's position in Asia proceeds from the World War II settlement, the suzerainty over Japan, the commitment in Korea and the developing security architecture of the Cold War. But in truth the United States has been a major East Asian power for a hundred years, ever since, as Assistant Secretary of the Navy, Teddy Roosevelt almost singlehandedly engineered the Spanish–American war in which the US took possession of the Philippines, an act which, among other things, determined that the US would become a great naval power of the Pacific. And Washington has shown itself, for more than a hundred years, to be well able to use a combination of force, diplomacy and economic clout to protect what it regards as vital interests in Asia.

But Kissinger argues that in the end Wilson's idealism, though hopelessly misapplied, better reflected America's belief in the universality of its own principles and the obligation of America to promote those principles around the world. One of Kissinger's most powerful and important insights is, despite his own deeply cynical cast of mind, that idealism is virtually always a central element in the making of American foreign policy. This is one reason why American foreign policy is so often so unpredictable to outsiders. It doesn't always travel along normal national interest or balance-of-power lines. You will never understand American foreign policy, Kissinger argues, unless you understand the political significance of idealism as a force in the making of that policy.

Of course America is still a nation state and is forced at times to play balance-of-power games. But idealism, or at least some partial obeisance to idealism, has to be factored into even such calculations as those.

It would be wrong to suggest that Kissinger is cynical about America itself. Born a German Jew, he suffered a brutal childhood in the early years of Nazi rule and has every reason to love the animating ideas of America. Indeed, the tension between, on the one hand, Kissinger's natural central European, realpolitik, deeply analytical inclination and, on the other, his unsuppressed immigrant's love of America is a highly creative dynamic in his writing and thinking on Ameican foreign policy.

In *Diplomacy*, Kissinger provides a strong defence of Nixon's actions in Vietnam. When Nixon came to office 500 000 American troops were stationed in Vietnam. Even if he had wanted to, he could not have withdrawn them overnight. To have tried to do so could easily have produced chaos and panic, massive loss of American life and perhaps even an unbearable, ongoing hostage situation. Three years later, there were only 20 000 American troops in Vietnam, the cost of the war for America had been slashed and the South Vietnamese were handling the military situation relatively well. In a deeply unpopular view, Kissinger argues that South Vietnam could have continued in this way had it continued to receive American air support, or even perhaps merely logistic and economic support, as Nixon had envisaged. The congressional Democrats, the vandals of Vietnam, made sure that this was impossible.

That day at the Nixon Centre, however, Kissinger was less worried about the general historical justification he makes for Nixon's Vietnam policies, which is a justification generally against criticism from the Left. Instead, that day, he seemed to be seriously troubled by, and making a genuine effort to grapple with, criticism from the Right—that America had sold out its allies in South Vietnam. No doubt this reflected the composition of his audience—it was the Nixon Centre after all—but it also seemed that this was the one criticism which could really sting Kissinger and indeed which has often troubled Asians, not least former citizens of South Vietnam.

'Our tragedy was our domestic situation,' Kissinger told his audience. It was also the tragedy of the South Vietnamese.

And it was the tragedy of 50 000 American servicemen. A few days after the seminar at the Nixon Centre I took a cab down to the Vietnam war monument and walked along its shining black wall, pausing to read some of the names. In a nation so verbally fluent, so full of noise and entertainment and countless momentary distractions, I found a rare sense of peace and reverence. There was quiet at the Vietnam monument. Here and there a single person, or a small family group, had stopped to meditate on a particular name, a brother or a son or a husband, in some cases a father, whose name had been memorialised forever in a unique honour role. One middle-aged woman was quietly weeping. At a few points at the base of the monument someone had left flowers. One or two people took photographs of the name of their family member who had fallen in the line of duty. There is now a deep reverence for this memory in America and it is not before time. While Washington bungled its Vietnam commitment in countless ways, and while the question of its ultimate desertion of the South Vietnamese will never be answered satisfactorily, the conflict also embodied the enormous sacrifice in blood and treasure the United States was willing to make to a security commitment in South East Asia.

For at least the last 50 years commitment has been the key motif of America's involvement in Asia—commitment to Asian security, commitment to allies, commitment to certain values. These values Americans are often happy to call American values. But they believe American values should be universal values—not that they want to impose American cultural norms on Asia exactly, although it sometimes rather seems like that. But if pushed, most Americans concerned with Asia will argue that human rights, democracy, political and religious freedoms—things they identify as American values—are also universal values.

America has promoted these values in several ways. One is by war—the Japanese were not allowed to establish suzerainty over East Asia. They were stopped by American force of arms. Undoubtedly America went to war on the Korean peninsula to advance and protect its own national interests as it saw them, but it also was genuinely motivated by a desire to keep faith with the South Koreans, to offer them a chance of democracy and self-determination. Often the US has had to work with unpleasant allies, and the South Korean leadership at the time of the Korean War were hardly model democrats, or democrats of any kind for that matter. But America always pressures its allies to do better in terms of democracy and human rights, so that over time most American allies, such as South Korea or Taiwan, do become democracies and do respect their citizens' human rights.

The other main method of promoting and disseminating American values is through American technology and American popular culture. It is difficult when writing these days to think of a single literary reference with which it can be assumed that most of the writer's audience, even in predominantly English-speaking nations, will be familiar. This is a very different situation even from the 1960s, when Martin Luther King could deliver his magnificent 'I Have a Dream' speech, full of Biblical echoes, knowing that not only would an American audience have an ear attuned to such references, but so would most literate English-speaking international audiences. Now not even the Bible, much less Shakespeare or any lesser work from the great classical canon of the West, has that kind of universal recognition. But many elements of American popular culture do have that kind of almost universal recognition factor, even across vast and disparate cultures. It is easy to write journalism full of references to the film *Titanic*, or to such television shows as *The Simpsons*, or even older numbers such as *Dallas* or *Dynasty* or *The Bold and the Beautiful*. Michael Jackson, or even Oprah Winfrey, are undoubtedly easier references for most people to relate to than King Lear or Hamlet. All over Asia, from the truly trashy to the genuinely first rate, American popular culture is consumed in vast quantities. And it all gives a version, however distorted at times, of the American dream.

But perhaps the most effective method of spreading American values in Asia has been the oldest and the simplest of all—the power of example. This works in two ways, one of which is through the observations and experiences of that vast number of Asians who have lived in the United States and watched its raucous democracy, astonishing wealth and universal human rights in action.

It also works through the experience of the even greater numbers of Asians who have seen and experienced the American presence in Asia directly.

On almost the last stop of my journey through the United States I took a cab across the Potomac to Roslyn, Virginia, not far from the Pentagon, to talk to a man who for me, and for many others, symbolises perfectly the strength of American commitment to Asia, and who also demonstrates by his own life the power of example.

Rich Armitage is a barrel-chested, bald-headed, raspy-voiced Georgian. Years of daily workouts have given him biceps like titanium girders, he is relatively short but bulky, his bullet-head seems to sink into his oversize shoulders, a replacement tooth glistens. Yet he has the intellectual subtlety of a thin, reedy, policy-wonk in horn-rimmed spectacles. And, put simply, he has the heart of a lion.

From 1967 to 1973 Armitage served in the American Navy,

including three tours of duty in Vietnam. From 1973 he served as a military adviser to the South Vietnamese. Later he rose to be Assistant Secretary of Defence for International Security in the Reagan and Bush years. He is perhaps best known to Americans as Colin Powell's best friend. He is part of that permanent governing class in American national security, that class which knows all the secrets and has influence all the time, in government or out.

I have known Armitage since the late 1980s, and for me he is the ideal American. Rumbustious, informal, intellectually full of substance but without pretension, direct, democratic but fiercely committed to basic ideals, he has laid his life on the line for these ideals more than once, and in a sense does so every day. There is not a sliver of light between what he says and the way he lives.

Armitage was committed to the cause of the South Vietnamese but opposed to the way Washington waged the war. It seemed to him stupid to use American soldiers to fight a Vietnamese war when there were plenty of Vietnamese soldiers willing and able to do the job. This view emerged, not from an unwillingness to help an ally, but from a deeper respect than most Americans had for the capability and commitment of the South Vietnamese. And from a much more genuinely collegial view of what allied relationships should be.

I now put it to him, on a bright and brilliant day in his Virginia office, that Hollywood had depicted South Vietnamese soldiers almost universally as cowards. Armitage's response to Hollywood's slur is characteristic: 'As far as I'm concerned that's total and utter bullshit. In the units I saw they were as good or as bad as their leaders' (by which he means the South Vietnamese officers, not their American advisers).

'They had balls as big as anyone's. They were as good as American GIs.'

That is a big statement from a man profoundly in love with America's military traditions and profoundly protective of America's military honour.

But, he points out, there are special difficulties for a democracy in fighting a totalitarian dictatorship in war. At its most simple, the totalitarian dictatorship can inflict vastly more pain on its own people without the government falling. That gives it far greater manoeuvrability.

After the Paris peace agreements on Vietnam Armitage resigned his commission. He did this for several reasons but chief among them was his desire to stay in Vietnam and serve as a military adviser, which is what he did. The US was restricted to a small number of formal military personnel, so if he was going to stay that was the only way it could be accomplished.

In March 1975 he was back in the States, but had just returned from a visit to South Vietnam where he could see that it was going to hell. He ran into a friend in the Pentagon who asked him to go back and organise the evacuation of the South Vietnamese navy, a mission that Armitage, filled with concern for his old South Vietnamese allies, readily undertook. He went back to South Vietnam on 24 April on the last Pan Am flight in. His journey in, like so much of his experience in Vietnam, was almost ludicrously heroic. He had been told by American intelligence that Saigon would not fall until some time in May, a fatal miscalculation (Saigon fell on 30 April) which hampered all manner of American efforts. At times on his journey into the interior of South Vietnam he was confronted by South Vietnamese troops desperate to get out, at least one of whom pulled a gun on Armitage and demanded to be taken with him. Well, you can come with me, Armitage told him, but I'm going in, not out.

The Ford administration in Washington had primarily in mind for this evacuation exercise the destruction of matériel that could possibly be of use to the North Vietnamese. Instead, Armitage organised a vast flotilla of boats to take out South Vietnamese navy personnel and their families. It was a desperate and terrible business; in the days leading up to the evacuation they were constantly being shelled. Many times Armitage should have been killed in the process.

Eventually, just before the fall of Saigon, Armitage had got nearly 30 000 South Vietnamese out of the country and into the South China Sea. In some ways that was only the beginning of the problem. He saw Soviet aircraft observing his flotilla and was worried about the possibility of being attacked again from the air. He had sick and wounded people with him. Eventually he made contact with an American naval vessel in the area and told an astonished captain to check his authority with the Pentagon and then provide protection for the group's trip to the Philippines. The Ford administration was not looking for refugees from this process but really had no alternative but to comply with Armitage's request. The Philippines' then president, Ferdinand Marcos, was so discombobulated that after they all arrived in the Philippines he had Armitage put under a form of house arrest for a few days—to show the North Vietnamese that the whole amazing operation was not some conspiracy the Philippines had cooked up. Virtually all the people Armitage took out of Vietnam ended up in the United States.

The whole action was so completely American—heroic, extraordinary, responsible, relying on the honour and initiative of a single individual, a redemption of a debt, an obligation freely entered into and subsequently borne with courage and complete commitment.

'The great majority of the people who came with us were civilians,' Armitage recalls, 'family members, anyone who could get on [the boats] got on. My government was unamused at the arrival of these 30 000 extra problems. I was told to deny the [South Vietnamese naval] units to the enemy. I thought I would do that by getting them to the Philippines. They were the first wave of the boat people.'

And Armitage's judgement on it all now? 'It was the right thing to do in my lights. We [Americans] generally do the right thing, after exhausting all the other possibilities.'

Of course, a commitment like this shapes and defines a life. Armitage subsequently sponsored about ten separate Vietnamese families as immigrants to the United States. But Vietnam changed his life in another, unexpected way as well. Armitage and his wife have two children of their own, now grown up. But they have also adopted six children, who have taken their names and become in every sense part of their family. Three of these kids are African-Americans. Altogether, the Armitages have fostered more than 30 children for different periods of time. And again it is all directly down to Vietnam.

Armitage recalls: 'I was spending a lot of time in Thailand at Arunyaprathet [a town near the border of Thailand and

Cambodia which became famous as a major refugee camp] after the fall of South Vietnam. I found a little girl there who had been left totally alone, no relatives, nothing. I had enough sway with the Thais to organise it so that my wife and I were going to foster her back in the US. But then at the last minute an uncle or something turned up and said to me: 'I know you can offer her a lot more than I can but you've got to remember, I've lost my whole family, she's all I've got.' So I agreed to that. But then my wife and I were surprised to find just how much we'd set our hearts on fostering that little girl. Later a woman rang my wife and asked whether we'd be interested in fostering here in the US. Now we've had more than 30 kids in fostering situations.'

Some of those kids had crack-addicted mothers or had been otherwise hard to place in foster care. Armitage says he didn't set out to change the world with any of this. Having a biracial family has been fun, he says, and has involved his learning about the different grooming styles for African-Americans—but even there he didn't particularly have making any racial statement in mind. It's just the way it happened. Armitage is a truly colour blind conservative. He hates racism; he also hates responses to racism that further exaggerate the fact of race. He tells his children a simple lesson in dealing with racism, one found in his friend Colin Powell's autobiography: 'Don't let their problem become your problem.'

I have often discussed race with Armitage and find him absolutely committed to racial equality, to judging each individual by his or her merits rather than assigning them any preconceived qualities based on race. But he is also impatient with the traditional liberal responses on race, which often trap people in negative stereotypes or even seek to exploit such stereotypes. The racial situation is mixed in the United States, he says, but overall he thinks race relations are getting better.

Armitage's optimism is a key to his personality. It is one of the reasons he's a Republican rather than a Democrat—he believes Republicans are more optimistic than Democrats. It is one of the most American things about him, the unshakeable faith that you can make a difference, that you can make things better.

While we are talking Colin Powell rings, and Armitage's

secretary is popping in and out as her boss tries to return a call to a former prime minister of Jordan. It is perhaps this familiarity, this ease, with power that has occasionally made Armitage the centre of bizarre conspiracy theories. Ross Perot, businessman and failed presidential candidate, nominated Armitage as, would you believe, an agent of the Vietnamese Communist Party concealing the existence of American MIAs (servicemen missing in action) in Vietnam. Perot spouted a vast range of other accusations at Armitage, all of them wholly groundless. It is a feature of conspiracy theories to sometimes turn reality absolutely upside down, so that some Americans once thought Eisenhower, a war hero and in later life the very embodiment of avuncular Republican conservatism, a communist agent. Armitage took Perot's temporary attentions stoically enough but hit back several times in the press with devastating critiques of Perot.

Armitage has been at the centre of countless, crucial issues between the US and Asia. He acted as the Bush administration's negotiator with the Philippines over whether the US bases at Subic Bay and Clark Air Field would be maintained or closed. After a tortuous and tough negotiation Armitage finally succeeded in getting an agreed position with Cory Aquino's Government, but the Aquino Administration could not get the deal ratified by the Philippines Senate and the bases ultimately closed.

Armitage's recollection of the motive for trying to hang on to the bases is instructive: 'Had it not been for Japan, Singapore and Australia we would not even have tried to negotiate staying there.' His point is that with the end of the Cold War there was no strict military need for the bases in the Philippines and the US defence budget was under pressure and coming down. But the American security order in the Pacific was still critically important. Washington did not want to give the impression, to allies or to potential adversaries, that it was losing heart for the commitment. So it decided to stay on in the Philippines and to make it clear to the whole of Asia that it was willing to do so. This was despite Armitage's own doubts, and his feeling that perhaps Philippines–US relations would best be served by the closure of the bases, so that all the post-colonial neuralgia in that relationship could be dissipated.

'We talked about the alliance, but for them [the Filipino

politicians] it was just a matter of money. I said to them I don't like dealing with cash register diplomats. Now they have to take the blame or the credit for their own situation themselves.

'We got an agreement with the Philippines Government eventually but they couldn't get it through their Senate. It caused tremendous conflict in the Philippines. But everyone in Asia knew that this was not the doing of the United States. And then others in Asia stepped up to the plate in terms of offering port access to US ships.'

Thus, although in the end the US lost its bases in the Philippines, Armitage made it clear to everyone in Asia that this was not a sign of declining American commitment to Asian security. That commitment, the clear reaffirmation of that commitment, as Armitage clearly saw, was crucial, both to America's standing in Asia and to the reality of Asian security itself.

The other great strategic initiative with which Armitage was intimately associated was the development and application of the Reagan Doctrine.

The Reagan Doctrine, which was crucial in ending the Cold War, held that just as the Soviet Union gave financial and other support to insurgent movements in nations that were friendly to the United States, so the US would help movements challenging undemocratic regimes aligned, formally or informally, with the Soviet Union. The Reagan Doctrine had its most obviously effective application in Afghanistan. The effort to support forces resisting Soviet occupation of Afghanistan enjoyed bipartisan support in America. On the other hand the Reagan Doctrine had its most controversial application in Central America, where President Reagan's determination to help the anti-Sandinista Contras was bitterly opposed by the Democratic majority in Congress.

The strategic purpose of the Reagan Doctrine was twofold: to give moral and material support to forces fighting for freedom in contested countries; and to radically raise the cost to the Soviet Union of maintaining its empire. At least in the second of these aims it was devastatingly effective. In its sense of self-confident competition with the Soviets, in its abandonment of the equivocations of détente and the left liberal consensus of the 1970s, it was classically Reagan. Combined with the missile defence systems envisaged in Reagan's Strategic Defence Initiative, which was derided by the experts but taken deadly seriously by the Soviets, it presented an America moving way ahead of the Soviets in strategic competition. It gave full weight to Washington's huge superiority in economic and technological resources over Moscow.

Armitage, having served on Reagan's interim foreign policy advisory body before the presidential inauguration and then taken up a senior position in the Pentagon, played a central role in formulating congressional testimony on the Reagan Doctrine and giving it a coherent rationale.

'It was just a given that we were going to take it to them [the Soviets] everywhere. From the first day on we started undermining them in Eastern Europe. Reagan was the culmination of 50 years of American strategic policy. He brought about a victory over the Soviet Union. The other thing Reagan brought was a sense of America's optimism. He got up every morning rarin' to go. He was a very necessary president for that time.

'The Reagan Doctrine grew out of opposing an expansionist Soviet Union wherever and whenever. But it was not a case of my enemy's enemy is my friend. Assistance had to be appropriate. We wouldn't work with the Khmer Rouge in Cambodia, for example. But we made it clear to the Soviets that no battlefield was beyond our reach or beyond our interest. The arguments about it had to do with how you opposed the Soviets in certain cases.'

Ironically, Armitage says, the bipartisan support for applying the doctrine in Afghanistan overlooked the fact that it was always pretty clear that, when the Soviets left, the Afghanis would fall on each other. Whereas the policy in Central America, which excited fanatical opposition in Congress and more widely, was actually a policy with a much broader moral intent—in that Washington was determined to leave behind political arrangements that were better, more democratic, than those which went before. And, without reprising all the tortuous arguments about Washington's long intervention in Central America, it is true that the Reagan and Bush administrations did pressure their Central American allies to behave in a more democratic fashion.

The Reagan Doctrine certainly played a part in demoralising the Soviet Union. From the perspective of today that may seem an historical triviality—that the Soviet system was always destined to implode, to be crushed by the weight of its own internal contradictions. The inevitability of eventual Soviet collapse, an understanding of the Soviet Union's essential brittleness, was always Reagan's personal view, but in this he was in a small minority, even among fellow Cold War warriors. Here a leap of the historical imagination is required. For much of the Cold War it was by no means clear who was going to be the eventual victor. For many years the amount of territory and population around the globe that owed at least nominal allegiance to one of the two great poles of the communist system grew steadily. In many ways the Soviets seemed to have a clarity, and certainly a ruthlessness, of purpose which the West lacked. But their system was internally decadent in a fatal fashion. And the challenge that Reagan threw out to them was simply too great.

Armitage's judgement? 'I think the real cost of the Reagan Doctrine to the Soviet Union was more political and psychological than economic—just to find that the regimes they were supporting were doing so badly in so many ways.'

Armitage hasn't worried too much about Asian values because he is so utterly colour blind himself and regards human values as universal. He has deeply internalised America's universalist promise to mankind: that these values are open to anyone. But he does acknowledge the political consequences of differing cultural inclinations: 'We tend to emphasise the idea of the rights of the individual; Asian societies tend to go straight to societal rights. That gets translated into families first, then relatives, then the clan.' Nonetheless, he points to the numerous Asian democracies as obvious proof that democracy is not inimical to Asian culture.

But he likes the American idea of citizenship and believes that America's diversity is one of its great strengths. He worries that anti-Americanism could make a comeback in Asia, and declares: 'The absolute need for American leadership in Asia is a *sine qua non.*'

Armitage is the straightest man I know. He also seems to enjoy life more than almost anyone I know, by which I don't mean that he indulges in extravagant or gross pleasures, but that he's on good-humoured terms with the world and with himself. One day in Washington I rang up Rich for a coffee. We met on a Saturday morning because he was busy during the week participating in a war simulation for the Army. The Army had asked him to play the role of president in this simulation. As he drove me back to my hotel in the centre of the District, I asked: 'How did it feel to be president?'

He looked at me and grinned. 'It felt pretty damned good!'

As I left Washington for home I knew that no investigation of Asian values could possibly have been undertaken without considering that great force in history, America's friendship with Asia. The United States is the most powerful nation in Asia, economically, militarily, culturally, politically. The manner in which it exercises that power will have a huge bearing on Asia's success, and on America's success too.

The path for America in Asia should never be too confusing. If it pays attention to its own essential and historical values, America will fulfil Asia's every wish for its behaviour in the region. But of course for this to happen the idea of America's historic role in Asia needs to beat in the hearts of men, it needs to give life to friendships across the Pacific, to human beings who share ideals as well as interests.

For interests are permanent, but friendships can be broken.

14

ASIAN VALUES ON THE ROAD AGAIN

AND SO WE HAVE come to the end of our journey. Still we are unable to state precisely, in a neat formula, what Asian values are. Mind you, greater minds than ours, both Asian and Western, have tried to in the past, without much success. One of the greatest formula-makers for Asian values was Indonesia's founding president, Sukarno. He provided at least three ideological constructs for values to guide his society. In some respects the most appealing was Marhaenism. This was based on a poor farmer, probably apocryphal, whom Sukarno said he had met; a man named Marhaen. The doctrine was meant to embody the concern of Sukarno, and by extension the Indonesian state, for the fate of poor farmers and for the central position that such folk should occupy in the concerns of the nation.

Marhaenism was interesting because it represented an Indonesian attempt to find an indigenous version of socialism, and socialism of a relatively Marxist kind. Naturally, in an overwhelmingly rural society as Indonesia was when Sukarno ruled, it was a bit silly to talk of the historical role of the industrial proletariat. So Sukarno, who was trying, albeit in a rather slapdash fashion, to create an Indonesian version of socialism, sensibly substituted Marhaen and all he represented for the rhetorical device of the working class, or the proletariat. Marhaenism, however, did not last.

Sukarno also gave us guided democracy, another attempt to indigenise external values. Sukarno found Indonesia's experiment with open, real democracy in the 1950s to be messy and difficult to manage. His solution was to return to a more authoritarian form of government, with himself at its apex. Yet he did not completely destroy civic society. Indeed, intense competition and factionalism between the communists and the military, and organised Islam, continued during the guided democracy period. But that need not detain us here; the point is that Sukarno was again trying to construct an alternative with an indigenous flavour, one that embodied the tradition of consultation in the word 'democracy' and the tradition of leader-centric civil society in the word 'guided'.

Sukarno's most important such effort was undoubtedly the creation of Pancasila as the official state ideology of Indonesia, a concept which his successor Suharto embraced wholeheartedly and which formed the official ideology of Indonesia throughout the Suharto period. As we saw in Chapter 3 on Indonesia, Pancasila is a vague formulation which requires belief in one God—but does not make Indonesia an Islamic state—and then adds democracy, social justice, humanism and nationalism as additional desirable civic virtues. It was too vague to have much meaning apart from its central purpose of finding a religiously acceptable compromise which did not leave Indonesia either as a wholly secular state or as an Islamic state.

In this way Pancasila did serve an at least partly useful purpose but it was also used crudely to deny the legitimacy of Islamic political activism for much of the Suharto era. And other than that it was vague and vacuous, so much so that even though the government required organisations to accept it as their official ideology, even though compulsory courses were held on it for civil servants, it never really acquired any animating force of its own.

That is why this book has not been much concerned with such official formulations but rather has travelled the more unpredictable route of investigating what Asians regard as Asian values.

It should not be thought that Sukarno and Indonesia were unique in providing such formulations of desirable civic virtues. Singapore in 1990 introduced a White Paper on Shared Values. These values were: nation before community and society before self; the basic unit of society to be the family; community support for the individual; consensus instead of contention; and racial and religious harmony. These are actually a pretty fair reflection of the values that most Singaporeans would approve and share. Yet the particular formulation in the White Paper didn't really take off and achieve a life of its own.

The mainland Chinese are of course without peer in constructing endless slogans and neat ideological formulations. When I lived in China for a period in the mid-1980s the chief state invocation was: 'Marry late, have one child, support the four modernisations!'

Yet being, (formally at least), a Marxist state made China so prone to ideological lurches that even the people designated by the state to explain the ideology tended to try to hedge their bets—as I found when interviewing officials from the Marxism-Leninism-Mao Zedong Thought Institute. The latest great guiding slogan, 'Socialism with Chinese Characteristics', seems at least as vacuous and plastic as Pancasila, and derives its consequence more from the government's decision to use it to license certain activities than because it is an authentic wellspring of cultural life.

Such examples of more or less failed slogans do not invalidate the idea of Asian values. Rather they actually confirm the idea, in two crucial ways. First, the fact that governments are groping to give expression to what they regard as their national genius, their enduring, distinctive national culture, in a modernising context indicates a realisation that there is something of value, and something that people want to keep, in their indigenous culture. There are, in other words, Asian values. And secondly, if paradoxically, the very failure of a slogan to capture and contain those values indicates that they are living, breathing cultural forces, too subtle, too slippery, above all too alive, to be captured by a document designed by a government committee.

That is the situation of most nations, not just Asian ones. Very few people in very few countries know many of the words of their Constitution, for example.

The United States is an exception, mainly because its most important prismatic documents were forged in warfare and struggle. My own purely subjective assessment is that the three greatest American documents of this kind are the Declaration of

Independence, the Gettysburg Address and Martin Luther King's 'I Have a Dream' speech. And it is instructive that these three magnificent statements of American values issued from, respectively, the War of Independence in the 18th century, the Civil War in the 19th century and the civil rights struggle in the 20th century. One great defining document per century is actually a pretty good batting average for any nation. And of course these American documents embody universal as well as American values.

Only the Declaration of Independence could remotely be seen as emerging from a government committee of the type that drafted Singapore's Shared Values paper. The other two came from the individual hands of American political geniuses at the highest pitch of mortal struggle over fundamental issues. Even in these cases, the power of America's popular culture, and the conscious commitment of its education system to promulgating and immortalising these documents, have had a lot to do with their wide dissemination. Of course, no amount of government promotion would have worked had each of these not been a superb statement of human values in itself. But America's position as the dominant generator of popular culture in the world—the numerous movies featuring Abe Lincoln, for example—is not irrelevant here.

Asia too has produced its memorable wordsmiths of freedom and democracy and more broadly of transcendent human values—José Rizal, Kim Dae Jung, Mahatma Gandhi, Benigno Aquino, Sun Yat Sen, Lu Xun, Aung San Suu Kyi and countless others. And these, as well as championing different ideas of freedom, have represented different sets of values. The idea that there is no such thing as Asian values must mean that José Rizal, Kim Dae Jung and the rest are not Asians.

And this, again, is only to consider the hotly contested arena of politics. Can anyone who has read the hauntingly beautiful novels of Malaysia's K. S. Maniam, the densely allusive works of Korea's Yi Mun-yol, the vast historical tapestry constructed by the Philippines' Francisco Sionil José in his Rosales saga novels, really believe that they are not communicating Asian values?

That too many in the West, especially the United States, have been deprived of the pleasures of reading any of these novelists is a sign that the globalisation of culture is not yet global enough.

Everybody in the world who reads will read novels about New York, but very few people outside Malaysia will read a novel about Kuala Lumpur. The people who suffer most from this are not Asians, who are starting to turn on to both their own national literary tradition and those of their neighbours, while of course, like everyone else on the globe, having access to the traditions of Manhattan and Hollywood. No, the people who suffer most from the non-global nature of the sources of globalisation of popular culture are those in the United States, and in the West more generally, who are deprived of so much of the fabulous diversity and genius of such a big stream of the human family.

To overcome this widespread deprivation, as I say, globalised culture will need to become more truly global. And technology is probably helping in this. The vast increase in the power of information technology allows a single cultural product, like the splendid movie, *Titanic*, to achieve an astonishing worldwide acceptance, so that even China's president, Jiang Zemin, is blown away by Kate Winslet and Leonardo DiCaprio's romance. But the new information technology also allows fine differentiation, the development of market niches; as well as audience agglomeration you get differentiation. The Taiwan market wants Taiwan movies. Satellite television for India needs to have, as well as a bit of *Melrose Place* and *Beverly Hills 90210*, Indian soap operas and Indian versions of *MTV.*

Information technology first of all allows groups and individuals within a nation to communicate with each other. Then it allows communications across nations. With any luck at all, this process is going to enrich the cultural diets of us all in the decades ahead. In particular, the vast cultural treasure-houses of Asia are waiting to be explored, by Asians and Westerners alike. For such exploration to be successful, Westerners especially must learn much, much more about Asian values. And for this purpose, and in their own interests, many in the West are going to need a new openness in the way they think about Asia. They are going to have to accept some Asian categories of intellectual and political life, rather than always trying to fit Asia into the neat prejudices and formulas of Western political discussion.

This is the case also because, notwithstanding the regional economic crisis of the late 1990s, East Asia will gradually make its way back on to the main stage of global history. Its economies will again come to grow more rapidly than most Western economies. It will resume the trajectory of catching up, although of course catching up is going to take a long time. But even if it were rapid, it need not fill the West with fear, just as its delay due to the economic crisis ought not fill the West with phoney and transient triumphalism. It just means that eventually Chinese culture, Japanese culture, Korean culture, even Indonesian and Thai culture, and of course Indian culture too, will have to have more weight in world affairs because their respective national economies will have more weight. It's wrong though, to be an economic determinist in thinking about this. Nothing is absolutely inevitable. The extraordinary international success of Indian literature in English demonstrates that the power of cultural virtuosity can operate independently of generally poor economic performance (notwithstanding the Indian economy's recent exciting improvements). Culture can succeed even when economics fails.

Be that as it may, the basic point is that the West needs to shake itself up in its perceptions of Asia. This applies particularly to the United States because the US is by a vast distance the most powerful nation in the world, and certainly the most powerful national influence in Asia. Yet it applies with even greater poignancy, greater pressing urgency, to Australia because Australia is the one society of generally Western derivation that lives on the edge of East Asia and ought therefore to make itself, of all the Western nations, by far the most expert on Asia.

Sam Huntington included an extraordinary passage about Australia in his book, *The Clash of Civilizations and the Remaking of World Order*. In this book he describes Australia as a classically 'torn' country, a country which cannot decide whether it is part of one civilisational grouping or another, in this case the West or Asia. Huntington argues that Australia's prime minister in the early 1990s, Paul Keating, tried to get Australia to defect from the West and join Asia. This move is unlikely to succeed, according to Huntington, because the majority of Australians don't want it and the Asian elites also don't want it. Keating, according to Huntington, constantly offended his Asian interlocutors with his coarse language and rough political manner, characteristics of Australians which Asians naturally dislike.

Huntington sees Australia as irretrievably culturally cut off from the Asian mainstream by its dialectical and sometimes didactic ways. He accepts a general view of Asian values, describing Asians as 'subtle, indirect, modulated, devious, non-judgemental, non-moralistic and non-confrontational'. Australians, on the other hand, he says, are 'the most direct, blunt, outspoken, some would say insensitive people in the English-speaking world'.

Keating's mistake, Huntington argues, was to give more weight to economics than culture. But Huntington has a solution. Referring to Keating's desire to end Australia's gossamer-thin remaining link to the British monarch and become a full-fledged republic, Huntington proposes the exciting and radical idea that Australia should align itself with the United States!

Huntington's analysis is so wrong on so many fronts it is in its way a little breathtaking. But its chief service is to show how comprehensively misunderstood Australia's efforts to engage with Asia can be by those without an intimate knowledge of Australia.

For a start, Huntington's facts are ropey. Like many democratic leaders, Keating was extremely rough in dealing with domestic opponents, but he never behaved that way when dealing with international leaders. Most hard-edged democratic leaders are like that. Keating famously had a close friendship with former Indonesian president Suharto, a very Asian leader. Huntington might just as easily have figured the inter-cultural ramifications of that friendship into his simplistic culture as destiny calculus. Similarly Filipino politics, and certainly the Filipino press, are more raucous than the Australian variety but that hardly disqualifies the Philippines from participation in the Asian region.

But all that in a sense is trivial. What is much more important is that Huntington seems to have entirely misunderstood the nature and content of Australia's engagement with Asia under Keating, especially in its strategic dimension. Australia is already aligned with the United States, not least through a formal military alliance. Keating was the strongest champion of APEC among any national leader in the Asia-Pacific. And his whole purpose in that endeavour was to tie the US into Asia.

Keating believed, and passionately argued, that Australia's Asian engagement amplified and enhanced its connection with the United States, that Australia became of more use and interest to Washington because of its deep involvement with Asia, while at the same time becoming of more use and interest to Asia because of its deep, intimate links with the United States. Australia has been a formal ally of the US since shortly after World War II. The alliance is unbroken and no one was more devoted to it than Keating.

Indeed, Keating's successor, John Howard, has taken up a similar theme with a different verbal formulation, that Australia does not have to choose between its geography and its history. Very few Australians who argued for an intensified Asian engagement saw this as coming at the expense of Australia's alliance or broader connections with the United States. Certainly, Keating did not. So Huntington's entire construction of Australia's Asian engagement is misplaced.

Rather, and this is really where Australia is a fascinating case, the more Australia commits itself to the conscious New World ethos that the United States has historically championed, the more it is enthusiastic about the Asian embrace. It is an ambivalence in Australia concerning the ethos of being explicitly and normatively a New World nation that has contributed so much to making Australia timid and unsure about its embrace of Asia.

Ronald Reagan once said that Australia would be the America of the 21st century. Reagan was paying Australia a handsome compliment and there is certainly a strand of Australian politics and traditional development thinking which would agree with Reagan's aspiration for Australia.

In any event, the bottom line is, in an almost exact reverse of Huntington's analysis, if Australia became more like America, with all its optimism and self-belief, and all its openness to new ideas and new people, it would embrace Asia much more deeply, not least through an expanded immigration program.

Many of the representative Western responses to Asia, especially to Asia's extraordinary economic success in recent decades and then its shuddering economic crisis, have been extremely unsatisfactory in their explanatory power, their value as forecasts of what is likely to happen and the reflection they offer of Western values.

Let's take a few examples.

Chalmers Johnson, Karel Van Wolferen and the rest of the school of revisionist scholars on Japan gave the strong impression that there was something fundamentally illegitimate about Japan's previous economic success. Theirs was the mercantilist theory of Japanese economics, that somehow economics had other rules when undertaken by the Japanese. Skating over all the great cultural difficulties the Japanese had to confront when they entered the American market after World War II they then saw any cultural difficulties Americans had in the Japanese market as entirely illegitimate and unfair. They massively overestimated the power of the Japanese Government. But before the regional economic crisis they also helped give respectability to a lot of American animus towards Japan. In so far as other Asian nations were seen as emulating the Japanese model the animus was directed at them too.

Sam Huntington, whose book *The Clash of Civilizations and the Remaking of World Order* has figured in the discussions in these pages, at least had the virtue of taking Asian cultures seriously. But if anything he took them too seriously. His thesis was, in approximate terms, that culture is destiny, especially geopolitical destiny. And he saw both Confucian cultures and the Japanese culture as inherently in competition with the West, led naturally by the United States. His response was a version of 'circle the wagons'. If economists traditionally give culture too little weight, Huntington gave it too much, and distorted it by treating it simplistically and deterministically (despite the genuine and great erudition of his work, and his deserved high standing as a scholar).

Huntington's view was in a sense a kind of Calvinism of geopolitics. Free will was lost and predestination ruled. Societies, unlike individuals, could no longer choose their friends and enemies—that was all determined by culture. Yet the contrary examples were endless. Could Japan and the United States really not be allies because they were of different cultural origin? What a depressing and terrible fate for humanity! Wasn't there a way in which cultures, and multitudinous voices within cultures, could be in dialogue with each other that was not only dynamic but constructive? In any event, his prognostications seemed to be all wiped out by the regional economic crisis.

Francis Fukuyama, in his original essay *The End of History* and his subsequent book *The End of History and the Last Man*, was the opposite of Huntington. For Huntington, in the post–Cold War world, ideology was nothing and culture everything. Fukuyama read precisely the opposite lesson from the same data—that culture was nothing, or next to nothing except for a few nations still 'trapped in history', but the ideology of liberal democratic capitalism was everything and that all the world would converge on the one political and economic model.

I found the temper of Fukuyama's arguments much more appealing than those of Huntington, but really they were no more satisfactory as explanations for the real world as it really existed. The end of communism did not mean the end of ideological conflict, especially ideological conflict within societies as opposed to between societies. The world did not converge upon a shining single model, not least because the world was too dynamic and the international financial system too powerful and capricious. But, for the purposes of this discussion, the main fault I find with Fukuyama, though his writing is dazzling and his thesis in many ways appealing, is that it gives insufficient weight to Asian values—that is, to the traditions, genius and distinctiveness of the Asian societies that were apparently going to be swept up in the end of history.

Fukuyama repeats this mistake in an otherwise highly perceptive essay on the Asian economic crisis in the February 1998 issue of *Commentary*, a New York journal published by the American Jewish Committee. This essay, 'Asian Values and the Asian Crisis', is actually one of the best, and least triumphalist, interpretations of the crisis to appear in America. Like many other Western analysts Fukuyama attributes too much of the idea of Asian values to just two leaders, namely Lee Kuan Yew and Dr Mahathir, although he also says that the concept had great appeal to China's leadership. However, he does at least acknowledge a wider constituency in Asia for Asian values, commenting: 'In part it reflected the genuine pride felt by many people in the region at the stunning success of their economies over the previous two generations.'

At its heart, though, Fukuyama's argument against the idea of Asian values is that Asia is diverse and no one set of values can be said to encompass all of Asia. But, as I have argued in this book, that is really a footnote to the debate on Asian values, a tedious bit of definitional throat clearing. No one with any knowledge of Asia has ever argued that there is one set of easily encapsulated values that can be applied across the whole of Asia.

Fukuyama's essay is notable for three other important insights. First, he analyses the Asian economic crisis mainly in economic terms, avoiding the facile and unenlightening idea that the crisis was caused by Asian values. Many American commentators seem to hold the peculiarly strange and contradictory notion that Asian values do not exist and yet, while not existing, caused the economic crisis. One sees this in countless references to the 'dark side of Asian values' in many American business and political journals.

Second, Fukuyama makes the point that many Asian societies had relatively low levels of corruption given the rapid development they experienced and the extensive power wielded by their bureaucrats.

However, his most important and interesting insight—a little reminiscent of Kishore Mahbubani's in *Can Asians Think?*—is that Asian values may have their greatest significance not in politics but in social relations. Dealing primarily but not exclusively with North East Asian societies he points out that many East Asian societies, have experienced rapid and sustained economic growth without the breakdown in marriage, the rise in teenage pregnancies, drug use, youth alienation and so on that are often observed in the United States and in the West more generally. He attributes this in part to Asia's much lower stress on individualism but also, crucially, to the entirely different expectations of women in most Asian societies, where they are still expected to spend many if not most of their career years on full-time home making and child raising.

Fukuyama then goes on to argue that the economic reforms required to make Asia competitive again will likely destroy the segregated expectations of the sexes and therefore destroy Asian social exceptionalism. In my view it is far too early to make such a call.

But, more broadly, Fukuyama does not confront the implications of his important and intriguing insight. If Fukuyama is right then feminism in the West, and the abandonment in the West by women of their traditional roles, have contributed a great deal to all the social pathologies of marital breakdown and the like. This need not necessarily lead to a conservative call for a re-creation of the 1950s but does suggest that some questioning of the dominant social liberalism in the West might be in order and that Asian societies offer an interesting point of comparison. If Asian values were accepted more readily as a politically neutral but culturally rich concept, it would be easier for some dispassionate comparative analysis of this kind to figure in more mainstream Western discussions.

Fukuyama's ideas provoke another interesting reflection. During the 1980s and 1990s the Left in the West was virtually disappearing as a political force. Mainstream left-of-centre parties, such as the Democrats in the US, Labour in Britain and Labor in Australia, were still politically competitive but only at the expense of becoming de facto conservative parties. But hardly anyone on the Left looked to any Asian societies for inspiration or even comparison. Yet Japan for example offered much that at first blush the Left in the West should have liked—heavy government intervention in the economy, strong social solidarity, strong communalism, a full acceptance by corporations of their social obligations to their employees, indeed the construction of employment as essentially a social contract between company and individual, and an overall social and familial solidarity that saw very few people completely marginalised or alienated from their own society. This sounds like a left-wing communalist's dream. The problem of course was that accompanying all this, in fact underlying it, was a strong acceptance of traditional authority, especially patriarchal authority residing in the male head of the household.

Thus the patterns of social authority in East Asian societies were anathema to the Left in the West, even though those patterns of authority underlay an overall communalism which at the very least should have been of intense interest to the Left. It raises the question: Is effective communalism, effective social solidarity, only possible in situations of very strong authoritarianism? I don't know the answer to that question but the fact that it was hardly ever debated on the Left shows that, like the

Right, the Left assumes that all the answers exist only in the West and there is absolutely nothing, apart from the sterile and anachronistic rhetoric of anti-colonialism, to be learned from Asian societies.

All of these intellectual deficiencies in the West derive from a failure to take Asian values seriously.

There are other examples of unsatisfactory Western responses to Asia. There was a school of thought, especially in the United States, that saw China as emerging rapidly as a serious strategic competitor with the US. This school became especially prominent as Japan's economic performance started to fade and the need to find a new enemy, a new threat, now that the Soviet Union was gone, became more acute. This was always more a tribute to China's potential rather than its power. It overstated China's ability to offer that strategic competition.

And finally there was a diverse range of purely economic theories purporting to explain the rise of Asia, and therefore the whole of Asia.

Of these the most entertaining in some ways was provided by the renowned international economist-celebrity, Paul Krugman. In 1994 in the journal *Foreign Affairs* Krugman published an article entitled 'The Myth of the Asian Miracle'. In it he argued that there were two basic ways for a society to become more wealthy. One was to increase productivity; that is, to increase the efficiency with which the various factors of production were deployed. The other was to increase the *quantity* of the factors of production that were deployed—factors such as land, labour and investment. East Asia's impressive economic growth, he said, came about almost entirely from the second method.

By involving whole communities of previously marginalised people, and especially women, in the modern economy, Asian societies had been able to massively increase the quantity of labour they deployed. At the same time, because of the rush of Western investors, as well as their own high savings rate, they had been able to massively increase the quantity of investment in their economies. But really, Krugman argued, they had shown very little increase in efficiency or productivity. Therefore, as the rate of increase of quantity of factors of production could not possibly be maintained, their overall economic growth would soon slow.

Like everything Krugman writes, the article was a highly entertaining, even witty, one. He is one of very few economists in the world (in history?) to have mastered the tone, the style, of conversational informality of the best type of popular op-ed journalism, while maintaining the substance of serious analysis.

Krugman also compared Asian economic growth to early Soviet bloc economic growth, which was similarly based on mobilising additional factors of production.

At the time, Krugman's thesis was harshly criticised through-out Asia, including by me. The main criticism was that the measures he relied on for calibrating increased productivity were seriously inadequate. As Lee Kuan Yew tartly riposted, to believe Krugman's thesis you had to equate Singapore Airlines with Aeroflot!

Apart from technical questions about the measurements of productivity that Krugman used, more generally the thesis was, at the very least, highly counterintuitive. It was simply impossible to believe that the gleaming streets and perfect ease of Singapore, or Singapore Airport especially, did not contain gains in efficiency. Moreover, so much of East Asia's economic growth had been fuelled by exports—which had passed the ultimate efficiency test, the test of price on the global market.

All of this, in a sense, is by the by. What is most relevant for our purposes here is that, when the economic crisis hit in 1997, Krugman's article was immediately hailed as the prophetic tract that had foretold the disaster. Of course, it was nothing of the sort and Krugman, more than any of his acolytes, had the intellectual honesty to point this out. His article had predicted a gradual slowing of high rates of growth as it became impossible to keep adding new factors of production. If his thesis had been borne out the slowing of Asia would have been gradual and would have occurred at different times in different Asian societies. His thesis had absolutely nothing to do with the sudden outbreak of a debilitating financial crisis.

What is interesting about all this, from the point of view of this argument, is how enthusiastically Krugman's article was seized on by so many Western commentators. The more Krug-man told them he hadn't predicted the Asian crisis the more they lauded him for having predicted the Asian crisis. What that enthusiasm among the Western commentariat suggests is an almost obscene desire to hear bad news about Asia, or, if that is impossible, at least explanations of good news about Asia that are to Asia's discredit. 'See, there really was no miracle, the Asians can't do it after all' seemed to be the unattractive Schadenfreudish tone of much comment.

Krugman went on to become one of the more creative thinkers trying to come to grips with the Asian crisis. His writings acknowledged that the economic crisis inflicted much more damage on some of the Asian economies than was warranted by the economic fundamentals. An element of panic had overtaken the markets in the most furious months of the crisis, so that the very real danger for an investor of being the last one out the door made the panic self-fulfilling. It was the very fear of collapse that brought about collapse. As analysts pointed out, to understand what was happening in Asia it would be necessary to think of the United States losing not just the $200 billion in foreign investment it attracts but also a trillion dollars in sudden capital outflow. In such a circumstance many formerly good loans would become bad loans and many banks and other credit-providing institutions would struggle.

Other economists failed to get Asia right because they were imprisoned by the limitations of their discipline. This sort of economics approach looks on nations as mere masses of economic data which are fed into a model that produces, at the other end, various policy commands. This seemed particularly the case with the International Monetary Fund in its early response to the Asian economic crisis. At first it advised Indonesia, Thailand and South Korea to slash spending and increase their Budget surpluses, or eliminate their deficits. And this in economies radically contracting! The policy response seemed to be one minted in Latin America where profligate government spending—not unhedged foreign loans and a consequent financial system crisis— was the problem. At one stage the IMF negotiated a program with Indonesia that involved 50 simultaneous structural reforms.

This is all familiar territory and the IMF has been widely criticised for these policy responses. The relevant point for our considerations is the way in which economists were immune to the particularities of the Asian nations involved. No one seriously familiar with Indonesia and its thin, brittle civil service could possibly imagine 50 major structural reforms being implemented simultaneously. There was an intellectual arrogance among Western policy makers, which again arose from the conceit that all wisdom was contained in Western disciplines, such as economics, rather than a portion of it, at least, residing in the history, culture and values of particular Asian nations.

The World Bank, in its famous report on the East Asian miracle in 1993, was much better because at least it looked at the diversity of the tiger economies, as well as those things that they had in common. There was at least an acknowledgement that the distinct experiences of each nation had to be taken into account.

The intellectual failures of the West in its policy responses to the Asian crisis reflect also a sad and disturbing decline in area studies at Western universities, especially American universities. Area studies, the examination of individual nations and regions of nations, have lost credibility and standing in American universities, and this is one of the most worrying developments of all. Instead of examining, say Indonesia or even Japan in a holistic way, as an integrated society, the study of each nation takes place piecemeal across many discipline-centred departments. Thus a bit of Indonesian literature is discussed in the literature department. A module of Indonesian history is offered in the history department. Indonesia figures a little in a development economics option in the economics department. And so on. But nobody is really studying Indonesia and therefore nobody really understands Indonesia.

A bright graduate student might choose to write his or her dissertation on Indonesian literature. But then if that graduate student goes to work for the university they will most likely find themselves in a heavily theoretical department, in which their Indonesian literature will at best be used merely to illustrate exotic and almost entirely self-referential literary theory. In time our graduate student will lose touch with the Indonesian language, and eventually with Indonesian literature. Lots of people will know a lot about literary theory, but nobody will know anything in much depth about Indonesian literature.

It goes rather further than worries about literature. The United

States once found itself with very little area knowledge of a society with which it was becoming deeply involved, namely Vietnam, and it was not a pleasant reality.

These academic fashions paralleled the operations of the US State Department in the first Clinton administration. Its traditional area agencies declined in influence and specialist functional agencies were in the ascendant. Thus the running on China policy was for a time made by the human rights bureau, the running on North Korea policy by the non-proliferation folks. But the problem is that to know a society in depth you have to study its history, its politics and its economics—in short, its culture, its values.

Of course, not knowing much about Asia has never been a bar to Western politicians, in particular, having a lot to say about Asia. One of the most entertaining cases of this is Christopher Patten, the last British governor of Hong Kong. The book he wrote afterwards, *East and West: China, Power and the Future of Asia*, is highly instructive in this regard.

Patten devotes an entire chapter to Asian values, of which he is uniformly critical and dismissive. He makes his overall judgement clear early on: 'Asian Values has been a shorthand for the justification of authoritarianism, bossiness and closed collusion rather than open accountability in economic management.' Much of the chapter is devoted to Lee Kuan Yew, whom he seems particularly to dislike. Yet it is worth noting at once that Singapore has had less 'closed collusion' and lack of 'open accountability in economic management' than almost any other society on Earth. In matters economic Singapore is a paragon of accountability and transparent procedures. This kind of broad-brush attack on Asian values is immensely unsophisticated.

But what Patten's book as a whole demonstrates is a lack of real familiarity with Asia. He had made only a handful of visits to mainland China and he hadn't been to Taiwan at all until after he left Hong Kong. Nor, by his own account, was he a scholar of Asia. He'd had an interesting experience as governor of Hong Kong, which certainly offered some insights and was worth recording. But would a politician who had been, say, the governor of Gibraltar but had hardly ever travelled to Europe or studied European history or culture feel so confident about making gross generalisations and vast historical judgements about Europe? Doesn't this misplaced confidence tell us something about the unjustified sense of omniscience on the subject of Asia among Western blathermouths generally?

Much of Patten's book reads like a somewhat better than usual parliamentary speech at Westminster. In that sense it reminds me of some of Hilaire Belloc's later books, which he dictated more or less off the top of his head. The words are rhetorical, sometimes repetitive, at the level of bar-room discourse modestly learned. The expression is sometimes orotund.

Patten's major point about Asian values is the old, old, old one that Asia is diverse and therefore cannot be said to hold common values—an argument really designed to stop further discussion rather than explore the subject. Patten enjoys quoting some Asians against Asian values, but enjoys quoting some Asians against authoritarianism even more. And because he simply equates Asian values with authoritarianism he thinks that seals the argument. Yet in the heart of the chapter in question lies its most delicious contradiction. Patten quotes Malaysia's former deputy prime minister, Anwar Ibrahim, who had once told *Newsweek*:

Does Sun Yat-sen represent Asian values? Of course he does. He was a democrat and he believed in freedom of the press. And the media played a role in Sun's revolutionary era. The Philippines, Indonesia, Malaysia, Vietnam, Thailand—they all had similar experiences. The founding fathers always subscribed to moral fervour and traditional values—very Asian at that—but certainly they were great democrats.

Patten seems not to realise the meaning of the very words he has quoted here. Anwar is defending Asian values, and calling Sun Yat-sen to his side, as well as the independence leaders of several South East Asian nations. So Anwar in fact is making the much more sophisticated and Asian case that Asian values are not just, not even, about authoritarianism. Patten simply cedes possession of the term to those he then derides as authoritarians. If you equate Asian values with harsh authoritarianism it is easy to argue against them. But it is the ultimate case of constructing a straw man for the purpose of knocking it down. It is akin to

Orwell's metaphor of not really thinking but rather bolting together a series of slogans, a kind of Meccano-set approach to language and reason.

Having said that, there are some attractive passages in the book where Patten argues that certain Asian societies (particularly Hong Kong under Patten it seems) may offer useful lessons for Western policy makers. That is not the primary burden of his argument, but even that much of an acknowledgement is welcome.

Naturally, the Western argument in favour of democracy is persuasive, as are Asian arguments in favour of democracy. I believe in democracy because it is the best system of government, it most truly accords with the nature of man and it best respects the human rights of people. But democracy cannot always be successfully imposed at a moment's notice. Moreover, no democracy is perfect and many of the most stable democracies have numerous undemocratic features, while many authoritarian nations have genuinely consultative features. This is not to argue that we should get lost in a swamp of relativism but that we should afford due recognition to the uniqueness and challenge of each nation's individual circumstances.

Moreover, despite what American spokesmen in particular often claim, democracy is neither sufficient nor necessary for economic progress and development. (That democracy was necessary and perhaps sufficient seemed to be the nub of Al Gore's infamous speech in Kuala Lumpur in 1998, dealt with in Chapter 5 on Malaysia.) The Asian economic crisis made things clear. Consider the following.

The crisis hit Indonesia very hard, Indonesia was not a democracy at the time, therefore (some commentators say) democracy must be the answer. But it also hit South Korea and Thailand very hard, and they were democracies already before the crisis occurred. Being democracies didn't prevent their being hit.

Singapore and Hong Kong were less adversely affected by the crisis than most other East Asian economies. Yet Hong Kong has never been a democracy, and Patten, for one, would not accept that Singapore is a liberal democracy of the type he prefers. China also weathered the crisis better than most and it definitely was not a democracy. But then so did Taiwan and it was a democracy.

Elsewhere, Russia throughout the 1990s has been a genuine

democracy by the normal test. Its elections were real and the elections determined the government. Yet Russia's economic performance during the decade was catastrophic.

So what does all this actually tell us? It says that there is no simple correlation between democracy and economic performance.

Prior to the regional crisis there was one other important Western school of interpretation of Asia—the economic boosters school. Certainly there were plenty of books on the Asian economic miracle, an output that was entirely justified at the time by the magnitude of the region's economic achievement and the transformation it brought in people's lives and in whole societies. Many such boosters underplayed the dangers of unhedged foreign debts, the rickety nature of some of the region's financial systems and the particular dangers of real estate and other asset bubbles. Nonetheless, even in hindsight there are arguments in mitigation. The region was punished by the financial crisis far more than the economic fundamentals justified. Since there was such a large element of panic in the crisis, since so much of it was consequent on a loss of confidence, it was inherently unpredictable. Still, the region was 'overboomed' during the boom times.

Virtually all of the Western approaches to Asia examined in this chapter suffered from one gross deficiency: they all greatly underestimated the role and power of America in Asia. This of course was much more the case before the onset of the economic crisis. It was truly pathetic at times during that period to hear American spokesmen maundering on about Asia's wickedness in trade or some other contested area of policy, to see George Bush leading a troupe of persecuted American businessmen to Japan because American business was so downtrodden that it could not succeed any other way, to see Mickey Kantor's ridiculous posturing statements that trade policy would never again be subordinated to anything else, as though the idea that America might have strategic interests, or even human values, to put into the mix as well as trade was a shocking thought.

One final area in which the West, the United States in particular, needs to do some serious rethinking in its relationships with Asia is the perennially vexed question of human rights.

Of course basic human rights are universal. This derives in a most straightforward fashion from the universality of human nature. Of course a human being in Shanghai should enjoy the same human rights as a human being in San Francisco. And of course civil and political rights must always be tempered by the rights of society as a whole. Amnesty International and the Pope, for example, believe that state executions of criminals are a violation of human rights. The United States believes that execution is a legitimate part of state policy. The difference is conscientious. Neither Amnesty International and the Pope, on the one hand, nor the United States, on the other, is in bad faith. But it seems to be impossible that the US could ever accept that anyone who disagrees with it on human rights is not in bad faith.

Asian countries often believe that human rights is a stalking horse for other, much more venal, American interests. There was a time before the regional economic crisis in Asia when the US was threatening to make certain types of trade conditional on South East Asian nations accepting US-approved labour standards. The hypocrisy of this sort of position is breathtaking—what were labour standards like in the US when it had the per capita GNP of Indonesia, for example?

Such positions also represent what has become an ugly trend in international diplomacy—the almost raw use of power by rich white nations against poor, third world nations, in part to determine their political arrangements. The power of the US is so absolutely vast that it carries with it a special responsibility to install respect for the rights of other nations as a paramount consideration.

Indeed, this injunction is one half of the central tension in human rights diplomacy in the modern world, the tension between the undeniable universality of human rights and the legitimate rights of nation states, the presumption of non-interference in other nations' internal behaviour. Of course human rights are universal and the fact that the US is so often and so powerfully concerned with human rights in many different parts of the world is one of the great civilising features of the global system. It is greatly to the credit of the US and goes to the heart of why the US is such a great and good nation.

But the rights of nation states should not be put at nought

either. For the principle of extra-territoriality, and the presumption of non-interference in other states' internal behaviour, is the only thing that stands between the independence of the weak and the tyranny of the strong.

What factors should influence countries like the US, Australia, the democracies of Western Europe in forming their human rights diplomacy towards the nations of Asia?

First of all, while not making the false assumption of equating human rights with economic prosperity, there ought to be an *a priori* recognition that economic development is very often the best, sometimes the only, method of improving actual human rights on the ground. Human freedom expands with economic development almost independently of whether the political system becomes more democratic. Of course, it is possible to find examples in history—the economic development of Germany under the Nazis, say—when this has not been the case. And human rights in general might be improving while certain minorities face increased persecution. But overwhelmingly it has been the case that greater prosperity has meant greater freedom. First, the state has more largesse to dispense as patronage and is therefore less likely to expropriate a debilitating portion of the property of its citizens in order to pay off a favoured class, such as the military.

Secondly, economic independence creates greater political space, even if democracy does not reign. If a small trader in Shanghai has the money to buy a television or radio set and listen to overseas broadcasts he is by that fact alone more free. If he has the money to supplement the education of his children and to provide for primary health care for his parents, by those acts alone he is more in control of his own life, and has greater personal space, independent of the state. But if what you're looking for out of your human rights diplomacy is emotional gratification, promoting long-term economic development won't give it to you.

When dealing with human rights abuses, degrees of severity must be taken into account. These are often not 'nice' distinctions, they are often unpleasant distinctions, but they must be made nonetheless. A single unjustified death in the justice system is unconscionable if you regard every human life as sacred. But is there a government in the world that has not presided over a single unjustified death? A single death does not make a regime the equivalent of Hitler's Germany. If you are dealing with Hitler's Germany you have no option but total opposition; but nowhere in Asia, not even in North Korea, are we dealing with Hitler's Germany. All human rights abuses are obnoxious but overblown rhetoric can distort what is often a complex situation.

Further, what response is likely to be most effective? Even a nation as powerful as the US must sometimes confront the reality that, short of war and invasion to topple a particular regime, it cannot fundamentally improve the human rights situation. In such cases making a moral statement may still be worthwhile, but such statements can also mislead internal players about likely future actions. There is often a case for benign neglect. There is also a case for offering political criticism and opposition but not trade or other sanctions. This may not be hypocrisy but merely a means of staying true to core values while recognising what is likely to be most effective in the real world.

Then it is worth asking what the voices within the society under consideration are asking outsiders to do. It is wrong to think the only voice to listen to is the Government's, but equally it is wrong to assign a power of policy veto over the West to one favoured dissident, as appeared to happen in the 1990s with Myanmar's Aung San Suu Kyi. Some Chinese dissidents may support the withholding of Most Favoured Nation trading status (now called normal trading status) to China on the basis of its human rights abuses. But as Hong Kong's Martin Lee, an impeccable democrat, has observed, this is akin to saying to an abusive husband: 'If you don't stop beating your wife I'll kill her.'

It is also legitimate to consider what domestic politics in the West demands, but too often in Asia the actions and words of US spokesmen look as though they are crafted primarily for the TV audience at home and not for the reality they are allegedly confronting.

It is also reasonable to ask what are the national interests of the nation making the response. Human rights activists in the West sometimes adopt an absurdly purist tone which is ignored when real compelling interests are at stake (few seriously argued, for example, that the lack of democracy in Kuwait made

Operation Desert Storm immoral) but which distorts the debate in other cases.

What are friends and neighbours saying and doing? Asia is home to numerous exemplary democracies—India, the world's biggest democracy, Japan, the world's second biggest economy, South Korea, Thailand, the Philippines and others. In each of these countries policy is subject to intense domestic scrutiny and debate. Isn't it reasonable for nations outside the region occasionally to seek the advice of regional democracies on human rights diplomacy?

What is the real morality of penalties and inducements? North Korea has a bomb, so it gets billions of dollars of aid; Myanmar has no bomb and a charismatic dissident leader, so it not only gets no aid but effectively gets isolation and even some sporadic sanctions. The grosser inconsistencies damage the overall credibility of human rights diplomacy.

Finally, one of the most important questions is this: In which direction is the regime moving? If it is moving in a liberalising direction, even if from a highly authoritarian base and at a slow pace, there is an overwhelming case for working with rather than against it.

A single test case illustrates the real complexity of human rights diplomacy. In 1990 Aung San Suu Kyi won a democratic election in Myanmar (Burma as it was then called) but was not allowed to take office. For a long period she was kept under house arrest. Aung San Suu Kyi is undoubtedly a splendidly admirable person and her captors thoroughly deplorable. But as a result she was given a kind of power of moral veto over Western policy towards Myanmar. The West tried to isolate Myanmar and occasionally imposed sanctions of varying degrees of severity. The consequences for the people of Myanmar have been appalling. Economic development has been retarded. Rangoon has moved to a tight strategic embrace with China which has transferred billions of dollars of weaponry to Myanmar. Washington has lost what had been a relatively cheap involvement in an anti-poppy-growing program. Myanmar, one of the poorest nations in the world, does not have the wherewithal to eradicate its poppy industry by itself even if it had a wholly admirable government. Instead it has become an important link in the supply chain of heroin to the West. At the same time the country is experiencing, and helping to spread, an alarming HIV-AIDS epidemic. So what has the policy of isolation and sanctions actually achieved beyond a few good sound bites and photo-ops for the usual troupe of posturing Western politicians?

If the policy had been to assist Myanmar's economic development during that period it would have been impossible for the West to have had less influence on human rights in Myanmar. But tens of thousands, perhaps many more, of Myanmar's people would have had decent paying jobs with all the increase in freedom that that brings. Washington would undoubtedly have had a continuing involvement in an anti-poppy program and the world would have been able to help much more with anti-AIDS efforts.

So what did the so-called moral human rights policy achieve? Whose interests did it serve? Aung San Suu Kyi, admirable figure that she is, should never have been allowed effectively to veto Western policy. This is all wrong. It is about the power of a television image and not the power of reason or good policy.

The human rights debate needs to be much wider and much more sophisticated, and Western nations need to walk with a lot more humility in their approach to Asian nations over human rights.

Much of this chapter has been devoted to discussing the failings of Western intellectual approaches to Asia. But most of this book has been devoted to exploring Asian approaches to Asian values. And in human rights as in other areas it is how the debate plays out in Asia that will ultimately be most important.

It is sheer folly to think that Asian values will not be among the most important subjects for critical analysis and understanding throughout the entire world in the decades ahead. The debate that counts most will not be the Western debate—though it is important that the West understand more and preach less—but the debate within Asia itself.

It is a newly re-engaged debate, rich and full of meaning. The economic crisis notwithstanding, Asian values are on the road again.

INDEX